Catering for Large Numbers

Stephen Ashley

Sean Anderson

Butterworth-Heinemann

Sydney, London, Oxford, Boston, Munich, New Delhi,
Singapore, Tokyo, Toronto, Wellington

1993

BUTTERWORTH-HEINEMANN

AUSTRALIA   BUTTERWORTH-HEINEMANN 271–273 Lane Cove Road, North Ryde 2113
                   BUTTERWORTH-HEINEMANN 18 Salmon Street, Port Melbourne 3207

UNITED KINGDOM   BUTTERWORTH-HEINEMANN LTD   Oxford

USA   BUTTERWORTH-HEINEMANN   Stoneham

National Library of Australia Cataloguing-in-Publication entry

---

Ashley, Stephen.
  Catering for large numbers.
Includes index.
ISBN 0 409 30642 8.
1. Quantity cookery. I. Anderson, Sean. II. Title.
641.57

Inquiries should be addressed to the publishers.

Cover design and illustration by Yolande Bull.
Typeset in Palatino and Optima by Post Typesetters, Queensland.

Printed in Australia by Star Printery Pty. Ltd.

Foreword

Catering for large numbers is a unique art, and so it is appropriate that a text should be devoted especially to it. This publication has been designed with Australian conditions in mind, making it particularly useful for both teaching purposes and for use in large-scale catering establishments.

It is no longer acceptable to simply produce a large amount of food for a large number of people. Large-scale caterers must be aware of factors such as healthy menu planning, nutrition, hygiene, presentation of food, budgeting and costing, and ordering of foodstuffs. The first section of this book provides information about all these matters, and also includes ordering and costing sheets and checklists, which will be extremely useful for caterers preparing food for large functions or for large institutions. The second section of the book contains a wide and varied selection of recipes with ingredients listed in quantities appropriate for 25, 50 or 100 people.

The authors of this book, with a combined catering experience of 24 years, have written a clear and easy to follow text which will be invaluable for students and professional caterers alike.

Phil Armitt
Dip Teach (Tech.)

Contents

Recipes

Preface

Catering for Large Numbers is designed as a reference book for caterers working in large-scale catering operations and for students, and will be useful for those preparing food for banquets and large functions, as well as in such diverse settings as office complexes, health care facilities, factories, universities, colleges and schools. It is hoped that this book will benefit both experienced caterers and caterers new to the industry.

The authors wish to thank Meredith Wilson and Marianne Evans for their many hours of hard work and support during the preparation of this book, Mark Feetham, John Gallagher and Phil Armitt for their expert advice, Pam Lines for the graphics, Lyndal Sayer for the illustration concepts and Yolande Bull for their execution, Simon Hawkswell for the photograph of the authors, and the staff of Butterworths for making publication possible. Thanks are also recorded to the Australian Meat and Livestock Corporation for permission to publish the colour photographs of cuts of beef, veal and lamb, and the Australian Pork Corporation for permission to publish the colour photographs of cuts of pork.

A special thank you is extended to Peter van der Kwaak, who was responsible for bringing the authors together.

Catering for Large Numbers is dedicated to the authors' families.

September 1992
Sydney

Stephen Ashley
Sean Anderson

1
Methods of Cookery

- Roasting
- Baking
- Stewing
- Boiling
- Steaming
- Grilling
- Frying
- Sautéing
- Microwaving
- Suitability of Meats for Different Cooking Methods

Roasting

Roasting is the modern equivalent of spit-roasting which is the process of cooking meat in front of an open fire. The juices from the meat are caught in a drip tray and spooned back over the meat to keep it moist, the same method used today in basting.

Roasting today occurs in a variety of ovens. A convection/fan forced oven is most commonly used in large scale catering. Every oven performs differently. An uneven displacement of heat is a major cause of anxiety to a chef using a particular oven for the first time. If one side of the oven is hotter than the other, a fluctuation of a few degrees from the desired setting may occur. If a 7 kg rump of beef is placed in an oven at a temperature setting of 150°C, the cooking time should be approximately 4 hours, but the oven may in fact be a few degrees hotter

1

than the last oven mastered at the same temperature. This temperature difference over a period of 4 hours will overcook the meat and therefore produce a finished product of lesser quality. Only experience can combat this. A chef who is using an oven for the first time should take extra care when monitoring the food's progress. It takes only a short amount of time to master even the most eccentric of ovens. The temperature setting must be left to the chef's discretion.

Heat displacement is another major problem with an unfamiliar oven. This problem is easily solved by rotating the roasting tray 180 degrees each time the food is basted or otherwise checked to assess its progress. Rotation will ensure that a joint cooks evenly.

An oven is unlimited in its capacity to cook foodstuffs. It can be used to cook a freshly prepared dish or to heat a pre-prepared frozen dish. When timed correctly and when storage space for hot foods outside the oven is limited, an oven can permit extra foods to be kept at the correct temperature until required.

Ovens should be maintained hygienically. The lower tray which protects the food from the actual flame may be easily removed for cleaning. Ovens should be thoroughly cleaned at least once a week. When more than one oven is at a chef's disposal, it is practicable to clean the ovens on different days and to prepare a menu which does not involve using the oven to be cleaned on that day. For ovens that need heavy duty cleaning, the bottom catch tray, shelves and shelf supports should be soaked overnight in an industrial cleaner. Aluminium foil covering the catch tray will save time. For ovens that are used constantly, replace the foil daily. The price of the foil will always be less than the price of hired labour to soak and scrub.

REMEMBER: Food particles left in an oven will burn and may impair the flavour of foods cooked thereafter.

To prevent frying and overcooking of the lower portion of the roast, which can lead to difficulties in carving, meats being roasted should always be kept clear of the fat in the bottom of the roasting tray. This can be done in a number of ways:

   (a) by using a wire rack which usually keeps the meat approximately 2 cm from the base of the roasting pan;

   (b) spreading rough-cut carrots and onions under the meat; or

   (c) making a trivet from bones on which to stand the meat.

All visible sinew should be removed from the meat before cooking commences. The meat should then be placed in the desired size pan, fat side up. The fat of the meat, supplemented by a little extra oil, will liquefy during cooking, thus basting the meat and keeping it moist. The recommended seasoning should then be added.

Poultry to be roasted should be placed in the pan breast side up. Because of the lack of fat on poultry, surplus pork fat may be used to assist the basting procedure. This is called barding. The pork fat may be draped over the bird or stitched through the bird by securing the fat to two needle-like instruments. The latter method, which is the classical way of barding, is very time-consuming, and since its effect is not noticeably superior, it is not recommended where a large number of birds are to be cooked. Draping pork fat over poultry will produce the same result as meats placed in the oven fat side up. The pork fat will liquefy and keep the bird moist. The required seasoning should be rubbed on to the bird after adding the fat but before the addition of any bacon rind. There is also another form of keeping meat moist during cooking. In this method, known as Pique, fat is pushed through the outer layer of the meat, just piercing the flesh, before cooking begins. This method is reserved for premium cuts of meat such as fillet and tenderloin.

It is commonly but incorrectly thought that joints of meat to be roasted must first be sealed in an oven hotter than the recommended temperature to retain the natural juices. This method actually increases shrinkage. Meat should be placed in an oven preheated to the required temperature. This method will completely seal the meat in a very short time by closing the pores and preventing the juices from escaping, thus ensuring a moist finished product. During the cooking process, regular basting is advised. This also allows the meat's progress to be monitored.

NOTE: This guideline does not apply to the cooking of a whole fillet of beef, veal or lamb. It is recommended that the fillet be seasoned and sealed in a hot pan or under a grill and then transferred to the oven to complete the cooking process.

Cooking times for different meats are as follows:

Beef	30 minutes per kg and 30 minutes over (*RARE*)
	35 minutes per kg and 40 minutes over (*DONE*)
Lamb	40 minutes per kg and 40 minutes over (*DONE*)
Veal	50 minutes per kg and 50 minutes over (*DONE*)
Pork	50 minutes per kg and 50 minutes over (*DONE*)
Poultry	30 minutes per half kg

NOTE: If meats have been stuffed, an extra 5 minutes per half kg must be added.

White meats, such as poultry and pork, must be thoroughly cooked because both are potential sources of harmful bacteria if undercooked.

Baking

Baking is a combination of dry heat from the oven, complemented by moisture from the evaporation of the liquid in the food being cooked.

In most conventional ovens there is an internal heat difference of approximately 5–10°C. Therefore, as explained in the section on roasting, a sound knowledge of the oven is required. Temperature control is essential for baking. The heat in the oven is controlled not only by the thermostat, but also by the position in which the food is placed. The higher the shelf used, the hotter the temperature will be.

The ideal type of oven for baking is a convection oven — also known as a fan forced oven. This type of oven contains an internal fan which circulates the heat and eliminates heat fluctuation.

Certain other products can be prepared ('cooked off') and then finished in the oven. A finishing glaze on Duchess Potatoes is obtained by this method.

Stewing

Stewing is one of the most nutritional methods of cookery because all the goodness of the foodstuff is retained and incorporated into the dish. The ingredients complement each other enhancing the overall flavour.

This method of cooking is generally applied to the more fibrous cuts of meat. Different cooking methods for different cuts of meat will be explained at the end of this chapter. Compared to other cooking processes, stewing is ideal for the lesser quality cuts of meat. The extended cooking time allows the connective tissues holding the meat together to break down. This ensures a tender and palatable finished product.

The ingredients for stewing are cooked together in a small amount of liquid, such as stock, covered with a tight fitting lid and brought to the boil. After boiling point is reached, any scum that has risen to the surface should be removed with a ladle and the lid replaced. The stew should then be simmered slowly, either on the stove or in the lower part of the oven. Meat to be stewed should be lightly fried before being added to the stew to seal the pores and retain its juices.

Boiling

Boiling is defined as the cooking of food in liquid that has reached a temperature of 100°C, the liquid being either water or suitable stock. Once boiling point has been reached, any scum should be removed and the temperature controlled by lowering the heat to a simmer. For the cooking of certain foods extra care should be taken to monitor the rate of the boil because the difference between a light and a rapid simmer is slight.

Salted or pickled meats should be placed in cold water or stock and brought to the boil. Other meats should be placed in boiling liquid in order to retain the full taste and moisture of the meat. In the case of salted and pickled meats, it is important to extract as much of the salt or spices as possible, so the pores must be left open as long as possible. Poultry should be treated in the same way as salted and pickled meats.

Boiling is also an ideal way to cook the lesser quality cuts of meat because the long cooking time allows the connective tissues to break down and the meat to become tender. Because it is essential not to cook the food too quickly, the temperature of the liquid must be monitored carefully.

If required, seasoning may be added to the liquid to help flavour the meat. When skimming the surface ensure that the seasoning remains in the pot.

Boiling is an effective form of cookery for a variety of foods such as pastas, eggs, soups, stocks, sauces and vegetables.

Vegetables that are grown above the ground, for example greens, should be covered by (salted) boiling water. Below ground vegetables, such as potatoes, are usually denser and should be placed into cold liquid and brought to the boil. The exception to this rule is new potatoes which are usually placed into boiling water. When boiling point is reached, any scum should be removed and the liquid reduced to a simmer until the vegetable is cooked. Care should be taken not to boil the vegetable too quickly because this will cause it to break up.

NOTE: Cooking times for various foods are given in the relevant recipes.

Steaming

A steamer is a very useful piece of equipment, and few modern kitchens are without them. Steamed foods are often more palatable than foods cooked using other methods. In the same way as with stewing and boiling, lesser quality foods benefit because colour is maintained and little moisture is lost.

Steaming is an efficient and effective way of cooking most vegetables, especially those that are cooked whole, for example potato, squash and corn on the cob. Cooking fish in a steamer guarantees a nutritious result.

If a steamer is not available, a large pan and a colander can be used instead. Place the pan containing a little water on the stove and position a colander on top. Bring the water to the boil and place the food to be cooked in the colander. Cover with a lid. Now you have a steamer.

The moist heat factor must be taken into consideration when steaming food. So, for example, when cooking sponges and puddings ensure that they are well protected from condensation. Lightly greased greaseproof paper is ideal for this purpose.

NOTE: Due to the extremely high temperature of steam, especially under pressure, extra care must be taken with this method at all times.

Grilling

This method of cooking requires heated elements either above, as in a salamander, or below, as in a charcoal grill. The short cooking time required for grilling necessitates the use of only good quality cuts of meat. When cooking over the heat in a charcoal grill or on a grill plate, the meat should first be sealed on both sides on a hot part of the grill and then transferred to a cooler part for the duration of the cooking process. Foods cooked on a charcoal grill have a distinct taste and appearance which can not be achieved by any other form of grilling. If this effect is required, metal bars may be purchased. These are heated and placed onto the meat in order to sear it. This is time-consuming, however, and is not practical where large quantities of meat are to be grilled.

A salamander grill is a stock-in-trade appliance in every kitchen for the cooking of prepared foodstuffs placed on a tray such as bacon, tomatoes and mushrooms. The final stages of cooking, for example glazing, are effective under a salamander because the process can be easily monitored.

Meats to be grilled should be seasoned and lightly covered with oil. This protects them from direct heat and prevents burning. Fish must always be coated with at least a light covering of flour. The required seasoning should be incorporated into the flour.

Grilling is a healthy way of cooking food because all the oil is drained from the meat. If a salamander is used to cook fatty foods the grilling tray should be drained regularly.

Frying

Because oil can reach extremely high temperatures, frying is a very quick method of cookery and care should be taken when cooking foods in this way. Extra care should be taken when deep-frying since the whole article is submerged and all sides are subjected to the same intensity of heat.

When deep-frying foods, a basket should be used whenever possible, and if not, a spider (a web-shaped wirer tool) should be kept handy for the removal of excess food.

Top quality oils or compounds are essential for the best results. Old oils/compounds fail to reach the required temperature, soak into the food and impair the flavour, and will not result in a crispy finish. Oils/compounds must always be strained after use to remove any particles that will burn the next time they are used. This will also extend the life of the oils/compounds considerably. The life span of oils/compounds is also determined by the number of times they are subjected to high temperatures. In between cooking, the temperature of the oil/compound should be reduced. When oils/compounds darken, smoke at low temperatures or bubble, they must be replaced. Always keep oils/compounds containers safe. Old oils/compounds should be replaced into their original containers and sealed ready for collection. Never pour old oils/compounds down drains. Once they have cooled, they may solidify and block them. It is also environmentally unacceptable to dispose of oils/compounds in this way.

When a large batch of food requires frying, be sure not to cook too much at any one time since this will reduce the temperature of the oil/compound and result in the food absorbing too much oil/compound. It must be remembered that the initial heat will seal the food, preventing absorption of oil/compound. When oil/compound is not at the right temperature it will be absorbed until the correct temperature for frying is reached. Greasy food is not a good result.

Tougher cuts of meat are not suitable for deep-frying because the short cooking time does not allow for the breakdown of connective tissues, and the meat will remain tough. This can be overcome in certain circumstances with the use of a meat tenderiser. A meat tenderiser is a metal mallet with small blunt spikes protruding from the head. The entire piece of meat should be firmly hit with the tenderiser to break down the connective tissue. This method is effective in the preparation of schnitzels. Having said this, it is still wise, where possible, to avoid deep-frying lesser quality cuts of meat.

Ideally all foods to be deep-fried should have a protective covering of some kind, be it batter, breadcrumbs or simply flour. This prevents overcooking, seals in any juices that may cause the oil/compound to spit and also adds interest and texture difference to the dish. Note that this does not apply to some potato dishes, for example sautéed potatoes.

When deep-frying fish, a protective coating of some sort is required. This applies also to shallow-frying. The coating improves the colour and presentation of the cooked fish. Oils/compounds that have been used for shallow-frying must be discarded after use and the pan cleaned thoroughly.

Cooking times vary according to the thickness of the food, and extra consideration is needed if the food is raw. Actual frying commences when the oil/compound reaches a temperature of 140°C. At this temperature the food will move about in the oil/compound. Cooking times and temperatures will be provided in the relevant recipes.

When shallow-frying food, the presentation side should be placed into the pan first because this side will always look the best. It should then be turned and cooked to acquire the desired result. Oils/compounds for shallow-frying can be used with the addition of a little butter to enhance the flavour. When cooking for large numbers, margarine with a little salt added can be used instead. There is a myriad of flavoured oils on the market for various uses and results. The choice is yours.

Saut'eing

The difference between saut'eing and shallow-frying food is that, generally, when saut'eing, a minimum amount of oil/compound is used and the foodstuff is regularly agitated or tossed. When used for meat, saut'eing is usually reserved for the better quality cuts.

Microwaving

Microwave ovens are inefficient for large-scale catering and they are not suitable for mass production of meals. Therefore, microwave cooking is not covered in this text and none of the recipes provided involve its use.

Suitability of Meats for Different Cooking Methods

	Stewing and casseroles	Grilling	Boiling	Roasting
Beef	Chuck	Fillet	Brisket	Silverside
	Round	Sirloin	Corned	Topside
	Skirt	Rump	Silverside	Sirloin
	Topside	T-bone	Round	Fillet
		Rib eye		Rump
Lamb	Chops	Cutlets	Tongue	Shoulder
	Neck	Chops	Mutton cuts	Leg
		Forequarter		Loin
		Fillet		Fillet
Pork	Chops	Chops	Trotters	Leg
		Fillet	Ham	Loin
			Chump chops	Forequarter
				Fillet

2

Food Production Systems

■ Cook and Serve System: On Site: Conventional
■ Cook Chill System: On Site: Conventional
■ Cook Freeze System: On Site: Conventional
■ Cook Chill: Central Production Unit

Cook and Serve System: On Site: Conventional

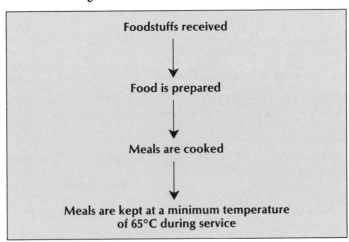

The cook and serve system is the most widely used of all food production systems. It involves one operation serving one outlet. The preparation, cooking and service of the finished product are carried out on the one site. Timing is an essential factor. Foods must be coordinated so that they are ready for consumption by the recipient as close to service time as possible. They should be kept constantly at the required temperature throughout service except for certain items on an *à la carte* menu.

In addition to the standard equipment in the kitchen, this type of food production requires hot and cold holding bays, for example hot and cold bainmaries, hot boxes etc, which will hold prepared dishes at the required temperature. This equipment can be permanently based or mobile for a delivery service. A complex establishment, such as a hospital, may have annexes on the grounds which need supplying with food from a base kitchen.

Transportation in this type of system will be by heated or refrigerated mobile carts or by insulated trays. Dishes can be made up at service areas from items boxed separately. Insulated trays may be made up at the base location and then transported to the required destination.

Minimal capital outlay is required for setting up this system of food production. Most major operations will already have some kind of system in use, and modification will usually be minimal. Financial outlay will largely be due to maintenance, replacement and servicing of existing equipment.

Good management skills are required to keep operating costs to a minimum. A strict budget must be adhered to. Labour costs are usually high because trained staff are necessary for each shift (where a shift system applies). This system of food production may be restricted in its operation depending on the availability and size of equipment and the cost of labour.

Cook Chill System: On Site: Conventional

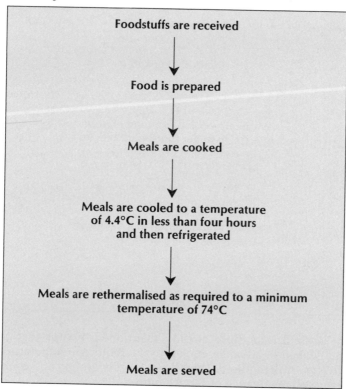

Foodstuffs are received

↓

Food is prepared

↓

Meals are cooked

↓

Meals are cooled to a temperature
of 4.4°C in less than four hours
and then refrigerated

↓

Meals are rethermalised as required to a minimum
temperature of 74°C

↓

Meals are served

This system of food production, like the cook and serve system, requires one operation serving one outlet. The difference with this system is that the prepared and cooked foodstuffs are chilled to the required temperatures and then stored in the refrigerator. Prior to meal service they are rethermalised to the required temperatures.

The advantages of conventional cook chill are that highly trained staff are required for only one shift per 24 hours, since foods can be prepared by a chef working one shift and then rethermalised to the required temperatures as needed.

The quality of the foodstuffs can be monitored by the chef and in most cases portions are controlled. Costs are variable, depending on the efficiency of the management within the operation. Labour costs are reduced because less skilled staff are required and bulk purchasing of foodstuffs is maximised.

Cook Freeze System: On Site: Conventional

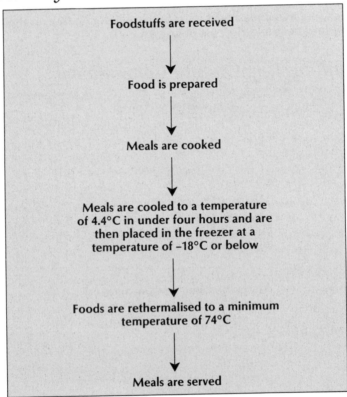

Foodstuffs are received

↓

Food is prepared

↓

Meals are cooked

↓

Meals are cooled to a temperature of 4.4°C in under four hours and are then placed in the freezer at a temperature of –18°C or below

↓

Foods are rethermalised to a minimum temperature of 74°C

↓

Meals are served

This system is similar to those already mentioned, except that the food is prepared and cooked in advance, cooled to the required temperature and then placed in a freezer until required. This allows for preparation and cooking of pre-planned meals well in advance of service time.

Staffing costs are reduced because highly trained staff are not always required.

Rethermalisation occurs just before service and the temperature is maintained in the same way as the cook serve system. Quantity control of foodstuffs is essential because food cannot be refrozen after thawing, and excess wastage will result in a reduction in profit.

Cook Chill: Central Production Unit

Cook chill, using a central production unit, is the system whereby the preparation, cooking and rapid chilling of foods and then refrigerating until required is carried out at one central production site. The food is then distributed to satellite operations for rethermalisation.

This system is often used by airlines in their meal preparation. Produced in a central kitchen, meals are then distributed to aircraft where rethermalisation is carried out.

Handling of food is thus kept to a minimum and staffing is reduced because meals can be prepared in advance, and highly trained staff are not required in all areas of preparation. Meals can be prepared well in advance in an eight-hour shift and weekend or lengthy shifts are eliminated. As a result, labour costs are kept to a minimum.

Control of each ingredient is able to be monitored from the central kitchen using recipe cards, thus ensuring quality and consistency of meals. Budget controls are further maintained in this way.

The Method

1. Foods are prepared and cooked to the stage of 'just done'.

2. They are then packaged into suitable containers or casings and while still above sterile temperatures, chilled rapidly.

3. Refrigeration follows at a central location.

4. Distribution is carried out and the foods are stored in refrigerators until required.

5. They are then rethermalised in containers or casings just prior to service.

6. Foods can be refrigerated whole or divided, depending on requirements.

7. After rethermalisation, the foods should reach a minimum temperature of 75°C. Divided or plated foods are brought to this temperature in approximately 40 minutes. Gentle and even heating allows for retention of nutrients and for better presentation of the dish.

8. Foods prepared in this way can be reheated in bulk for cafeteria-style operations and then portioned. Alternatively, they can be 'plated-up' at the central location prior to distribution, or distributed and then 'plated-up' cold prior to rethermalisation.

9. Bulk reheating can be achieved using standard kitchen equipment such as ovens, convection ovens and steamers. When rethermalisation is complete for pre-plated meals, hot beverages and chilled products may be added to the tray.

Advantages of the Centralised Cook Chill System

1. A minimum number of staff is required — one shift can produce the meals for three or more shifts.
2. There is minimal handling of foods.
3. The nutritional value of foods is retained.
4. Foods can easily be monitored for quality and consistency.
5. Kitchen space of the receiving operation is reduced.
6. Serving temperatures are ideal.
7. Foods are served to the standard required by the chef.

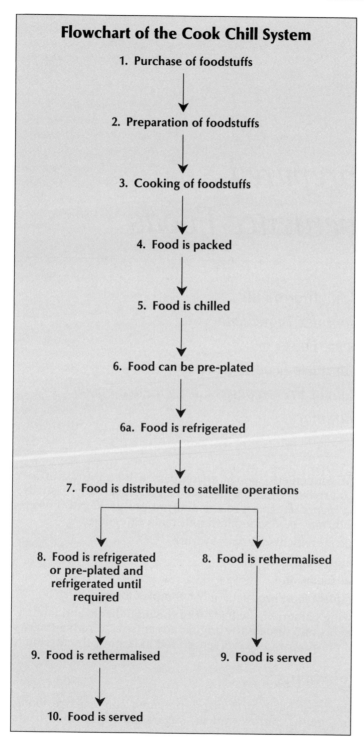

Flowchart of the Cook Chill System

1. Purchase of foodstuffs

2. Preparation of foodstuffs

3. Cooking of foodstuffs

4. Food is packed

5. Food is chilled

6. Food can be pre-plated

6a. Food is refrigerated

7. Food is distributed to satellite operations

8. Food is refrigerated or pre-plated and refrigerated until required

8. Food is rethermalised

9. Food is rethermalised

9. Food is served

10. Food is served

3

Pre-prepared Convenience Foods

- *Basic Ingredients*
- *Complex Ingredients*
- *Basic Foods*
- *Complete Food Products*
- *Role of Pre-prepared Convenience Foods*
- *Summary*

Pre-prepared convenience foods encompass a broad array of accessible and convenient ingredients that large-scale caterers use daily. Usually, they have undergone a manufacturing process and are pre-packaged. Pre-prepared convenience foods may be divided into four main categories:

(a) basic ingredients (simplest form);

(b) complex ingredients;

(c) basic foods; and

(d) complete food products (most complex form).

The following paragraphs will identify the ingredients and foods which make up each category and discuss the origins, advantages, disadvantages and roles of each type of pre-prepared convenience food in large-scale catering today.

Basic Ingredients

These are the most basic form of pre-prepared convenience foods. Examples include flours, grains, pulses, cereals, sugars, nuts and dried fruits. They are generally products in their raw state that have undergone a simple form of processing.

This type of convenience food is the forerunner of the more complex pre-prepared convenience foods. It was not so long ago that small communities were producing their own flours and grains and every household baked its own bread. These basic ingredients are still produced in a similar way today, but caterers receive them in a ready-to-use state.

Caterers all over the world use basic ingredients. No kitchen would be complete or properly equipped without them. A wide selection of flours, pulses and grains is available to cater for individual preferences. Without basic ingredients, caterers would find it difficult to provide a service.

Basic ingredients are now considered to be an integral part of any catering operation; they are no longer regarded as convenience foods.

Complex Ingredients

These are a slightly more complex form of pre-prepared convenience foods. Included in this group are, for example, beef and chicken powdered stock bases, ready-made sauces, tinned fruits in syrup and tinned vegetables. These products have usually undergone a more complex manufacturing process and are often a combination of ingredients.

A fairly recent addition to the pre-prepared convenience food group, complex ingredients have been made possible by science and improved methods of preservation and storage. Because they save production time, complex ingredients are regularly used in the catering process, and many are now considered to be necessities, for example, tomato puree and powdered stock bases. As manufacturers continue to produce new products, more and more of these types of convenience foods will be used in large-scale catering operations.

A disadvantage of using these ingredients is that there is some loss of control over the finished dish. For example, a powdered stock base will add a different flavour to foods than a freshly made stock. Also, since they are expensive, their cost should be compared with labour and production costs before purchase.

It is likely that in the next 10 years most ingredients in this category will be considered essential ingredients or foods.

Basic Foods

This category of pre-prepared convenience foods has developed in response to society's demands. It includes a wide range of foods which have been pre-prepared purely for convenience and which can be delivered daily. For example, butchers provide different cuts of meat, which reduces labour costs and also provides greater choice of presentation. Fish and seafood suppliers provide ready prepared gutted and filleted fish, cooked, peeled prawns and seafoods. Prepared vegetables are available from vegetable suppliers. Bakers are able to supply a great variety of different breads and pastries. These products are usually combined with other ingredients to produce a finished dish.

Some advantages of using this type of pre-prepared convenience food are that preparation time is reduced and consistency in quality is easier to achieve. On the other hand, it is easy to rely too heavily on pre-prepared products, which may undermine the chef's creative flair. Cost must also be considered — does the budget for labour and stock allow for fresh ingredients? If the fresh ingredients are within budget, but are time-consuming to prepare, it is wise to purchase the pre-prepared convenience food alternative instead.

Complete Food Products

These are a relatively recent innovation and are the most complex form of pre-prepared convenience foods. They are generally fully prepared dishes, requiring only minimal preparation and handling before service. Examples include lasagnes, meat pies, beef wellingtons, chicken kievs, and dessert dishes such as gateaux and cheesecakes.

Complete food products are invaluable in the catering process, since they provide a guaranteed finished product at a reduced labour cost. However, they do not have a 'home-baked' quality, and the caterer has minimal control over their presentation and taste. In addition, they are expensive because the manufacturer's production costs and packaging are incorporated into the price. It may be just as, or more, cost-effective to use fresh products.

Role of Pre-prepared Convenience foods

The role of pre-prepared convenience foods in large-scale catering is discussed below using three examples of popular dishes. All three dishes can be produced completely from pre-prepared convenience foods/ingredients. It is not suggested that they should be produced this way, but this method should be compared with using fresh ingredients taking into consideration storage, preparation time and labour costs. It is important to strike a balance between the two extremes in large-scale catering.

Entree

Penne Pasta in a Sauce of Tomato and Basil

    Ingredients

Penne pasta	preparing homemade pasta is very time-consuming when compared with using the convenience alternative, which requires only minimal handling and preparation
Tomatoes	using tinned peeled tomatoes saves preparation time and they can be stored for long periods of time prior to use
Tomato puree	an essential ingredient found in every kitchen today
Onion	can be purchased dried, or in powdered form
Garlic	can be purchased pre-prepared and dried, and can be stored for long periods of time

| Basil | like garlic and onion, it can be purchased chopped and dried |
| Parmesan cheese | available pre-prepared and grated |

Main Course

Individual Steak and Mushroom Pies

Ingredients

Meat	prepared at the required size by your butcher
Onions	can be purchased dried or in powdered form
Mushrooms	sliced and then dried, or tinned or pre-cooked and frozen
Stock	prepared using powdered stock base
Pastry	pre-prepared, rolled and frozen
Egg mix	
Eggs	powdered
Milk	powdered

Dessert

Strawberry Cheesecake

Bought prepared and frozen complete with cream and strawberry garnish.

Summary

The intention in this chapter has been to stress the importance of pre-prepared convenience foods in large-scale catering. Most large-scale caterers use pre-prepared convenience foods in some form on most occasions. In their simplest form, they have become essential ingredients, and in the near future the more complex forms of pre-prepared convenience foods/ingredients will be regarded in this way. In large busy catering operations time is a key factor, and working against the clock can be stressful. The use of pre-prepared convenience foods can reduce time and stress.

Pre-prepared convenience foods may be used without jeopardising the required standard of food production. When considering whether to use pre-prepared convenience foods or fresh products, the following factors should be taken into account:

(a) daily capacity of the available labour force;

(b) budget constraints; and

(c) time constraints.

To maintain a high standard of food production try to modify the use of pre-prepared convenience foods from the basic and complete food groups. Remember, however, that it is better to use some pre-prepared convenience foods to achieve an acceptable finished result, than to use fresh ingredients without the time or staff to prepare them.

Lastly, always try to add a personal touch to each dish: for example, a fresh and well-presented garnish.

4
Hygiene

- Introduction
- Personal Hygiene
- Basic Kitchen Hygiene
- Basic Food Hygiene
- Temperature Guide
- Kitchen Cleaning Program

Introduction

Hygiene is the science concerned with the maintenance of health. It involves maintaining a high standard of cleanliness within the workplace, and includes careful storage, preparation and food service.

Following hygienic procedures will assist in minimum spoilage and contamination of food. Harmful bacteria, such as salmonella, will render food unfit for consumption. If contaminated foods is consumed, it is likely to cause some form of food poisoning with symptoms of nausea, vomiting, stomach cramps and diarrhoea. Attacks can be very severe, especially for the young or the elderly whose immune systems do not function to full capacity.

Hygiene plays a very important role in the catering industry and there are laws and regulations to ensure a national high standard. Caterers are obliged to adhere to the established regulations. A professional, well-managed kitchen/catering operation is easily recognised by its standard of hygiene. Poorly presented staff and unclean equipment are a result of bad management.

Food poisoning is the accumulation of harmful bacteria in certain foodstuffs. Salmonella bacteria, such as that found in chickens, or clostridium welchii contained in the soil, can be transferred to foodstuffs and may ultimately pass into the digestive system/stomach of humans. If products are not refrigerated, cooked or reheated correctly, harmful bacteria will rapidly multiply to a stage where the health of the consumer will be at risk. It is the sole responsibility of the chef that bacteria not be given the opportunity to multiply. Harmful bacteria will multiply at temperatures between 5-60°C.

Always strive to maintain the highest standard of hygiene at both a personal and company level. Kitchen equipment requires thorough and consistent cleaning. This applies even when a particular piece of equipment is not being used regularly. Certain bacteria are airborne and may settle on equipment. Given the required conditions, they will multiply rapidly. As well as eliminating bacteria, constant cleaning will ensure that all equipment operates effectively and to a standard which is consistently hygienic. Regular maintenance will also increase the working life of all kitchen equipment.

Floors should be kept as clean as possible, not only for hygienic reasons but also for the safety of people entering or working in the kitchen. A slippery floor and hot liquids can be a lethal combination in any kitchen. It is the responsibility of the chef or managers on duty to take the necessary precautions to protect the safety of their clients and employees.

Three main areas of hygiene need to be considered:

(a) personal hygiene;

(b) basic kitchen hygiene; and

(c) basic food hygiene.

It is most important that every kitchen devise a daily and weekly cleaning schedule which covers every item of equipment and includes regular cleaning. A weekly cleaning schedule covering most equipment in a modern commercial kitchen appears at the end of this chapter.

Personal Hygiene

1. Always strive to maintain the highest possible standard of personal hygiene. Hair should be well groomed and tied back if long. Fingernails should be cut short and kept clean. Any cuts should be covered with a waterproof dressing.

2. Always maintain uniform/work clothing in a clean state and have clean replacements on hand in case of accidents.

3. If an employee is suffering from any kind of ailment or infection, a person in charge should be informed immediately. Work should be suspended until a doctor has given the sick person authority to re-enter an area of food preparation.

4. Suitable protective gloves should be worn when directly handling foodstuffs.

5. Smoking should not be permitted in any catering establishment.

6. Employees should not handle food after touching their face or hair.

7. Minimum jewellery should be worn in the kitchen or when handling food.

8. Staff should regularly wash their hands thoroughly with soap and hot water.

9. Work clothes should not be worn outside the catering area.

Basic Kitchen Hygiene

1. A regular weekly cleaning program, such as the one set out at the end of this chapter, should be introduced and followed rigorously in every kitchen.

2. Dishwashing machines should operate at a minimum temperature of 77°C.

3. Refrigerators should operate at 4°C or below.

4. Freezers should operate at –18°C or below.

5. Warming counters should operate at a minimum temperature of 65°C.

6. The four items of equipment mentioned above must be fitted with a thermostat to monitor correct temperatures.

7. A hand basin with a good supply of hot water, soap and disposable towels should be available to staff to wash their hands between tasks. This basin should not be used for any other purpose.

8. No animals should be allowed in the food preparation area.

9. Surfaces that come into direct contact with food should be cleaned after use.

10. Chopping boards should be cleaned, particularly following the preparation of raw foods.

11. All food storage containers should be sealed and airtight.

Basic Food Hygiene

1. Foodstuffs should always be checked before use to ensure that they are fit for consumption.

2. Always monitor use by dates on foods and ensure that food stocks are consumed on a rotation basis, otherwise known as 'stock rotation'.

3. Never use crockery that is chipped or cracked because this provides a place for bacteria to breed. Damaged crockery should be wrapped in newspaper before disposal.

4. Only freeze foodstuffs once. Food, when thawed, should either be cooked, refrigerated or discarded.

5. To avoid cross-contamination, which occurs when harmful bacteria cross from one source to another and continue to multiply, staff should always wash their hands between jobs, and knives, chopping boards and benches should be cleaned after each foodstuff is prepared.

6. Raw and cooked foods should be stored separately in the refrigerator and freezer.

7. Raw meats should always be stored below cooked meats or foods.

8. All foodstuffs must be stored at least 75 cm above the ground to allow proper ventilation and easy access. This procedure may also assist in deterring dust mites, cockroaches and vermin from infecting products.

9. All foods should be maintained at the required temperature, whether frozen, refrigerated or in a food warmer etc.

10. Foods cooked but not consumed must be chilled to 4.4°C or less in under 4 hours.

11. Stockpots should never be left cooking overnight, and any stock to be retained for future use should be chilled to 4.4°C or less in under 4 hours.

12. Foods should be kept in the refrigerator and removed only when necessary.

Temperature Guide

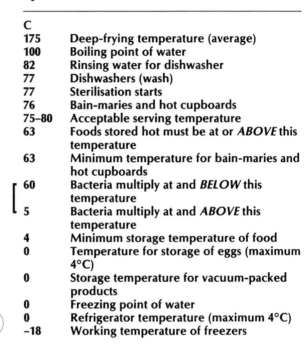

DANGER ZONE FOR BACTERIAL GROWTH

C	
175	Deep-frying temperature (average)
100	Boiling point of water
82	Rinsing water for dishwasher
77	Dishwashers (wash)
77	Sterilisation starts
76	Bain-maries and hot cupboards
75–80	Acceptable serving temperature
63	Foods stored hot must be at or *ABOVE* this temperature
63	Minimum temperature for bain-maries and hot cupboards
60	Bacteria multiply at and *BELOW* this temperature
5	Bacteria multiply at and *ABOVE* this temperature
4	Minimum storage temperature of food
0	Temperature for storage of eggs (maximum 4°C)
0	Storage temperature for vacuum-packed products
0	Freezing point of water
0	Refrigerator temperature (maximum 4°C)
–18	Working temperature of freezers

Kitchen Cleaning Program

Item	When to clean	Method of cleaning
Food preparation surfaces	After each use	1. Prepare solution of hot water, cleaner and sanitiser or according to manufacturer's instructions. 2. Wipe all excess debris directly into a bin using a dry cloth. 3. Wipe surface thoroughly using a cleaning pad if needed. 4. Rinse well with hot water and dry with a clean cloth.
Chopping boards	After each use	1. Prepare solution of hot water, cleaner and sanitiser or according to manufacturer's instructions. 2. Remove any excess debris by wiping with a dry cloth. 3. Using solution, wipe or scrub with a cleaning pad until clean.

Item	When to clean	Method of cleaning
Chopping boards	After each use	4. Rinse thoroughly with warm water. 5. Allow to dry thoroughly before reusing.
Slicers, mixers peelers, etc	After each use	As above except: 1. Soak all removable parts in suitable solution and scrub. 2. Dry thoroughly and double-check that machine has been reassembled correctly.

NOTES:
1. When cleaning slicing machines a blade cover/guard should always be used.
2. Staff members cleaning or operating machinery should be properly trained in operation and cleaning procedures.
3. Disconnect power supply before commencing cleaning program.

Item	When to clean	Method of cleaning
Floors	Daily or as required	1. Prepare solution according to manufacturer's recommendations using a cleaner, degreaser and hot water. 2. Make sure floor has been well swept. 3. Apply solution with a clean mop. 4. Mob floor a second time using hot water. 5. Mop up any excess water with a clean dry mop. 6. All people who have access to the kitchen should be warned that the floor is damp and slippery. 7. Allow to air dry.
Bain-maries and hot cupboards	Daily or as required	1. Remove all debris by using a dry cloth. 2. Make solution of cleaner, sanitiser and hot water according to manufacturer's instructions. 3. Wipe all surfaces inside and out. 4. Rinse thoroughly with clean hot water. 5. Allow to air dry.

NOTE: Wet bain-maries should have water changed daily, and sufficient water should cover the heating elements.

Item	When to clean	Method of cleaning
Sink, washing pots, pans, trays, general kitchen equipment	As required	1. Fill sink with hot water and sufficient detergent following manufacturer's instructions. 2. Fill a second sink with clean hot water. 3. Scrape any loose debris into a bin. 4. Place items into sink containing detergent and scrub with a brush or cleaning pad. 5. Rinse in sink containing clean hot water. 6. Allow to drain and dry with a clean cloth.
Dishwasher	Daily or as required	1. Remove, clean and rinse power rinse arms making sure all nozzles and spray tips are free from any particles that may cause a blockage. 2. Remove and clean scrap tray. 3. Clean pump screens.

Item	When to clean	Method of cleaning
Dishwasher	Daily or as required	4. Check and clean overflows. 5. Scrub curtains. 6. Rinse all the above thoroughly in hot water containing a cleaner and sanitiser or according to manufacturer's instructions. Allow to air dry. 7. Refit and refill machine double-checking that all components are fitted correctly. 8. Chemical solutions used by the dishwasher should be checked regularly.

NOTE: Polish exterior of dishwasher when necessary.

Item	When to clean	Method of cleaning
Microwave oven	As required	1. Prepare solution of cleaner, sanitiser and hot water according to manufacturer's recommendations. 2. Remove all excess debris using a dry cloth. 3. Remove plate and clean thoroughly with solution. 4. Wipe all surfaces inside and out with solution. 5. Rinse well with warm water. 6. Wipe oven and plate dry with a dry cloth.

NOTE: Disconnect power supply before commencing cleaning program.

Item	When to clean	Method of cleaning
Ovens and grills	Weekly or as required	1. Spray warm oven or grill with designated cleaner and leave to stand for 15 minutes or according to manufacturer's instructions. 2. Wearing suitable gloves and goggles, scrub surfaces until all dirt is removed. 3. Rinse thoroughly with hot water. 4. Allow to air dry with doors open.

NOTE: Check that pilot lights have not been extinguished and relight if necessary.

Item	When to clean	Method of cleaning
Boilers and steamers	Weekly or as required	1. Prepare solution of cleaner, sanitiser and hot water according to manufacturer's instructions. 2. Wipe all surfaces inside and out with solution. 3. Rinse with hot water. 4. Allow to air dry.
Drains and gullies	Weekly or as required	1. Prepare a solution with hot water, a degreaser and sanitising agent according to manufacturer's instructions. 2. Lift drain covers out and scrub well with solution making sure any debris caught in grid does not enter the drainage system. 3. Swill out drains with a degreaser. 4. Remember to always replace covers and rinse with hot water.

Item	When to clean	Method of cleaning
Refrigerators	Weekly or as required	1. Prepare solution of hot water and sanitiser or according to manufacturer's instructions. 2. Wipe all surfaces including shelving bars, supports, and plastic door seals. 3. Clean walls thoroughly. 4. Rinse with warm water. 5. Mop floors and dry.

NOTE: It is best to remove all foodstuffs from refrigerator prior to cleaning to avoid contamination. Food should not be left out for too long so make sure enough time is allowed to complete the task after it is begun.

Item	When to clean	Method of cleaning
Extraction hoods and canopies	Weekly or as required	1. Prepare solution of hot water and degreaser or to manufacturer's instructions. 2. Wipe all surfaces with solution. 3. Rinse thoroughly with warm water. 4. Remove filters and soak and scrub thoroughly in solution 5. Rinse well in warm water.

NOTE: Allow to dry and polish if necessary.

Item	When to clean	Method of cleaning
Fat fryers	Weekly or as required	1. Disconnect fryer or turn off the power supply. 2. When oil is cool, drain fat and remove any debris by hand. 3. Make up sufficient cleaning solution containing a degreaser and hot water. 4. Fill fryer with solution, reconnect and boil for 15 minutes without overflowing. 5. Switch off and disconnect the power supply. 6. Scrub all sides with a stiff brush and empty solution from fryer. 7. Rinse fryer with clean warm water. 8. Allow to air dry. 9. Refill with fresh or filtered oil. 10. Clean baskets in the sink using same cleaning solution.

NOTE: Relight pilot light where appropriate.

Item	When to clean	Method of cleaning
Waste bins	Weekly or as required	1. Prepare solution as for manufacturer's instructions. Solution should contain a sanitiser and degreaser in hot water. 2. Wash inside and outside of bins with solution. 3. Rinse with warm water. 4. Allow to air dry.
Walls	Weekly or as required	1. Prepare solution according to manufacturer's instructions using a degreaser, sanitiser and hot water. 2. Use cleaning pad to scrub. 3. Be sure to give extra care to areas between tiles. 4. Rinse with warm water using a clean cloth or mop.

5
Nutrition

- Introduction
- The Five Basic Food Groups
- Fats
- Carbohydrates
- Proteins
- Minerals
- Vitamins
- Liquids
- Fibre
- Nutritional Value and Calorific/Kilojoule Content
  of Foods

Introduction

Nutrition is an aspect of catering which is becoming an increasingly popular source of conversation. Feeding the body the correct chemicals found in food enables it to function effectively. It is imperative that a chef has a sound knowledge of food content and the role it plays in the efficient functioning of the human body.

Nutrients assist the body in many ways. They help to maintain body temperature, aid skin and tissue repair, strengthen bones, and when excess quantities are stored can be utilised as the body requires. A balanced diet which incorporates a sufficient level of nutrients will aid and enhance the body's immune system. Particular attention to the diet during periods of exhaustion will speed the recovery process.

When preparing foods for quick meals, such as those sold at many takeaway outlets, good nutrition can sometimes be overlooked. Those preparing these types of foods should still consider healthy dietary requirements.

Meals served to the same people every day, as in the case of a company canteen, require considerable forethought by the chef in relation to nutrition. The chef is obliged to offer a well-planned and balanced menu that is nutritionally sound.

Nutrients are measured either in kilojoules or calories. The average man will require approximately 12,180 kJ (2900 calories) per day. The average woman will require approximately 8820 kJ (2100 calories) per day.

People's intake of kilojoules differ. Young adolescents require a relatively high intake of kilojoules to assist physical development. Athletes also need extra kilojoules because they are rapidly burning energy. Without the appropriate daily requirements fatigue will result. Alternatively, people who over-consume kilojoules will store the excess energy as fat. A chef has an unstated responsibility to consumers.

A chef's knowledge of the nutrients and kilojoule content required by the body will enable the chef to make informed decisions about an appropriate menu for a particular establishment. A menu prepared for office staff will vary from that prepared for a college canteen, where there is greater physical activity.

Many people are led to believe that pre-prepared or frozen foods have practically no nutritional value. This is untrue. Most manufacturers aim to maintain the nutritional value of the foods they produce. The chef is ultimately responsible for retaining a food's natural goodness.

Foods must therefore be prepared and cooked correctly. Fresh foods that are incorrectly prepared and cooked will lose their nutritional value.

The Five Basic Food Groups

The five basic food groups are:

(a) dairy products — milk, cheese, yoghurt, etc;

(b) meats;

(c) vegetables and fruits;

(d) cereals and breads; and

(e) fats — butter, margarine and oils.

A combined balance of food from each of the five groups will provide the body with its daily nutritional requirements. The goal of a chef is to provide this balance.

Below is a list of essential nutrients, where they are found, and how they assist body functioning.

Fats

These are found in oils, butter, margarine and most other dairy products. Meat also contains certain amounts of fat although it is not always visible. Fats provide heat and energy.

Carbohydrates

These are found in sugar, potatoes, breads, cereals and preserves. Carbohydrates supply half the amount of energy of fats and provide heat and energy.

Proteins

These are found in meats, dairy products, nuts, beans, fish, eggs, cheese and certain fruits and vegetables. Proteins aid the welfare of muscles, skin, the nervous system and blood. They are essential for body growth and development, therefore a high intake is particularly important for young children and pregnant women.

Minerals

Calcium

Calcium is found in milk, tinned fish, cheese and is high in broccoli. It is usually only found in small quantities so it is important to be aware that milk and cheese are the main sources of this mineral. Calcium controls muscle movement and helps to strengthen bones and teeth.

Iron

This is found in oatmeal, eggs, meat (especially kidneys, heart and liver), dried nuts and fruits. Iron helps the blood carry oxygen.

Phosphorus

Phosphorus is found in dairy products, meats, chicken, fish, nuts and eggs. It helps strengthen bones, aids in the release of energy from carbohydrates and stabilises the body's acid base.

Sodium and Potassium

These are found in most natural foods. Most of the body's sodium is provided by added salt (sodium chloride). Sodium and potassium help to control muscle movement, control fluid balance within the body and regulate blood pressure.

Vitamins

Vitamin A

Vitamin A is found in dairy products, liver, rockmelon, and a small proportion is also found in potatoes. Vitamin A assists in the welfare of the eyes, nose, throat, lungs and also aids digestion.

Vitamin B

Vitamin B is found in wholemeal products, nuts, meats, fruit and vegetables, milk, liver and kidneys. Vitamin B aids the nervous system, digestive system and the eyes.

Vitamin C

Vitamin C is found in fruits and raw vegetables especially citrus fruits and capsicum. Vitamin C helps the body fight disease, strengthens veins, helps the body's binding process, and ensures that gums stay healthy and bones remain strong. The plant form of vitamin C is known as beta carotene.

Vitamin D
Vitamin D is found in oily fish, butter, margarine and milk. Most of the body's intake of vitamin D is a chemical reaction to direct sunlight on the skin.

Vitamin E
Vitamin E is found in sunflowers, maize, cottonseed, soya bean oils, egg yolk, tuna, avocado, asparagus and broccoli. It helps to protect fats in cell walls.

Liquids

More than 60% of the body is comprised of water and every food contains a certain amount. The body will usually absorb about 1–1.5 litres per day depending on weather conditions and degrees of physical activity. Fluids are continuously leaving the body, and losses need to be replenished because it is the fluids in the body that maintain its correct temperature.

Fibre

Fibre is essentially a carbohydrate but it holds little energy value. It is the indigestible part of certain fruits and vegetables, cellulose and grain coverings. When consumed, it is only partly digested, the bulk passing through the digestive system helping to stimulate the bowels to function normally. It is now a necessary part of the daily diet.

Nutritional Value and Calorific/Kilojoule Content of Foods

	Nutritional values in		
Food	Calories	Kilojoules	Main nutrients contained in
FRUITS AND VEGETABLES			
Apples	60	252	Carbo, vit C
Apricot	45	189	Carbo, vit A, C, fibre
Asparagus	10	42	Vit C, E
Avocado	210	882	Fat, vit C, A
Aubergine	15	63	Vit C, iron
Banana	85	357	Vit C, fibre
Bean, broad	45	189	Carbo, vit C, A, iron, fibre
Bean, green	35	147	Vit C, A, fibre
Beetroot	30	126	Folate
Broccoli	20	84	Vit C, A, E, fibre, iron
Brussel sprout	36	151	Vit C, A, iron, fibre
Cabbage	25	105	Vit C, A
Capsicum	25	105	Vit C
Carrot	40	168	Vit A, C, fibre
Cauliflower	25	105	Vit C, iron, fibre
Celery	20	84	Vit C
Cherry	50	210	Carbo, vit C, iron

Food	Nutritional values in Calories	Kilojoules	Main nutrients contained in
FRUITS AND VEGETABLES — cont.			
Corn, sweet	90	378	Vit C, B, protein, fibre, carbo
Cucumber	10	42	Vit C
Grapes	40	168	Carbo, fibre, vit C
Grapefruit	25	105	Carbo, vit C
Kiwifruit	50	120	Vit C, iron
Leek	24	101	Vit C, iron, fibre
Lemon	25	105	Vit C
Lettuce	20	84	Vit C
Lime	20	84	Vit C
Lychee	70	294	Carbo, vit C, iron
Mango	65	273	Carbo, vit A, iron
Mushroom	10	42	Vit B, iron, folate, phosphorus
Onion	23	97	Vit C
Orange	25	105	Vit C, carbo, iron
Passionfruit	45	189	Vit C, fibre, carbo
Pea	75	315	Vit C, fibre, iron
Peach	35	147	Vit A, C, carbo
Pear	48	202	Carbo, fibre, vit C
Pineapple	40	168	Vit C, carbo
Plum	40	168	Carbo, vit C, E, fibre
Potato	75	315	Vit C, potassium, carbo, phosphorus
Pumpkin	35	147	Vit A, C, carbo
Radish	10	42	Vit C
Rhubarb	20	84	Calcium, iron
Rockmelon	20	84	Vit C
Shallot	36	151	Vit C, folate
Spinach	28	118	Fibre, iron, vit A, C, E
Squash	7	29	Low carbo
Strawberry	20	84	Vit C, iron
Swede	38	160	Vit C
Sweet potato	140	588	Vit C, E, carbo
Tomato	15	63	Vit A, C
Turnip	23	97	Vit C
Watermelon	25	105	Vit C
Yam	135	567	Vit C, potassium, iron
Zucchini	15	63	Vit C
MEATS			
BEEF			
Fillet	215	903	Protein, fat, iron, vit B, phosphorus
Rump	240	1008	Protein, fat, vit B, iron, phosphorus
Silverside	165	693	Fat, protein, minerals, vitamins, iron
Sirloin	120	504	Fat, protein, vit B, iron
Topside	95	399	Fat, protein, iron, vitamins, minerals
Ribs	225	945	Fat, protein, iron, vitamins
Sausage	260	1092	Fat, protein, iron, phosphorus
VEAL			
Forequarter	130	546	Phosphorus, iron, zinc, protein
Leg	165	693	Phosphorus, iron, zinc

Food	Nutritional values in Calories	Kilojoules	Main nutrients contained in
MEATS — cont.			
VEAL — cont.			
Loin	115	483	Fat, protein, phosphorus, iron
Neck	130	546	Phosphorus, iron, zinc, protein
LAMB			
Chops	430	1806	Fat, protein, iron, phosphorus
Forequarter	310	1302	Fat, protein, iron, phosphorus
Leg	260	1092	Fat, protein, iron, phosphorus
Liver (lamb/beef)	215	903	Fat, vit A
Loin	360	1512	Fat, protein, iron, phosphorus
PORK			
Leg	240	1008	Protein, fat, zinc
Loin	320	1344	Protein, fat, iron, zinc
Rump	180	756	Protein, fat, iron, zinc
Topside	180	756	Protein, fat, iron, zinc
Forequarter	215	903	Fat, phosphorus, iron
Shoulder	240	1008	Fat, phosphorus, iron, magnesium
Bacon (middle)	410	1722	Fat, phosphorus, iron, zinc
Gammon	180	756	Protein, fat, phosphorus
Sausage	310	1302	Fat, protein, iron, phosphorus
POULTRY			
Chicken	230	966	Protein, phosphorus, iron
Eggs	160	672	Phosphorus, iron, fat, vit A, D
Turkey	170	714	Protein, phosphorus, iron, fat
FISH			
Bream	90	378	Protein, calcium, phosphorus
Cod	75	315	Protein, phosphorus
John Dory	83	349	Protein, calcium, phosphorus
Flathead	90	378	Protein, calcium, phosphorus
Flounder	65	273	Protein, calcium, phosphorus
Gemfish	95	399	Protein, calcium, phosphorus
Herring	230	966	Fat, protein, phosphorus
Jewfish	90	378	Protein, calcium, phosphorus
Leatherjacket	90	378	Protein, calcium, phosphorus
Orange Roughie	90	378	Protein, calcium, phosphorus
Perch	85	357	Protein, calcium, phosphorus
Salmon	180	756	Protein, fat, phosphorus
Salmon (canned)	155	651	Protein, fat, sodium, phosphorus
Salmon (smoked)	140	588	Protein, fat, sodium, potassium
Schnapper	90	378	Protein, phosphorus
Sole	80	336	Protein, phosphorus
Trout	135	567	Protein, fat, phosphorus
Tuna	135	567	Protein, fat, phosphorus
Tuna (canned)	110	462	Protein, fat, phosphorus
Whiting	95	399	Protein, phosphorus, sodium

Food	Nutritional values in		Main nutrients contained in
	Calories	*Kilojoules*	
SHELLFISH AND SEAFOOD			
Balmain bugs	120	504	Protein, fat, phosphorus
Crab	125	525	Protein, fat, phosphorus, sodium
Crayfish	70	294	Protein, calcium, phosphorus
Lobster	120	504	Protein, fat, phosphorus
Mussels	90	378	Protein, fat, phosphorus, iron, zinc
Octopus	70	294	Protein
Oysters	50	210	Protein, sodium, calcium, phosphorus
Prawns	110	462	Protein, fat, sodium, calcium, phosphorus
Scallop	110	462	Protein, sodium, potassium, phosphorus
Squid	85	357	Protein, phosphorus

NOTES
1. Vitamin A in plants is known as beta carotene.
2. All calorific values are approximate
3. All calorific values are based on 100 g serves.

6

Ordering of Foodstuffs

- ■ *Daily Record of Orders*
- ■ *Recommended Portion Sizes and Bulk Ordering Quantities*

Ordering the food is an important aspect of a catering operation. To be effective, a workable system is required. This often develops from a period of trial and error. Once installed, however, a system will prove to be invaluable.

A caterer dreads the thought of not having enough provisions, particularly if menus are altered at the last minute and no suitable alternative is available. Equally distressing is an over-supply of provisions that cannot be utilised, especially perishable goods with a limited shelf life.

It is wise to keep accurate records of all foodstuffs at the time of ordering. This will help build an accurate record of what has been ordered and will be an excellent reference when decisions are being made about what quantities to order in the future. To assist in the ordering procedure, a table of recommended portion sizes for meats, fish, fruits, vegetables and cheeses has been included in this chapter. Also included is a prepared ordering sheet (complete with a prepared vegetable order as an example) which can be copied and used as required. It is recommended that different sheets be used for each separate supplier, for example fruit and vegetables, meats and dry goods. The quantity and dates should be recorded whenever an order is placed. This will enable a check to be made if an order is incorrect at the time of delivery.

Lastly, always check that a delivery contains the precise amount and weight requested. Also, ensure that the product is of the expected quality. If a product is not satisfactory, do not hesitate to send it back to the supplier with a request for a prompt replacement. Remember, suppliers need your business, and they will go to great lengths to maintain your custom, particularly when bulk orders are involved. Be sure to compare the prices of different suppliers before making a commitment to purchase. A supplier will often be happy to reduce his or her prices to match those of another supplier if it means gaining a sale.

Daily Record of Orders

Supplier: Evans Fruit and Vegetables **Contact:** Jim Evans (Proprietor) **Telephone:** 888 8888

Item	Date 25/2																				
Alfalfa	1 kg																				
Apples, cooking	1 kg																				
Apples, green	2 kg																				
Apples, red	2 kg																				
Asparagus (bunch)	8																				
Avocados	6 kg																				
Bananas	2 kg																				
Beans, green	1 kg																				
Broccoli	4 kg																				
Cabbage	2																				
Capsicum, green	1 kg																				
Capsicum, red	1 kg																				
Carrots	6 kg																				
Cauliflower	1																				

Recommended Portion Sizes and Bulk Ordering Quantities

			Covers	
	Portion size	25	50	100
MEATS (uncooked weights)				
BEEF				
Fillet	110 g	2.75 kg	5.5 kg	11 kg
Rump	150 g	3.75 kg	7.5 kg	15 kg
Loin	150 g	3.75 kg	7.5 kg	15 kg
Silverside	100 g	2.5 kg	5 kg	10 kg
Sirloin	120 g	3 kg	6 kg	12 kg
Topside	100 g	2.5 kg	5 kg	10 kg
Chuck	140 g	3.5 kg	7 kg	14 kg
Ribs	150 g	3.75 kg	7.5 kg	15 kg
Mince	110 g	2.75 kg	5.5 kg	11 kg
Oxtail	250 g	6.25 kg	12.5 kg	25 kg
Kidney	90 g	2.25 kg	4.5 kg	9 kg
Liver	110 g	2.75 kg	5.5 kg	11 kg
Sausages	100 g	2.5 kg	5 kg	10 kg
Bones (for stock)	2 kg will yield 4 L of stock which is enough for 60 servings of a beef-based sauce			
VEAL				
Fillet	110 g	2.75 kg	5.5 kg	11 kg
Leg	110 g	2.75 kg	5.5 kg	11 kg
Loin	120 g	3 kg	6 kg	12 kg
Forequarter	120 g	3 kg	6 kg	12 kg
Shoulder	110 g	2.75 kg	5.5 kg	11 kg
Knuckle	120 g	3 kg	6 kg	12 kg
LAMB				
Fillet	100 g	2.5 kg	5 kg	10 kg
Leg	120 g	3 kg	6 kg	12 kg
Chump	140 g	3.5 kg	7 kg	14 kg
Loin	110 g	2.75 kg	5.5 kg	11 kg
Shoulder	110 g	2.75 kg	5.5 kg	11 kg
Rack and cutlets	2 to 4 cutlets per person approx			
Forequarter	110 g	2.75 kg	5.5 kg	11 kg
Chops	1 to 2 per person depending on size			
Shank	250 g	6.25 kg	12.5 kg	25 kg
Ribs	200 g	5 kg	10 kg	20 kg
Liver	110 g	2.75 kg	5.5 kg	11 kg
Kidneys	90 g	2.25 kg	4.5 kg	9 kg
Sweetbreads	80 g	2 kg	4 kg	8 kg
PORK				
Fillet	110 g	2.75 kg	5.5 kg	11 kg
Leg	100 g	2.5 kg	5 kg	10 kg
Loin	140 g	3.5 kg	7 kg	14 kg
Rump	140 g	3.5 kg	7 kg	14 kg
Forequarter	140 g	3.5 kg	7 kg	14 kg
Shoulder	120 g	3 kg	6 kg	12 kg

	Portion size	25	Covers 50	100

PORK — cont.

	Portion size	25	50	100
Chop	1 to 2 per portion depending on size			
Ribs	150 g	3.75 kg	7.5 kg	15 kg
Ham steak	100 g	2.5 kg	5 kg	10 kg
Back bacon	50 g	1.25 kg	2.5 kg	5 kg
Streaky bacon	50 g	1.25 kg	2.5 kg	5 kg
Sausages	100 g	2.5 kg	5 kg	10 kg

POULTRY

Chicken	One 1–1.5 kg chicken will yield 4 portions
Turkey	One 9–10 kg turkey will yield 50 portions
Duck	One 1–1.5 kg duck will yield 2 to 4 portions

NOTE: When serving poultry free of bone and skin we recommend a portion size of approx 70 g.

Breast	Allow 1 per portion
Thigh	Allow 1 to 2 per portion depending on size
Drumsticks	Allow 2 per portion
Wing tips	Allow 6 to 8 per portion
Bones (for stock)	6 kg to make 16 L of stock (50 soup serves)
	1 kg to make 3 L of stock (50 sauce serves)

COOKED AND CURED MEATS

	Portion size	25	50	100
Black pudding	80 g	2 kg	4 kg	8 kg
Bloodwurst	80 g	2 kg	4 kg	8 kg
Bologna	40 g	1 kg	2 kg	4 kg
Brawn	50 g	1.25 kg	2.5 kg	5 kg
Cabanossi	40 g	1 kg	2 kg	4 kg
Chicken roll	40 g	1 kg	2 kg	4 kg
Corned beef	70 g	1.75 kg	3.5 kg	7 kg
Devon	40 g	1 kg	2 kg	4 kg
Frankfurt	100 g	2.5 kg	5 kg	10 kg
Frankfurt	50 g (hot dog)	1.25 kg	2.5 kg	5 kg
Garlic sausage	60 g	1.5 kg	3 kg	6 kg
Ham	60 g	1.5 kg	3 kg	6 kg
Liverwurst	35 g	875 g	1.75 kg	3.5 kg
Kielbasa	40 g	1 kg	2 kg	4 kg
Mortadella	40 g	1 kg	2 kg	4 kg
Pastrami	35 g	875 g	1.75 kg	3.5 kg
Paté	35 g	875 g	1.75 kg	3.5 kg
Pies	1 per portion			
Salami	35 g	875 g	1.75 kg	3.5 kg
Saveloy	100 g	2.5 kg	5 kg	10 kg
Smoked beef	60 g	1.5 kg	3 kg	6 kg
Tongue	60 g	1.5 kg	3 kg	6 kg

FISH

	Portion size	25	50	100
A good approx size portion of fish on or off the bone is	100 g	2.5 kg	5 kg	10 kg
Smoked salmon	50 g	1.25 kg	2.5 kg	5 kg

			Covers	
	Portion size	25	50	100
FISH — cont.				
Tinned fish	70 g	1.75 kg	3.5 kg	7 kg
Bones (for stock)	6 kg to make 16 L of stock (50 soup serves)			
	1 kg to make 3 L of stock (50 sauce serves)			
SHELLFISH				
Calamari	100 g	2.5 kg	5 kg	10 kg
Crab	50–100 g per serve			
Lobster	50–100 g			
Mussels	120 g half shell	3 kg	6 kg	12 kg
Octopus	100 g	2.5 kg	5 kg	10 kg
Oyster	6 to 12 per serve			
Prawns	110 g	2.75 kg	5.5 kg	11 kg
Scallops	80 g	2 kg	4 kg	8 kg
Scampi	100 g	2.5 kg	5 kg	10 kg
VEGETABLES				
Alfalfa	2 g	50 g	100 g	200 g
Asparagus	60 g	1.5 kg	3 kg	6 kg
Aubergine	80 g	2 kg	4 kg	8 kg
Bamboo shoot	40 g	1 kg	2 kg	4 kg
Bean, broad	60 g	1.5 kg	3 kg	6 kg
Bean, French	60 g	1.5 kg	3 kg	6 kg
Bean, green	60 g	1.5 kg	3 kg	6 kg
Bean, runner	60 g	1.5 kg	3 kg	6 kg
Bean, snake	60 g	1.5 kg	3 kg	6 kg
Bean sprouts	60 g	1.5 kg	3 kg	6 kg
Beetroot	35 g	875 g	1.75 kg	3.5 kg
Broccoli	70 g	1.75 kg	3.5 kg	7 kg
Brussels sprout	70 g	1.75 kg	3.5 kg	7 kg
Cabbage	60 g	1.5 kg	3 kg	6 kg
Capsicum	20 g	500 g	1 kg	2 kg
Carrot	60 g	1.5 kg	3 kg	6 kg
Cauliflower	70 g	1.75 kg	3.5 kg	7 kg
Celery	40 g	1 kg	2 kg	4 kg
Corn, cob	Usually one 1 portion, half if very large.			
Corn, niblets	40 g	1 kg	2 kg	4 kg
Cucumber	30 g	750 g	1.5 kg	3 kg
Endive	60 g	1.5 kg	3 kg	6 kg
Leek	60 g	1.5 kg	3 kg	6 kg
Lettuce	1 and a half average-sized iceberg lettuces for 25 serves			
Mushroom	40 g	1 kg	2 kg	4 kg
Onion	40 g	1 kg	2 kg	4 kg
Parsnip	60 g	1.5 kg	3 kg	6 kg
Peas	50 g	1.25 kg	2.5 kg	5 kg
Potato	150 g	3.75 kg	7.5 kg	15 kg
Potato, sweet	70 g	1.75 kg	3.5 kg	7 kg
Pumpkin	60 g	1.5 kg	3 kg	6 kg
Radish	30 g	750 g	1.5 kg	3 kg

	Portion size	Covers 25	50	100
VEGETABLES — cont.				
Shallot	30 g	750 g	1.5 kg	3 kg
Snow peas	50 g	1.25 kg	2.5 kg	5 kg
Spinach	60 g	1.5 kg	3 kg	6 kg
Squash	60 g	1.5 kg	3 kg	6 kg
Turnip	60 g	1.5 kg	3 kg	6 kg
Water chestnut	40 g	1 kg	2 kg	4 kg
Yam	70 g	1.75 kg	3.5 kg	7 kg
Zucchini	60 g	1.5 kg	3 kg	6 kg
FRUITS				
Apple	120 g	3 kg	6 kg	12 kg
Apricot	100 g	2.5 kg	5 kg	10 kg
Avocado	100 g	2.5 kg	5 kg	10 kg
Banana	100 g	2.5 kg	5 kg	10 kg
Blackberries	90 g	2.25 kg	4.5 kg	9 kg
Blueberries	90 g	2.25 kg	4.5 kg	9 kg
Cherries	70 g	1.75 kg	3.5 kg	7 kg
Cranberries	80 g	2 kg	4 kg	8 kg
Currants, black	90 g	2.25 kg	4.5 kg	9 kg
Currants, red	90 g	2.25 kg	4.5 kg	9 kg
Dates	40 g	1 kg	2 kg	4 kg
Gooseberries	90 g	2.25 kg	4.5 kg	9 kg
Grapes	90 g	2.25 kg	4.5 kg	9 kg
Grapefruit	usually half per portion			
Kiwifruit	90 g	2.25 kg	4.5 kg	9 kg
Lemon	1 lemon will yield approx 13–14 slices for garnish			
		2	4	8
Lime	1 lime will yield approx 9–12 slices for garnish			
		3	6	12
Lychee	80 g	2 kg	4 kg	8 kg
Mandarin	usually 1 per portion			
Mango	usually half per portion			
Melon	110 g	2.75 kg	5.5 kg	11 kg
Nectarine	90 g	2.25 kg	4.5 kg	9 kg
Orange	usually 1 per portion			
Passionfruit	usually 1 per portion or 25–30 g pulp as accompaniment			
Paw Paw	90 g		2.25 kg	4.5 kg	9 kg
Peach	usually 1 per portion			
Pear	usually 1 per portion			
Pineapple	80 g	2 kg	4 kg	8 kg
Plum	90 g	2.25 kg	4.5 kg	9 kg
Raspberries	80 g	2 kg	4 kg	8 kg
Starfruit	90 g	2.25 kg	4.5 kg	9 kg
Strawberry	90 g	2.25 kg	4.5 kg	9 kg
Tomato, in salads	half			
Tomato, baked	half to 1			
Tomato, stuffed	1			
	1 tomato will yield 8–10 wedges for garnish			

	Portion size	Covers		
		25	50	100
CHEESES				
Brie	25 g	625 g	1.25 kg	2.5 kg
Caerphilly	20 g	500 g	1 kg	2 kg
Camembert	25 g	625 g	1.25 kg	2.5 kg
Cheddar	30 g	750 g	1.5 kg	3 kg
Cottage cheese	20 g	500 g	1 kg	2 kg
Cream cheese	20 g	500 g	1 kg	2 kg
Danish blue	25 g	625 g	1.25 kg	2.5 kg
Double Gloucester	25 g	625 g	1.25 kg	2.5 kg
Edam	25 g	625 g	1.25 kg	2.5 kg
Emmental	25 g	625 g	1.25 kg	2.5 kg
Fetta	20 g	500 g	1 kg	2 kg
Gorgonzola	25 g	625 g	1.25 kg	2.5 kg
Gouda	20 g	500 g	1 kg	2 kg
Gruyere	25 g	625 g	1.25 kg	2.5 kg
Jarlsberg	25 g	625 g	1.25 kg	2.5 kg
Red Leicester	25 g	625 g	1.25 kg	2.5 kg
Mascarpone	15 g	375 g	750 g	1.5 kg
Mozzarella	20 g	500 g	1 kg	2 kg
Parmesan	10 g	250 g	500 g	1 kg
Port Salut	20 g	500 g	1 kg	2 kg
Provolone	20 g	500 g	1 kg	2 kg
Ricotta	20 g	500 g	1 kg	2 kg
Roquefort	20 g	500 g	1 kg	2 kg
Stilton	25 g	625 g	1.25 kg	2.5 kg
Wensleydale	20 g	500 g	1 kg	2 kg

7
Menu Planning

Introduction

Professional menu planning plays a vital role in large-scale catering. Many catering operations are providing for regular, dependent customers, so it is imperative that well-balanced menus, which are appetising, nutritious and appropriate for the needs of customers, are provided.

Logically, menus must be prepared and produced within the company's budget. This chapter will cover the necessary criteria for effective menu planning.

Pre-planning of Menus

Menus should be created well in advance to allow enough time for the chef or manager to organise the purchase and delivery of foodstuffs. Always keep old menus for reference to prevent repetition. Planning in advance also allows available stock to be monitored so that it can be used before its expiry date.

Pre-planning of menus also assists in the preparation of staff rosters and in the efficient and cost-effective use of equipment. Special nutritional requirements need to be considered for some operations, for example, nursing homes and hospitals, where patients are dependent on the caterer's professional understanding of their dietary needs, so again pre-planning is essential.

Ideally, a menu should be planned at least one week in advance and it should cover one full week of meals. The adoption of a cycle menu which repeats every four, six or eight weeks is a widely accepted planning system. It minimises repetition, assists in staff utilisation and is cost-effective in the long run. Cycle menus will be discussed in greater detail later in this chapter.

Nutritional Requirements

Nutrition plays a very important role in menu planning. Meals must meet certain requirements: for example, food should not be overcooked, and good quality foodstuffs containing nutrients which provide energy, promote growth and repair body tissue should be used. Essential nutrients are:

(a) fats;

(b) carbohydrates;

(c) proteins;

(d) calcium;

(e) iron;

(f) vitamins;

(g) liquids; and

(h) fibre.

These are discussed in detail in Chapter 5.

The following factors need to be considered in the preparation of a nutritious menu:

(a) age of consumer;

(b) sex of consumer;

(c) workload of consumer; and

(d) climate. In cold weather extra energy is required to provide increased body warmth. This is obtained from foods containing a high level of fats and carbohydrates.

Large-scale catering is most commonly found in:

(a) educational institutions;

(b) health-care facilities; and

(c) business and industrial establishments.

Nutrition is particularly important for (a) and (b). Below is an outline of appropriate menu planning for each of the areas listed above.

(a) Educational Institutions

Food for educational institutions, including schools, colleges and universities, needs to be provided for large numbers of students at specific times of the day. Meals will be consumed by children, teenagers and adults and for students living on university campuses. Care must be taken to provide a nutritionally well-balanced selection of meals. Religious and personal preferences must also be respected. Vegetarian meals should be available.

(b) Health-care Facilities

Catering for health-care facilities, including public and private hospitals and nursing homes, is similar to that for educational institutions in that it is prepared in bulk and is provided at regular intervals. Food for the elderly and the sick requires well-balanced nutritional content essential for their well-being and/or speedy recovery, and there is a high demand for specialised diets. Budget restrictions must also be taken into account when pre-planning menus.

(c) Business and Industrial Establishments

Examples of these establishments are staff canteens and sports centres. Nutrition is not as important in these areas as in the areas discussed above, but it is important to provide a varied menu which allows consumers to choose the nutritional value of their meal.

Pleasing the Customer

Planning a menu and ordering and preparing the food does not guarantee the success of the meal, however. Customer satisfaction is dependent on a few further factors:

Customer Expectation

The customer's expectation must always be met. This means that the quality of the meal provided must be constant. Once customers have experienced a certain standard of food, they will expect this minimum quality of service every time. Portions and standards of service must be kept constant, and if they are increased, or standards of service improved, those increases or improvements must be maintained in the future.

Tried and Tested Dishes

Menus should include dishes that have been tried and tested, but new dishes should also be introduced to gauge their popularity. Try to provide a varied menu and avoid repetition of the same dish. A selection of dishes should be provided to cater for individual preferences: for example, vegetarian, low fat and cholesterol-free dishes.

Texture and Colour

Texture and colour are important in menu planning. Too much of any one texture or colour should be avoided because it will detract from the appearance and taste of the dish.

Flavour and Presentation

Flavour and presentation go hand in hand. Avoid combining strongly flavoured foods at any one service time. Also, be careful not to add too much salt. This can be added by consumers at their discretion. Aim to create a flavour which will appeal to a majority of consumers.

Garnishing

See Chapter 10.

Value for Money

It is important to provide value for money. Customers should complete their meals believing they have paid a fair price for the quality and quantity of the dish provided.

Taking into account budget restrictions, customer satisfaction should be the top priority of the chef and/or management when allocating available finances.

Staff and Equipment

The number and skill of the staff of a catering operation is important in the menu planning process. It is essential that a balance between the difficulty of service and the rostered staff be achieved — the intended standard of food should not be thwarted by poor staff organisation. Keep in mind that although it is cost-effective to limit staff numbers, increasing workloads will affect staff morale and capacity, and food may be poorly prepared or very late in reaching the customer, resulting in dissatisfaction and possible loss of patronage.

Staff should be kept informed about any new dishes and given information about the required preparation time. It is unsatisfactory to attempt to prepare a good Irish Stew, for example, in 30 minutes. On the other hand, if a meal is quick and easy to prepare, but the staff are not informed of this, they may be standing about with nothing to do.

The head chef, manager and second chef should discuss a menu before it is prepared to avoid possible confrontation during preparation time.

Equipment should not be overloaded so that it is prevented from operating to its maximum potential. For example, overuse of fryers will result in temperature loss and poor food quality.

Financial Considerations

Every large-scale catering operation is run on a budget. Some work to a weekly budget and others budget monthly. Certain operations require only a return for their stock, while others need enough income to cover labour costs, equipment repairs, etc. All catering operations aim to make a profit, however.

It is possible to achieve a professional standard of catering within a limited budget. The following suggestions are applicable to catering operations restricted to a tight budget:

1. Where possible, use a tried recipe that has been put on to a standard recipe card, being careful to watch out for ingredients which fluctuate in price.

2. Record the number of dishes produced and sold to gauge the amount of waste, and adjust the menu if necessary.

3. Monitor hired labour. If an operation is understaffed and the pre-planned menu cycle cannot be adhered to, temporary replacement dishes may not be cost-effective.

4. Aim to have over only a few portions of each prepared dish. These are suitable for staff meals.

5. Portion control must be agreed upon and strictly adhered to by all staff.

6. Use foods which are in season and/or when available at attractive prices. Use a supplier who will give information about price increases or reductions.

7. Keep an accurate record of stock rotation to avoid last-minute small orders which cannot be purchased at the discount rates applicable to bulk purchases.

Waste

There are four common areas of waste in large-scale catering operations:

   (a) *preparation of food:* this includes the peeling, coring, deboning, filleting and trimming fat from meat, fish, fruit and vegetables;

   (b) *cooking of food:* food with a high fat content, especially red meat, will reduce in weight as the fat breaks down;

   (c) *overproduction of food:* perishable foods cannot be reused and have to be discarded; and

   (d) *plate waste:* the food left by the consumer of the meal. This is a direct result of poor quality food or over-generous portion sizes.

Minimising Waste

The following methods of food ordering and preparation will minimise waste and so increase the profit margin of a catering operation.

1. Allow for a weight loss of 5% (approx) on fruit and vegetables and up to 10% (approx) on meats, especially if deboning is necessary.

NOTE: All vegetable and meat scraps should be used to produce stock which will save having to buy extra powdered stock bases.

2. Try not to use excessive heat when cooking, especially for red meat, because this increases shrinkage. Also, allow meat to rest for 5–10 minutes after cooking and before carving. This allows the meat's connective tissues to relax, which makes carving easier and the desired portions easier to obtain.

3. Keep a week's record of dish numbers provided and consumed, and gradually cut down dishes over-produced to find an accurate production figure. See the production and sales comparison sheet on p 51.

4. Careful ordering, customer counts and checking previous production and sales figures will keep overproduction of food to a minimum.

5. Count the returned plates and note the contents not consumed. This will indicate the popularity of the food and the most popular portion size. Keep this in mind for future menu planning.

Food Costing

It is important for caterers to know the cost of producing a dish because:

1. They have to work within budget restrictions.
2. It is useful to know whether individual dishes come within budget requirements.
3. It is important to know whether individual dishes make a reasonable profit and give customers value for money.
4. It is an indication of current trends and relevant costs.

If profit and loss margins are left unchecked, ineffective management and loss of control will result. To achieve profit targets, production and sales costs must be able to be calculated. A sample menu/recipe costing sheet has been provided in this chapter to help with these calculations. It is ideal for costing new dishes or for costing established dishes which have never been costed. A method of calculation to determine cost and sale prices is also given.

The example given is French Onion Soup. First, list the foodstuffs required for preparation. In the example, ingredients have been ordered for at least 25 portions, each a 250 ml serve. Slightly more than is required has been ordered to allow for a small amount of wastage in preparation and cooking and at time of service.

When a dish is being costed using the menu/recipe costing sheet (see p 48), it is important to record every ingredient, even seasonings. The name of the dish should be completed and the number of servings required; also record the date.

It is important to list each ingredient and the quantity purchased because it is the only way of achieving an accurate costing figure. All invoices from suppliers should be kept and used when calculating the cost of ingredients. Calculate the cost of individual ingredients and then add them together to give the total food cost. Divide this figure by the number of portions able to be served. In the example given, the total food cost needs to be divided by 25:

$$\frac{\text{Total food cost}}{\text{Number of portions}} = \text{Cost per serve}$$

$$\frac{\$7.38}{25} = 30 \text{ cents}$$

To calculate the selling price (that is the charge necessary to recover food costs and overhead charges), the gross profit percentage must be calculated. The gross profit figure for a successful dish generally covers costs and net profit. In the example given, the figure of 60% gross profit is being used. The equation for the required selling price is:

$$\frac{\text{Food cost} \times 100}{100\% - 60\%} = \frac{\text{Sales price}}{\text{per serve}}$$

The equation required to calculate the selling price for a portion of the example being used, French Onion Soup, is:

$$\frac{\text{Food cost per serve @ 30 cents} \times 100}{40} = 75 \text{ cents per serve}$$

The charge for each 250 ml bowl of French Onion Soup therefore needs to be 75 cents to meet budget requirements. Sometimes only food costs need to be recovered; other times profit percentages need to be calculated. By using the above formulas, production costs and sales prices can be calculated and menus can be confidently planned. When costings have been done, they should be transferred to a standard recipe card for the required production amounts, that is for 25, 50, 100, etc portions. A sample standard recipe card is shown on p 49. A production and sales comparison sheet is also provided: see p 51.

Portion Control

Portion control is defined as the serving of a controlled and pre-designated portion size at a certain food cost. Food costing can be accurate to the last cent, but if it is not followed up by accurate portion sizes, it becomes futile. If portion sizes are too small, there will not be value for money and customers may become resentful, sales may drop and wastage occur. If portion sizes are too large and food runs out before service is completed, customers will be dissatisfied, which may result in possible loss of sales, money and professional reputation.

For instance, using our costing for French Onion Soup, if over-generous portions are served, say 300 ml instead of the planned 250 ml serve, at 75 cents per serve, only 23 portions would be able to be served. Two customers would be left unsatisfied and $1.50 would be lost in revenue. If this is multiplied by a monthly amount, the numbers of unhappy customers and lost revenue start to become worrying. The chef will be forced to increase the ingredients required, causing a corresponding increase in cost.

Therefore portion control is extremely important when menu planning and costing is being done. Once portion sizes have been agreed upon by management, they must be adhered to by all staff, and supervision in this area is most important.

Equipment, such as scales, standard cups, glasses, soup bowls, pre-graded ladles, serving implements, flan and baking trays, and slicing machines help to control and implement portion sizes and portion control.

Planning a Healthy Menu

Nutritional requirements have been discussed earlier in this chapter and in Chapter 5 and these should be taken into account when preparing a healthy menu. A healthy menu is one which provides meals which are nutritionally sound and which contain foods from the major food groups. Meals should be balanced so that not too much sugary or fatty food is provided. For further information, see Chapter 5.

Nutritional requirements differ immensely, but, as caterers, it is important to be aware of healthy eating trends. It is now generally believed that a diet of lighter food, that is food with less butter, animal fats, polyunsaturated fats, oils, processed sugars and proteins such as are found in red meat, cheese and dairy produce, is better for continued health and well-being.

A reduction in the above foods should be offset against an increase in wholemeal breads and cereals, for example, wholemeal pasta and brown rice, and a higher intake of fresh fruit and vegetables, lentils and pulses. These foods are low in fat and do not contain large amounts of processed sugar. They also provide good quantities of fibre and are rich in essential vitamins and minerals.

By following the above suggestions, nutritionally sound and well-balanced meals which provide the appropriate energy/kilojoule intake can be provided. Healthy meals will also help avoid obesity, increased blood pressure, high cholesterol levels and other conditions common to people living a busy and often stressful lifestyle.

Recommended Food Intake

Food intake should consist of:

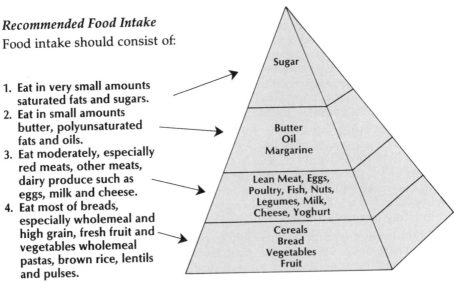

1. Eat in very small amounts saturated fats and sugars.
2. Eat in small amounts butter, polyunsaturated fats and oils.
3. Eat moderately, especially red meats, other meats, dairy produce such as eggs, milk and cheese.
4. Eat most of breads, especially wholemeal and high grain, fresh fruit and vegetables wholemeal pastas, brown rice, lentils and pulses.

Source: Australian Nutritional Foundation.

When planning a healthy menu, keep the following suggestions in mind:

1. Use lean cuts of meat that have been well trimmed.
2. Use minimum amounts of fats and oils when cooking.
3. Use low fat dairy products whenever possible.
4. Keep production of fried foods to a minimum.
5. Remember, people cannot be forced to eat healthy foods but healthy alternatives such as salads, fresh fruit and low fat spreads should be made available.
6. Try not to overcook food, especially vegetables, to minimise nutritional loss.
7. Try to incorporate more vegetable and fish dishes in place of high fat or red meat dishes on your menus.

Cycle Menus

Cycle menus are a very effective method of achieving well-balanced menus without repetition. The cycle menu is a set of weekly menus used, for instance, in a four, six or eight week rotation plan. After each completed sequence, it will generally be found that wastage will reduce, ordering of stock will become more efficient and staff will be more familiar with serving and preparing required dishes. When a cycle menu is being used, it is useful to keep an accurate record of portions and the amount of stock sold to assist in ordering.

Two factors need to be considered when using this scheme:

1. The menu should not be repeated too often, especially in residential establishments.

2. Introduce new dishes gradually and avoid repeating a dish if it is unpopular.

When using pre-prepared convenience foods in a catering operation, try to alter the dish in some way to give it a homemade look and taste, for example sprinkle some extra grated cheese and touch of oregano on top of a pre-bought lasagne. A powdered chicken stock can easily become a creamy chicken and leek velouté to be served with fresh chicken and mushroom pies. Pre-bought and pre-prepared desserts can also be improved with homemade sauces and garnishes. It is a good idea to experiment by trial and error to establish what will and will not work for the catering establishment.

An eight week cycle menu with a simple breakfast, lunch and dinner selection has been provided in Chapter 9.

Planning Sequence for Preparing Menus

When planning a menu, begin with:

    (a) main dishes;

    (b) vegetarian dishes;

    (c) salads; and

    (d) vegetables (and other accompaniments).

Structure the soups, entrees and desserts so that they complement other dishes on the menu. Try not to repeat any one item too often and always specify the availability of sauces and accompaniments where appropriate. Once this is done, check that your menu meets the catering operation's nutritional requirements and that the dishes will appeal to your customers. Ensure that no dish or food type is repeated and that flavours and colours harmonise. Consider how to garnish and present the dishes. Check that all dishes have been costed and that they meet budget requirements. Always prepare menus mindful of the capabilities of available staff and equipment.

Finally, advertise the menus in easy to read locations. Circulate copies around office blocks and on available noticeboards, indicating times of service and relevant prices, including specials. If a dish becomes unavailable, immediately remove it from the menu and offer an appropriate replacement.

MENU/RECIPE COSTING SHEET

DISH: .... DATE: ....

COSTING NUMBER: ....

Ingredients	Quantity	Price	Unit	Cost
			Total Food Cost	$
			Food Cost per Serve	$
			Gross Profit	%
			Food Charge	$

Comments/Special Remarks

STANDARD RECIPE CARD

NAME OF DISH .... REF. SOURCE .... PAGE ....

STYLE OF DISH .... COOKING TEMPERATURE(S) C° .... F° ....

FILE No .... COOKING METHOD ....

NUMBER OF PORTIONS .... PREPARATION TIME .... COOKING TIME ....

PORTION SIZE/COUNT .... TOTAL AMOUNTS ....

DISH COSTING

NAME OF DISH ....

No OF PORTIONS ....

PORTION SIZE ....

PORTION COST $ ....

DATE OF COSTING ....

COMMODITIES

ITEM	SPECIFICATION	No PART/SIZE	REQUIRED WEIGHT g/ml	% WASTE	USABLE WEIGHT	METHOD OF PRODUCTION	UNIT DESCRIPTION	UNIT COST	TOTAL COST $

TOTAL USABLE WEIGHT

LESS COOKED WEIGHT

LOSS IN COOKING

DISH PREPARED BY:

DISH COSTED BY:

TOTAL

STANDARD RECIPE CARD

NAME OF DISH ...French Onion Soup... REF. SOURCE ...Cat... for Lg Numbers...PAGE ..1..

STYLE OF DISH ..Soup/Entree... COOKING TEMPERATURE(S) C° ..N/A.... F° ..N/A.....

FILE No ....1.. Soups............ COOKING METHOD ....Frying/Boiling.................

NUMBER OF PORTIONS ..25......... PREPARATION TIME .15..mins. COOKING TIME .1–1¼ hours..

PORTION SIZE/COUNT ....250..mL...... TOTAL AMOUNTS ..6.25 L minimum required.....

COMMODITIES

ITEM	SPECIFICATION	No PART/SIZE	REQUIRED WEIGHT g/ml			% WASTE	USABLE WEIGHT			METHOD OF PRODUCTION
Butter/Marg			2	5	0		2	5	0	1. Peel onion and garlic and finely slice onion and finely chop garlic
Onions	White	Large	4			10%	3	6	0	2. Melt butter/margarine over a moderate heat in a suitably sized pan
Garlic	Fresh cloves			5	0	5%	4	7	.5	3. Add onions and garlic and fry until brown
Stock Powder	Beef		1	7	5		1	7	5	4. Mix stock powder and hot water thoroughly
Water	Hot		7				7			5. Add stock to cooked onion and garlic
Salt & Pepper	(Add to taste)									6. Bring back to the boil and lower heat
Croutons	Pre-prepared	Small	1	0	0		1	0	0	7. Allow to simmer (covered) gently for 1–1¼ hrs
Parsley	Fresh			7	5	33%		5		8. Remove any scum from surface and season
										9. Serve with a few croutons and a little finely chopped parsley

	TOTAL USABLE WEIGHT	7	L
	LESS COOKED WEIGHT	6.5	L
	LOSS IN COOKING	.5	L

DISH PREPARED BY:

Head Chef

DISH COSTING

NAME OF DISH ..French Onion Soup.............

No OF PORTIONS ...25...............................

PORTION SIZE .....250..mL.........................

PORTION COST $ ....30c..............................

DATE OF COSTING .....15.9.92.....................

UNIT DESCRIP-TION	$ UNIT COST			$ TOTAL COST		
kg	2	0	0	5	0
kg	8	0	3	2	0
kg	1	5	0	0	5	0
kg	9	0	0	1	5	8
L						
kg	1	0	0	1	0
kg	1	0	0	1	0	0
kg	2	0	0	5	0
				7	3	8

DISH COSTED BY: $

Head Chef

TOTAL

PRODUCTION AND SALES COMPARISON SHEET

	Monday		Tuesday		Wednesday		Thursday		Friday		Saturday		Sunday		Special Comments
	P	S	P	S	P	S	P	S	P	S	P	S	P	S	
Soups															
Entrees															
Main Dish															
Main Dish															
Main Dish															
Potato															
Vegetables															
Salads															
Cold Desserts															
Hot Desserts															

8
Banquets and Functions

- ■ *Introduction*
- ■ *The Running Buffet*
- ■ *Standard Table Setting*
- ■ *Planning*
- ■ *Pre-function Three Week Checklist*
- ■ *Banqueting/Function Staff and Equipment Checklist*
- ■ *Banqueting/Function Information and Charge Sheet*
- ■ *Banqueting/Function Equipment Checklist*

Introduction

'Banqueting' is a base term that covers many forms of catering. It often involves cooking for large numbers of people for a single occasion, such as a wedding reception, Christmas lunch or a director's boardroom meal. These types of functions are a regular occurrence in most catering operations and require maximum organisation by all staff involved. They are often scheduled into a chef's duties on top of his or her everyday workload.

To ensure the smooth organisation and execution of the activities involved in preparing a banquet, this chapter provides the following items:

(a) pre-function three week checklist;

(b) staffing and equipment checklist;

(c) function and information cost sheet;

(d) diagrams for the correct setting of a running buffet; and

(e) the correct arrangements for a sit-down place setting.

The most positive feedback comes from the provision of freshly prepared and well presented food and professional unpretentious service.

Always allow for the unexpected, such as unaccounted for guests arriving at the last minute. A few extra portions of food is the only way to prevent one of banqueting's greatest disasters — running out of food!

The disadvantages of catering for banquets revolve around portion control, which consequently makes ordering and budgeting difficult. This may be countered by having more expensive foods served by catering staff who can dish out prearranged portions.

To enhance presentation, have your chef carve the meat in full trade uniform.

The Running Buffet

If the function is for very large numbers, a running buffet can be set up on either side of the room. This will prevent congestion and speed up service, but it will require slightly more planning, equipment and staffing.

Running Buffet

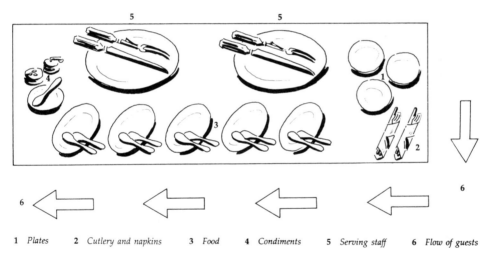

1 *Plates*   2 *Cutlery and napkins*   3 *Food*   4 *Condiments*   5 *Serving staff*   6 *Flow of guests*

The running buffet diagram above works from left to right (from the caterer's point of view). First, it displays a collection of plates, then cutlery, which, for convenience, should be neatly wrapped in a serviette. Bread rolls should appear next — these can be buttered prior to service or butter sachets made available to allow for customer preference. Then follow the food dishes, and the buffet should be completed with a selection of condiments, for example, cranberry sauce, mustard, etc. Serving staff stand behind the table.

To ensure that the left to right flow is maintained, ask the host to shepherd guests to the left-hand side of the buffet to queue and collect plates.

To make the buffet as attractive as possible, avoid food colours clashing, but also avoid a bland monochrome arrangement.

Establish prior to serving time what dishes are to be served by staff and inform them of the required portion sizes. Ensure that staff are aware of the name and ingredients of the dish so that they can answer any inquiries from guests. Assist any disabled guests where necessary.

The fresh bread or rolls should be warmed prior to service — the aroma is guaranteed to whet appetites! If hot food is being provided, plates should also be warmed to keep food warm until consumption.

Encourage guests to return to the buffet for a further helping if they wish. When it is clear that everyone has completed their meal, the table(s) should be cleared and dessert and coffee should be served. Make sure that enough food is reserved in the kitchen to cater for any late arrivals.

Standard Table Setting

The figure below shows the correct plate setting for a fixed course meal. Tables should be laid up correctly before a function commences.

Standard Setting for Three-course/Fixed-course Meal

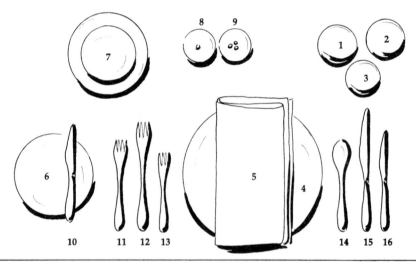

1	Water glass	5	Folded napkin	9	Pepper cruet	13	Dessert fork
2	White wine glass	6	Side plate	10	Bread and butter knife	14	Dessert spoon
3	Red wine glass	7	Butter dish on side plate	11	Entrée fork	15	Main course knife
4	Place mat (optional)	8	Salt cruet	12	Main course fork	16	Entrée knife

Waiting staff should always serve wine to the right-hand side of a guest. Likewise, the collection of empty glasses should always be from the right. There is some disagreement about the correct method of food service. Traditionally, food was served to the left and cleared from the right. Today, both serving and clearing tends to occur from the guest's right-hand side. Most catering operations will have an established system of service and clearing. It is recommended that this system be adhered to and that all staff be informed so that uniform service and clearing is achieved.

Planning

If a meal comprises two or more courses, plan to have entrees/starters and desserts which can be pre-prepared and stored in the refrigerator. This allows more time to concentrate on presentation of the main course.

Remember, do not hesitate to use pre-prepared, pre-packaged food — it saves time, and time control is the key to a banquet's success. Do try to add a creative touch to pre-prepared purchases though.

Never leave anything to the last minute! Plan carefully, and work within the limits of your kitchen, budget restrictions, staff and available time, and the banquet/function will be a success.

Pre-function Three Week Checklist

Three Weeks in Advance

1. Complete the banqueting/function staff and equipment checklist (see p 57) and also the banqueting/function information and charge sheet (see p 58) after liaising with the organiser of the function. Make sure you have all the information required on the sheet. Liaise with staffing agencies to book chefs/waiters/waitresses and any other staff required. When organising waiting staff, allow one waiter/waitress per 10 guests as a guideline.

2. The menu should be agreed upon by yourself and the organiser of the function bearing in mind your ability, budget and any special dietary requirements, for example, religious, health or vegetarian preferences.

3. Work out estimated costs on the banqueting/function information and charge sheet and inform the organiser.

Two Weeks in Advance

1. Order any required liquor/beverages for delivery not less than two days before the function date. A safe estimate when ordering wine is to provide one bottle between two people.

2. Order any china, crockery, linen, etc, by working through your banqueting/function equipment checklist (see p 59). Agree upon a delivery date, ideally the day before the function, to allow for any last minute changes or short or incorrect delivery. Around Christmas and midsummer, it is a good idea to order items one month in advance due to increased demands on suppliers.

One Week in Advance

1. Confirm orders for staff with agencies, and orders for liquor and equipment/crockery, etc.

2. Confirm numbers for function with organiser and time of function in case there have been any changes.

Three Days in Advance

Order any foodstuffs which require prior pre-preparation or cooking, for example, salmons which need to be dressed, hams which need to be cooked and dressed, etc.

Two Days in Advance

Order all other required foodstuffs, and ensure that suppliers can guarantee delivery of all the necessary items.

One Day in Advance

1. Check all foodstuffs for quality and correct quantity and reorder if they do not meet the required standards.

2. Check delivery of any hired goods for quality, breakages in transit and correct quantity.

3. Prepare as much of the menu as possible.

4. Refrigerate white wine and soft drinks if these are being served at the function, and ensure that a sufficient supply of ice is available.

Day of Function

1. Liaise with all staff involved with the function and inform them of all relevant details and their required duties, for example function time, type of service, alcohol, food to be served and any other necessary information.

2. Check tables and buffet table for correct settings.

3. If function involves buffet service, lay out food on the buffet table approximately 20–30 minutes before service begins. If it is a table-served meal, check with kitchen staff that the food will be ready at the designated time.

4. Confirm guest numbers by counting plates used during the meal to help with costing when the function is complete.

BANQUETING/FUNCTION STAFF AND EQUIPMENT CHECKLIST

Function Name: .... Cost/Ref No: .... Date/Time: ....

Location: ....

Liaise with: .... Contact Phone: ....

Theme: .... Cover: ....

Staffing Required:

	No. Required	Shift Times	Booking Confirmed
Chef	....	....	....
Kitchen Hand	....	....	....
Waiter/waitress	....	....	....
Wine waiter/waitress	....	....	....
Maître d'hôtel/Host	....	....	....

Agency: .... Contact Phone: ....

Contact Name: ....

BANQUETING/FUNCTION INFORMATION AND CHARGE SHEET

Cost/Ref No: ....

Function Name: .... Day & Date: ....

Location: .... Date Instructions Received: ....

Client: .... Contact No: ....

Contact Name: .... Cover: ....

Style of Function: .... Theme: ....

Start Time: .... Finish Time: .... Time Food Required: ....

Special Requirements: ....

Menu

Suggested Drinks

Items	Estimated Cost	Actual Cost
Food Cost		
Paper/Disposable Cost		
Liquor/Beverage Cost		
Ice Cost		
Hireage (inc. transport)		
Breakages		
Flowers		
Laundry		
Labour Cost		
Sub-Total		
Extras		
Mark Up		
Total Cost		

BANQUETING/FUNCTION EQUIPMENT CHECKLIST

Cost/Ref No: ....

Function Name: ....

Date & Time: ....

Location: ....

Equipment	Total No. Required	Amount in Stock	Amount Ordered	Ordered From	Completion Check Date
Entree Plate					
Dinner Plate					
Dessert Plate/Bowl					
Soup Dish					
Side Plate					
Salad Bowl					
Tea/Coffee Cup					
Tea/Coffee Saucer					
Coffee/Tea Pot					
Milk Jug					
Sugar Bowl					
Mint Plate					
Butter Dish					
Entree: Fork					
Knife					
Spoon					
Dinner: Knife					

59

Equipment	Total No. Required	Amount in Stock	Amount Ordered	Ordered From	Completion Check Date
Fork					
Spoon					
Dessert: Fork					
Knife					
Spoon					
Sugar Spoon					
Butter Knife					
Chopsticks					
Glasses: Red					
White					
Champagne					
Beer					
Soft Drink/Mineral Water					
Liqueur					
Coffee and Tea making facilities					
Hot Plate for Coffee/food etc					
Tea and Coffee and Condiments					
Cruet Set (salt & pepper)					
Table Cloth					
Napkin (cloth/paper)					
Place Mat					
Coaster					
Ashtray					

Equipment	Total No. Required	Amount in Stock	Amount Ordered	Ordered From	Completion Check Date
Candelabra					
Candle					
Centrepiece/Flower Arrangement					
Platter					
Bread Basket					
Black Pepper Grinder					
Corkscrew					
Serving Utensils					
Tongs					
Chopping Board					
Kitchen Knife					
Apron for Service					
Tea Towel					
Garbage Bag					
Table					
Chair					
Other Items					

9
Cycle Menus

Month 1. Week 1

	Breakfast	Lunch	Dinner
MONDAY	Cereals Orange Juice Poached Eggs Grilled Bacon Toast/Marmalade	Southern Fried Chicken Crispy Cheese Potatoes Greek Salad	Pea and Ham Soup Navarin of Lamb Croquette Potatoes Sautéed Zucchini with Tomato and Basil Chocolate Eclairs

TUESDAY	Cereals
	Grapefruit
	Pork Sausages
	Tomato au Gratin
	Toast/Honey
		Beef Spare Ribs in a
		   Smoky Barbeque Sauce
		Steamed Rice
		Coleslaw Salad
			Chicken and Rice Soup
			Pork Chops with Cider and
			   Cream Sauce
			Parmentier Potatoes
			Roasted Honey Pumpkin
			Minted Fruit Salad

WEDNESDAY	Cereals
	Apricot
	Fried Eggs
	Grilled Bacon
	Rolls
	Red Currant Jam
		Egg and Bacon Quiche
		Mixed Leaf Salad
		Creamy Vinaigrette
		   Dressing
			Potato and Leek Soup
			Chicken Kiev
			Boulanger Potatoes
			Grilled Herb and Cheese
			   Tomatoes
			Peach and Lemon Pie with
			   Whipped Cream

THURSDAY	Cereals
	Fruit Salad
	Savoury Scramble
	Chipolata Sausage
	Tomato
	Croissants
		Italian Meatballs in
		   Tomato, Parmesan and
		   Garlic Sauce
		Tagliatelle Tossed in
		   Butter and Basil
			Creamed Broccoli Soup
			Cottage Pie
			Minted Peas
			Braised Carrots
			Apple and Blackberry
			   Crumble

Month 1. Week 1 — cont.

	Breakfast	Lunch	Dinner
FRIDAY	Cereals Apple Rings Bacon Omelette Fried Potato Brown Rolls Raspberry Jam	Lemon and Dill Stuffed Trout New Potatoes Tossed Green Salad English Mustard Vinaigrette	Tomato and Basil Soup Lamb and Apricot Kebabs Saffron Rice Apple and Sultana Pie Vanilla Custard
SATURDAY	Cereals Mandarin Orange Pancakes Maple Syrup Toast/Jams	Ham, Mushroom and Pineapple French Bread Pizzas Waldorf Salad Sour Cream and Chive Dressing	Chilled Gazpacho Soup English Mixed Grill Lyonnaise Potatoes Lemon Meringue Pie
SUNDAY	Cereals Fried Eggs Grilled Bacon Tomato au Gratin Fried Bread Croissants	Roast Leg Lamb Roast Potatoes Baby Squash Green Beans Lemon and Rosemary Stuffing Mint Sauce	French Onion Soup Veal Parmigiana French Fried Potatoes Braised Mushrooms Banana Cake with Honeyed Cream

Month 1. Week 2

	Breakfast	Lunch	Dinner
MONDAY	Cereals Grapefruit Segments Ham/Tomato Omelette Corn Fritters Rolls Lemon Marmalade	Bacon and Sweetcorn Vol-au-vents Zucchini and Apple Salad with a Lemon Mayo Dressing	Chicken and Coriander Soup Grilled Garlic Steak Jacket Potatoes Topped with Sour Cream and Chives Whole Baby Carrots Lychee and Peach Crumble
TUESDAY	Cereals Orange Juice Poached Eggs Grilled Ham Toast/Raspberry Jam	Stir-fried Chicken with Cashew Nuts and Crisp Vegetables Steamed Rice	Pumpkin and Orange Soup Traditional Lamb and Vegetable Casserole Mashed Potatoes Banana Fritters
WEDNESDAY	Cereals Apple Rings Fried Eggs Grilled Bacon Baked Beans Crumpets	Fettuccine Bolognaise Garlic and Herb Bread Marinated Mushroom Salad	Cream of Asparagus Soup Lamb Cutlets Marinated in Lemon and Rosemary Parisienne Potatoes Apple Sponge with Homemade Custard

Month 1. Week 2 — cont.

	Breakfast	Lunch	Dinner

THURSDAY	Cereals
	Pineapple Rings
	Scrambled Eggs
	Pork Sausages
	Fried Potato
	Crusty Rolls
	Jams
		Almond Crusted
		  Chicken
		Roasted Parsnip Chips
		Potato and Chive Salad
			Celery Soup
			Beef and Ale Pie Topped
			  with Flaky Pastry
			Parsley Potatoes
			Peas à la Français
			Caribbean Rum Sponge

FRIDAY	Cereals
	Fruit Salad
	Boiled Eggs
	Cold Ham
	Corn Fritters
	Toast/Strawberry Jam
		Steamed Spanish Paella
		Tomato and Black Olive
		  Salad
		Cheesy Garlic Bread
			Chunky Vegetable Soup
			New York Style Meatloaf
			  with a Spicy Tomato
			  Sauce
			French Fried Potatoes
			Broccoli Florets
			Lemon Shortbread Biscuits

SATURDAY	Cereals Peaches Waffles Maple Syrup Croissants	Gourmet Burger Sesame Seed Bun Crispy Bacon Swiss Cheese Tomato and Pineapple Deep Fried Potato Skins	Minestrone Soup Chicken Satays Jasmine Rice Tomato, Cucumber and Coriander Salad Tropical Fruit Salad

SUNDAY	Cereals
	Pears
	Fried Eggs
	Grilled Gammon
	Baked Tomato
	Brown Rolls
	Orange Marmalade
		Roast Leg Pork
		Apple Sauce/Crackling
		Fondant Potatoes
		Braised Red Cabbage with
		  Sultanas and Apple
		Pureed Carrots
			White Onion Soup
			Marinated and Grilled
			  Perch
			Hash Browns
			French Beans
			Chocolate Profiteroles

Month 1. Week 3

	Breakfast	Lunch	Dinner

MONDAY	Cereals
	Apple Juice
	Scrambled Eggs au
	  Gratin
	Grilled Ham
	Toast/Jams
		Vegetarian Lasagne
		Crispy Herb Bread
		Cherry Tomato Salad
		  Tossed in Ginger and
		  Garlic Vinaigrette
			Leek and Chive Soup
			Sweet Lamb Curry
			Saffron Rice
			Lemon Blancmange and
			  Honeyed Cream

TUESDAY	Cereals
	Fruit Salad
	Ham and Cheese
	  Croissants
		Spinach and Fetta
		  Cheese Quiche
		Snow Pea and
		  Beansprout Salad
		Fresh Dill and Garlic
		  Dressing
			Mushroom and Garlic Soup
			Grilled Rump Steak with a
			  Pepper Sauce
			Italian Potatoes
			Zucchini Sticks
			Peach Crumble
			Almond Sauce

Month 1. Week 3 — cont.

	Breakfast	Lunch	Dinner
WEDNESDAY	Cereals Grapefruit Tomato Omelette Beef Sausages Rolls Lemon Marmalade	Seafood Vol-au-vents Carrot, Coconut and Sultana Salad	Brown Onion Soup Pork, Apple and Cider Casserole Steamed Acorn Squash Sautéed Potatoes Homemade Scones with Cream and Strawberry Jam
THURSDAY	Cereals Oranges Fried Eggs Grilled Bacon Tomato au Gratin Toast/Redcurrant Jam	Grilled Lamb Cutlets Chasseur Sauce Idaho Potatoes Cauliflower Floret Salad with Mayo and Satay Sauce Dressing	Chinese Noodle Soup Sweet and Sour Pork Steamed Rice Apricot and Cherry Strudel Crème Anglaise
FRIDAY	Cereal Pineapple Segments Poached Eggs Meat Patties Spaghetti in Tomato Sauce Croissants Orange Marmalade	Poached Cod Lemon and Parsley Sauce Buttered New Potatoes Peanut and Coriander Salad	Cream of Cauliflower Soup Greek Moussaka Cucumber and Tomato Salad Steamed Banana Pudding
SATURDAY	Cereal Rock Melon Pancakes Maple Syrup Rolls Jams	Chilli Con Carne Mexican Spiced Rice Sour Cream Guacamole Tortilla Chips	Seafood Chowder Chicken Burgers with Tomato, Avocado and Melted Cheese French Fried Potatoes Crème Caramels
SUNDAY	Cereal Sliced Peaches Grilled Gammon Fried Eggs Baked Tomatoes Toast/Honey	Roast Topside of Beef Roast Potatoes Lemon Carrots Braised Onions Yorkshire Pudding Gravy	Chicken and Mushroom Soup Veal Olives Duchess Potatoes Green Beans with Toasted Almonds Baked Apples with Honey and Sultana Custard

Month 1. Week 4

	Breakfast	Lunch	Dinner
MONDAY	Cereal Apple Rings Parsley Scrambled Fried Potatoes Chipolatas Fried Bread Croissants Raspberry Jam	Fettuccine Carbonara Green Leaf Salad Basil and Peppercorn Dressing	James Island Soup Hawaiian Ham and Pineapple Parmentier Potatoes Asparagus Spears Pear Flan with Whipped Cream

Month 1. Week 4 — cont.

	Breakfast	Lunch	Dinner
TUESDAY	Cereal Pineapple Juice Boiled Eggs Cold Ham Corn Fritters Brown Rolls Orange Marmalade	Salmon and Dill Fish Cakes Deep Fried Potato Curls Niçoise Salad Lemon Vinaigrette	Cream of Carrot Soup Chicken Wings with Texas Barbeque Sauce Corn on the Cob English Apple Pie Chantilly Cream

WEDNESDAY	Cereal
	Stewed Apricots
	Cheese Potatoes
	Spaghetti in Tomato
	  Sauce
	Toast/Jams
		Stuffed Jacket Potatoes
		  with a Creamy Sauce of
		  Leeks, Sweet Corn and
		  Crispy Bacon
		Apple and Celery Salad
			Cream of Sweet Corn Soup
			Beef Satay with Peanut
			  Sauce
			Jasmine Rice
			Creamed Raisin, Almond
			  and Rice Pudding

THURSDAY	Cereal
	Orange Juice
	Waffles
	Maple Syrup
	Croissants
	Jams
		Bacon and Sweet Corn
		  Puffs
		Cheesy Herbed Bread
		Green Leaf Salad
			Pumpkin Soup
			Hearty Irish Stew
			Parsley Potatoes
			Individual Passionfruit
			  Meringues

FRIDAY	Cereal
	Grapefruit Segments
	Ham Omelette
	Fried Potatoes
	Rolls
	Strawberry Jam
		Cod Steaks Deep-fried
		  in Beer Batter
		French Fried Potatoes
		Garden Peas
			Tomato and Chive Soup
			Beef Madras Curry
			Steamed Rice
			Crispy Pappadums
			Sultana Sponge with
			  Golden Syrup

SATURDAY	Cereal
	Oranges
	Fried Eggs
	Grilled Bacon
	Tomatoes au Gratin
	Toast/Lemon
	  Marmalade
		Paprika Chicken
		Provencal Sauce
		Lyonnaise Potatoes
		Cauliflower Polonaise
			Potato and Watercress
			  Soup
			Braised Lamb's Liver and
			  Bacon
			Mashed Potatoes
			Grilled Herbed Tomatoes
			Mixed Fruit Strudel

SUNDAY	Cereal Stewed Apple Poached Eggs Pork Sausages Grilled Ham Croissants Honey	Roast Chicken Sage and Onion Stuffing Roast Potatoes Sautéed Leeks Corn Niblets Gravy Sauce	Cream of Mushroom and Cheddar Soup Seasoned Veal Schnitzel Onion Sauce Spiced Cheese Potatoes Grilled Tomatoes Mixed Melon Salad

Month 2. Week 1

	Breakfast	Lunch	Dinner
MONDAY	Cereals Apple/Pear Salad Scrambled Eggs Meat Patties Brown Rolls Orange Marmalade	Crab and Asparagus Vol-au-vents with Mozzarella Cheese Potato and Shallot Salad Lemon and Chive Dressing	Pumpkin Vichyssoise Steak and Mushroom Pie Sautéed Potatoes Broccoli Florets Walnut and Apple Crumble with Vanilla Ice Cream
TUESDAY	Cereals Grapefruit Cold Ham Boiled Eggs Sliced Cheese Toast/Apricot Jam	Roasted Chicken Pieces Marinated in Soy, Honey and Ginger Apple and Sultana Salad Bound in Light Curry Mayonnaise	Lentil Soup Vegetable Moussaka Croquette Potatoes Sautéed French Beans Peach and Apricot Lattice Pie
WEDNESDAY	Cereals Apricots Waffles Honey Rolls Orange Marmalade	Quiche Lorraine Tomato and Oregano Salad with Thick Creamy Vinaigrette Dressing	Sweet Potato and Chive Soup Veal Cordon Bleu Boulanger Potatoes Steamed Baby Squash Golden Syrup Sponge
THURSDAY	Cereals Chilled Orange Segments Fried Eggs Sausage and Bacon Wrap Toast/Jams	Stir-fried Vegetables with Roasted Cashews and Pine Nuts Italian Style Cauliflower and Caper Salad	Crab Chowder Chicken à la King New Potatoes Tossed in Butter and Shallots Steamed Carrots Apple and Cinnamon Pie
FRIDAY	Cereal Pineapple Rings Poached Eggs Boiled Ham Brown Rolls Lemon Marmalade	Poached Cod with Parsley and Lemon Sauce Parsley Potatoes Green Salad with Chive Dressing	Creamy Tomato Soup Cornish Pasties with a mild Mustard Sauce Sautéed Potatoes Coconut Rice Pudding
SATURDAY	Cereals Orange/Passionfruit Juice Lemon Pancakes Maple Syrup Croissants Jams	Green Thai Chicken Curry Rice Braised in Chicken Stock	James Island Soup Swiss Style Veal Casserole Lyonnaise Potatoes Roasted Parsnips Bread and Butter Pudding

Month 2. Week 1 — cont.

	Breakfast	Lunch	Dinner
SUNDAY	Cereals Fruit Salad Fried Eggs Grilled Bacon Fried Bread Toast/Jam	Roasted Shoulder of Lamb Stuffed with Lemon and Rosemary Onion Gravy Roast Potatoes Braised Zucchini Steamed Spinach	Chunky Celery Soup Pasta Marinara Italian Salad Herb Vinaigrette Apple Fritters Vanilla Custard

Month 2. Week 2

	Breakfast	Lunch	Dinner

MONDAY	Cereals
	Pineapple Juice
	Savoury Scrambled
	  Eggs
	Fruit Loaf
		Pasta Brindisi
		Garlic and Oregano
		  Bread
		Tomato, Basil and Pine
		  Nut Salad
			Pumpkin and Sweet
			  Potato Soup
			Perch Fillets Poached in
			  Court Bouillon with
			  Hollandaise Sauce
			Noisette Potatoes
			Mushrooms Tossed in
			  Garlic and Chives
			Rice Pudding

TUESDAY	Cereals
	Oranges
	Cheese and Ham
	  Toasties
	Lemon Danish
		Stir-fried Beef with
		  Cashew Nuts and
		  Chinese Vegetables
		Steamed Rice
			Vichyssoise Soup
			Chicken and Asparagus
			  with Flaky Pastry
			Almond Potatoes
			Snake Beans
			Steamed Chocolate
			Pudding

WEDNESDAY	Cereals
	Pear and Peach Salad
	Ham Omelette
	Crumpets
		Traditional Italian
		  Lasagne
		Marinated Mushroom
		and Celery Salad
			Cream of Leek Soup
			Tandoori Chicken
			Saffron Rice
			Cucumber and Minted
			  Yoghurt Salad
			Banana Upside Down
			  Cake

THURSDAY	Cereals
	Grapefruit
	Fried Eggs
	Pork Sausages
	Boiled Mushrooms
	Crusty Rolls
	Apricot Jam
		Mexican Tacos with
		  Guacamole
		Sour Cream
		Grated Cheese
		Chilli Sauce
			Mushroom, Bacon and
			  Parsley Soup
			Steak Diane Casserole
			Duchess Potatoes
			Garden Peas
			Chocolate Mousse

Month 2. Week 2 — cont.

	Breakfast	Lunch	Dinner
FRIDAY	Cereals Apples Poached Eggs Tomato au Gratin Toast/Lemon Marmalade	Deep-fried Breaded Goujons of Haddock French Fried Potatoes	Chicken and Sweet Corn Soup Beef Madras Curry Steamed Rice Cauliflower and Broccoli Floret Medley Chocolate Blancmange
SATURDAY	Cereals Sliced Peaches Grilled Gammon Pineapple Fritters Baked Beans Brown Rolls Strawberry Jam	Vegetable Stuffed Baked Capsicum with Creamy Basil Sauce Parmentier Potatoes	Thai Style Soup Sirloin Steak Chasseur Baked Potato with Sour Cream and Chives Potato Salad Rhubarb Crumble with Custard Sauce
SUNDAY	Cereals Fruit Salad Scrambled Eggs Chipolatas Baked Tomato Crumpets	Roast Turkey Chestnut and Onion Stuffing Fondant Potatoes Roasted Onions Lemon Carrots	Mulligatawny Soup Bacon and Spinach Quiche Parisienne Potatoes Marinated Mushroom and Tomato Salad Coconut and Orange Sponge

Month 2. Week 3

	Breakfast	Lunch	Dinner
MONDAY	Cereals Apple and Pear Compote Scrambled Eggs Grilled Bacon Croissant/Toast Jams/Marmalades	Stir Fried Chicken with Cashew Nuts and Snow Peas Jasmine Rice Tomato, Cucumber and Oregano Salad	French Onion Soup Lamb Curry Basmati Rice Batons of Carrot Roast Pumpkin Homemade Anzac Biscuits
TUESDAY	Cereals Plums in Syrup Poached Eggs Sliced Grilled Leg of Ham Bagels/Toast Jams/Marmalade	Texas Style Ribs Cheesy Garlic Bread Tossed Mixed Green Salad English Mustard Vinaigrette	Chicken and Coconut Soup Roast Leg of Pork Sage, Onion and Garlic Stuffing Roast Potatoes and Onions Green Beans Plum Crumble Vanilla Custard
WEDNESDAY	Cereals Freshly Stewed Apple and Quince Fried Eggs Sausage and Bacon Wrap Crusty Rolls Jams/Marmalades	Mexican Chilli Con Carne Corn Chips Guacamole Sour Cream Boiled Rice	Cream of Mushroom Soup Chicken Satays Prawn Rice Tomato, Cucumber and Coriander Salad Apple and Sultana Strudel with Crème Anglaise

Month 2. Week 3 — cont.

	Breakfast	Lunch	Dinner

THURSDAY	Cereals
	Fresh Sliced Melon
	American Style
	  Pancakes with
	  Maple Syrup
	Wholemeal Croissant
	Toast/Jams
		Almond Chicken with
		  Basil Sauce
		Sautéed Parsley Potatoes
		Cauliflower florets
		Baked Cheese and
		  Tomatoes
			Potato and Chive Soup
			Australian Mixed Grill
			Idaho Potatoes
			Pumpkin and Nutmeg
			  Smash
			Banana and Blueberry
			  Lattice Pie with Vanilla Ice
			  Cream

FRIDAY	Cereals
	Peach Slices in Syrup
	Selection of Yoghurts
	Scrambled Spanish
	  Eggs
	Beef Sausages
	Lemon Pastries
	Toast/Jams/
	  Marmalade
		Grilled Cod Marinated
		  in Soy, Lemon, Chilli
		  and Coriander
		French Fries
		Celery, Walnut and
		  Tomato Salad
		Lemon and Chive
		  Dressing
			Sweet Corn and Crab
			  Chowder
			Curry Crusted Chicken
			  Breast with Lemon
			  Minted Yoghurt
			Saffron Rice
			Stir-fried Zucchini
			Rhubarb Crumble
			Brandy Custard

SATURDAY	Cereals
	Mandarin Segments
	Poached Eggs
	Grilled Gammon
	Baked Beans
	Brown Rolls
	Toast/Jams/
	  Marmalades
		Pitta Bread Pizzas
		Tossed Green Leaf Salad
		Oregano and Basil
		  Dressing
			Cream of Celery Soup
			Sirloin Steak Chasseur
			Italian Potatoes
			Sautéed Broccoli
			Honey Glazed Carrots
			Fruit and Cream Meringues

SUNDAY	Cereals
	Fresh Orange Juice
	Soft Boiled Eggs
	Blueberry Pancakes
	Maple Syrup
	Croissant
	Jams/Honey
		Cream of Pumpkin and
		  Nutmeg Soup
		Roast Leg of Lamb
		Rosemary and Lemon
		  Stuffing
		Steamed Broccoli and
		  Green Beans
		Roasted Potatoes
			Cream of Vegetable Soup
			Braised Steak in Ale and
			  Onion
			Lyonnaise Potatoes
			Buttered Leeks
			Stuffed Tomatoes
			Honeyed Bread and Butter
			  Pudding

Month 2. Week 4

	Breakfast	Lunch	Dinner

MONDAY	Cereals
	Apricots
	Poached Eggs
	Grilled Bacon
	Baked Tomato
	Toast/Jams
		Mushroom, Apricot,
		  Tomato and Capsicum
		  Kebabs Marinated in
		  an Asian Style
		Boiled Rice
			Potato Soup
			Lamb and Mushroom Kebabs
			Garlic Potatoes
			Steamed Cauliflower
			  Florets
			Pineapple and Cherry
			  Upside Down Cake

Month 2. Week 4 — cont.

	Breakfast	Lunch	Dinner
TUESDAY	Cereals Puréed Apple and Cinnamon Scrambled Eggs Sausage and Bacon Wraps Danish Pastries	Garlic and Swiss Cheese Burgers Deep-fried Potato Skins Apple and Mint Salad	White Onion Soup Traditional Steak and Kidney Pie Chateau Potatoes Crispy Green Beans Poached Pears in Red Wine Syrup
WEDNESDAY	Cereals Pears in Syrup Fried Eggs Crispy Bacon Muffins	Vegetable Roulade Mixed Green Leaf Salad Parsley and Dill Dressing	Brown Celery Soup Baby Trout Baked in White Wine and Lemon Juice Boiled Potatoes Sautéed Zucchini and Onion Chocolate Fudge Eclairs
THURSDAY	Cereals Orange and Lime Juice Bacon Omelettes Croissants/Jams	Macaroni Cheese with Chives Marinated Mushroom Salad Garlic Bread	Tomato and Rice Soup Blanquette of Lamb Herbed Potatoes Roasted Pumpkin Sultana and Custard Tart
FRIDAY	Cereals Chilled Melon Balls Poached Eggs Hash Browns Danish Pastries	Cod Steaks Baked in Parsley Sauce Topped with Cheddar Cheese Steamed Broccoli New Potatoes Tossed in Butter	Pumpkin and Orange Soup Minute Steak Schnitzel with Dijon Mustard Sauce Boulangère Potatoes Grilled Tomato with Cheese Mixed Fruit with Coconut Crumble Topping
SATURDAY	Cereals Grape Juice Boiled Eggs Pressed Ham Steaks Toast/Jam	Grilled Pork Chops with a Slice of Sage Butter Baked Mini Jacket Potatoes Corn on the Cob	Creamy Spinach Soup Chicken Maryland with Sweet Corn and Banana Fritters Sautéed Potatoes Mango Mousse
SUNDAY	Cereals Fruit Cocktail Pancakes with Golden Syrup Danish Pastries	Corned Silverside of Beef Onion and Mustard Sauce Roasted Potatoes Cauliflower Cheese Steamed Pumpkin	Tomato Soup Seafood Crumble French Fried Potatoes Green Beans with Toasted Almonds Apricot Flan with Whipped Cream

10

Garnishing

- ■ *Introduction*
- ■ *Suggested Garnishes*

Introduction

Good food presentation, enhanced by appropriate garnishing, plays a significant role in large-scale catering. Caterers should strive to market their food to its maximum potential. The use of 'marketing' may seem peculiar in large scale catering, but it exists, is effective, and is essential. A simple sprig of parsley is a marketing tool in itself. It is an attractive addition to a salad and will inevitably attract the eyes of an indecisive customer. It is, therefore, essential to be able to identify different techniques and styles of food presentation, and to realise their importance in the art of catering.

Garnishing is used to complement and enhance the appearance, and often the flavouring, of food. Garnishing adds extra colour to a dish. Colours should not clash and too many of one colour must be avoided. A dish should be aesthetically pleasing to catch the eye of the consumer. It is the initial visual impact of the dish that attracts potential customers. After all, we eat with our eyes first.

Aim for an appearance geared towards stimulating appetite and you will notice a return of clientele. Presentation, with an emphasis on colour balance, should be foremost in a caterer's mind. Use and improve your garnishing/presentation techniques in every aspect of the kitchen. Salads, sandwiches, desserts and cold buffets will certainly benefit from an attractive garnish.

A garnish can be as simple as croutons upon a steaming bowl of soup, or as complex as an ice carved swan on a buffet table. Bear in mind your customer's needs. Since a garnish is rarely eaten, be sure not to overdo it. Spooning away the grated carrot to find the chef's dish is not the objective of garnishing.

There are many simple and varied garnishes which can add individuality and colour to a dish. All too often parsley sprigs and chopped parsley are overexploited. With some forward thinking and innovation, alternative methods of garnishing and presentation of dishes can be developed.

First, consider which garnish will complement the dish. Fresh, chopped mint will not enhance the flavour of a hearty stew for instance. However, sour cream with a dash of paprika and chopped chives will certainly enhance its flavour as well as its colour and texture. A list of garnishes appropriate for different dishes is provided below.

Suggested Garnishes

For Breakfasts

Bacon: chopped, strips
Basil: chopped, sprigs
Capsicum: diced, sliced, strips
Lemon: wedges, slices, twists
Mint leaves: whole

Mushrooms: whole, sliced, diced
Paprika: sprinkled
Parsley: sprigs, chopped
Tomato: chopped, sliced, diced

For Soups

Thick

Capsicum: diced, chopped, rings
Carrot: grated
Chives: chopped
Cream
Croutons
Lemon: sliced

Natural yoghurt
Parmesan: grated
Parsley: sprigs, chopped
Sour Cream
Spring onion: sliced, strips, diced
Tomato: chopped

Creamed

Almonds: toasted
Bacon: diced, strips
Capsicum: sliced, diced, strips
Cheese: grated
Chives: chopped

Croutons
Mint: chopped
Mushrooms: sliced, diced, whole turned
Paprika: sprinkled
Parsley: sprigs, chopped

Other

Baked pitta bread strips
Carrot: strips
Celery: strips
Coriander leaves and sprigs
Crackers

Croutons
Crusty bread
Melba toast
Small sandwiches
Toasted bread

For Egg Dishes

Bacon: chopped
Capsicum: rings, strips, diced
Carrot: sticks
Celery: sticks, sliced
Cheese: grated
Chives: chopped
Gherkin: whole, sliced

Ham: chopped
Mushrooms: whole, sliced, chopped
Olives: whole, halved, sliced
Onion: rings, chopped
Paprika: sprinkled
Parsley: chopped sprigs
Tomato: sliced, diced, wedges

For Pasta Dishes

Bacon: chopped, strips
Basil: chopped, sprigs
Breadcrumbs: toasted
Capsicum: diced, sliced, strips
Cheese: grated
Chives: chopped, whole
Coriander: chopped, sprigs

Dill: chopped sprigs
Ham: chopped, strips
Oregano: chopped, leaves
Parmesan: grated
Parsley: chopped, sprigs
Tomato: sliced, chopped

For Seafood Dishes

Almonds: toasted
Capsicum: rings, strips, diced
Cucumber: twist, sliced, chopped
Dill: sprigs, chopped
Eggs: sliced, grated

Lemon: slices, wedges, twists
Mint: leaves, chopped
Mushrooms: whole, turned, sliced, diced
Paprika
Parsley: chopped, sprigs
Tomato: slices, wedges, chopped

For Vegetable Dishes

Almonds: toasted, slivered
Bacon: strips, chopped
Basil: chopped, sprigs
Capsicum: rings, strips, diced
Cheese: grated
Chives: chopped
Lemon: slices, wedges, twists
Mint: chopped

Mushrooms: sliced
Onion: chopped, rings
Oregano: chopped, leaves
Paprika: sprinkled
Parsley: sprigs, chopped
Tomato: wedges, sliced, chopped
Thyme: sprigs
Walnuts: crushed

For Meat and Poultry

Almonds: toasted whole
or slivered
Bacon: chopped
Basil: chopped, sprigs
Capsicum: rings, chopped, strips
Carrot: strips
Cheese: grated
Chives: chopped
Ham: strips, diced
Herb butter

Lemon: twists, wedges, slices
Mushrooms: whole, turned, sliced, diced
Onion: rings, diced
Orange: twists, wedges, slices
Parsley butter
Parsley: sprigs, chopped
Rosemary: leaves, sprigs
Tomato: sliced, wedges, diced
Thyme: sprigs

For Desserts

Almonds: toasted, slivered
Angelica
Cherries: glacé, halved
Cream: whipped
Icing sugar: dusted
Jelly crystals

Kiwi fruit: peeled, sliced
Mango: peeled, sliced
Mint: chopped, sprigs
Nuts: chopped
Starfruit: sliced whole, halved
Strawberry: sliced, halved, fanned

Illustrations of some salad cuts which make attractive garnishes are shown on pp 75-6. See pp 286-8 for instructions about how to prepare these garnishes.

Spun shallot

Radish flower

Turned mushroom

Chilli flower

Cucumber crown

Cucumber twist

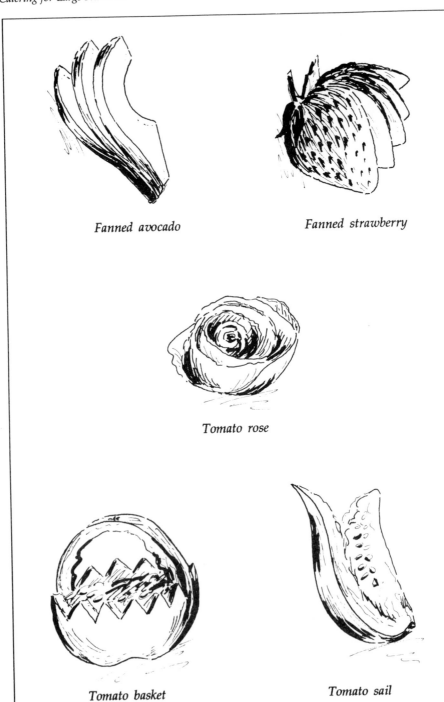

Fanned avocado

Fanned strawberry

Tomato rose

Tomato basket

Tomato sail

11
Use of Herbs

■ *Introduction*
■ *Herbs, Origins, Uses and Example*

Introduction

Herbs are a natural provision of tastes and colours. They can be used to give an outstanding flavour to any food when used correctly; they can also be used as attractive garnishes. There are no rigid rules governing their use because taste, regional preferences and availability all play their part when appropriate herbs are being selected.

Certain herbs have, over the years, become standard with particular western dishes, for example mint with any lamb dish, horseradish with beef, parsley with vegetables and oregano and basil with pasta dishes. Other herbs can, of course, be added to these dishes to give an individual taste. The chef must experiment with different herbs until the required flavour is achieved. To achieve a pleasant blend, herbs must be used sparingly: too much of one herb may have the adverse effect of overpowering the food which was meant to be enhanced.

Herbs make a bland dish exciting and delicious. They were a much revered commodity throughout the ages, and many famous travellers, for example Christopher Columbus and Vasco da Gama, took herbs and spices on their voyages to trade. Herbs were also in demand for their medicinal qualities, not to mention their use as a cover for rancid meat which people were forced to eat when fresh meat was scarce.

Herbs are best purchased fresh and whole, but pre-prepared and dried herbs are an ideal substitute and they have a longer lifespan. Their rotation in stock should be kept flowing because they have a limited shelf life; they quickly lose their colour and flavour. All dried herbs must be stored in airtight containers in a cool place away from direct sunlight. Provided fresh herbs are stored correctly, they can be very cost-effective. It is recommended that fresh herbs be wrapped in a damp cloth and refrigerated. The cloth should be moistened daily and a fresh one provided every two to three days. Fresh herbs will keep their colour and body for a long period when stored in this way. For large-scale catering, it is recommended that dried herbs be used for cooking and, if possible, fresh herbs for garnishing. This will strike the right balance between the use of fresh and dried herbs.

The next section contains a list of herbs, their country of origin, and suggestions for use. Note that although the list specifies the original country of origin of the herbs, they may nowadays be grown in many different countries.

Herbs, Origins, Uses and Example

Herb	Origin	Uses	Example
Allspice	South America	Pickling, white meat casseroles, soups, flavouring for desserts	Christmas Pudding
Anise	Middle East	Topping for crusty bread, also in the making of sweets and drinks	Anise Cookies
Basil	India	Any dish with tomato including soup and salads. Also used with zucchini, squash and spinach	Bolognaise
Bay	Mediterranean	Bouquet garni, stocks, sauces and soups. Good with any wet dish	Chicken Casserole
Caraway	America Europe	Pungent taste used in breads and confectionery	Caraway Cake
Chilli	America	Mexican, Italian and oriental cuisine	Chilli con Carne
Chives	Mediterranean China	Sauces, salads, soups and dips. Has a mild onion flavour	Potato and Chive Soup
Cinnamon	Sri Lanka	Chutneys, apple pie, apple sauce, pumpkin and zucchini	Cinnamon Bread
Cloves	China	Adds flavour to hams and fruits, also bread sauce	Honey Glazed Ham
Coriander	Mediterranean	Oriental dishes. Used with fish and poultry. Satay sauces, can be used in curries. Very sweet	Beef Satay
Dill	Mediterranean	Chutneys and pickles. Used with seafood. Garnish for salads and soups	Cucumber Salad
Garlic	India Egypt China	Mediterranean cuisine. Soups and marinades. Extremely versatile	Garlic Mushrooms
Ginger	Asia	Ingredient for curry. Used in cakes and most Asian dishes. Also acts as a tenderiser when used with meats	Ginger Bread
Marjoram	Mediterranean	Bouquet garni. Italian dishes in the absence of oregano. Used in stews. Goes well with poultry, fish and salads	Cottage Pie

Herb	Origin	Uses	Example
Mint	Mediterranean	Is now synonymous with any lamb dish, in jelly, sauce or stuffing. Used in drinks, chutneys and sauces	Minted Peas
Mustard	Mediterranean	Adds bite to most sauces. Served as condiment for beef and most cold meats. Must be used in moderation	Salad Dressings
Nutmeg	Sri Lanka	Ground and used in sweet dishes. Milk puddings. Good seasoning for pumpkin	Rice Pudding
Oregano	Mediterranean	Strong flavour. Used alongside bay and basil to make most Italian dishes. All tomato dishes. Sprinkled over salads	Lasagne
Paprika	Eastern Europe	Excellent garnish because of its deep red colour for any mayonnaise or white sauce dish. Good colour contrast when used with rice	Goulash
Parsley	Southern Europe	Bouquet garni. Soups and sauces for flavour and an excellent garnish when used either chopped or in sprig form for any dish	Parsley Butter
Rosemary	Europe Turkey	Used in conjunction with lemon for lamb dishes. Stuffings and pasta dishes	Rosemary Zucchini
Saffron	Asia Mediterranean	Because of the high cost of saffron, it is usually substituted by artificial colouring or the herb turmeric. Adds a yellow colour to rice and chicken. Used effectively for presentation purposes	Spanish Paella
Sage	Mediterranean	Powerful herb used mainly with poultry and pork as a stuffing	Sage/Onion Stuffing
Tarragon	Europe	Vinegars. Sauces, creamed soups. Complements most chicken dishes	Chicken Chasseur
Thyme	Mediterranean	Bouquet garni. Goes well with any savoury dish, soups, fish, chicken and stuffings	Savoury Durham Cutlets
Turmeric	India Africa	Curries, pickles and chutneys. Alternative to saffron	Curried Chicken

12
Sandwiches

- Introduction
- Basic Preparation of Sandwiches
- General Rules for Sandwich Making
- Filling Compatibility Chart

Introduction

Sandwiches are important in large-scale catering. They can be an alternative to many hot and cold dishes and be just as nutritious. They can also be real time savers.

The sandwich was created many years ago by a conscientious inventor, the Earl of Sandwich from England. He felt that too much time was being wasted in meal consumption, and he developed the concept of placing meat between two pieces of bread, which enabled him to eat as he played cards. The idea soon spread, and today the sandwich is an established food.

Everyone has a favourite sandwich. With its increased popularity, the choices of fillings and even types of bread used have reached mammoth proportions. A sandwich can be as basic as a 'cheese and tomato on white' to the more complex 'smoked salmon, creamed cheese and capers on a baguette'.

The origins of bread types (or filling cases) can be traced to various cultures. The foccacia bread is made from an Italian style pizza dough; Lebanese pocket bread is now being used as a casing for a variety of fillings; and Danish open sandwiches are another popular choice.

These types of sandwiches can provide a refreshing alternative for busy people 'on the go'. They are ideal for people who do not want to spend time eating a meal which will leave them weighed down and often fatigued.

When preparing a large amount of sandwiches, it is essential to provide a wide selection of fillings. Different types of breads and fillings create interest and will widen the appeal for prospective consumers. By using more than one filling in a sandwich, colour and flavour can be added.

Striking a balance between moist and dry fillings is important when preparing the perfect sandwich. While a moist sandwich can lose its shape and texture, a dry one can be difficult to swallow. For instance, a finely cut pickle or perhaps a slice or two of tomato added to a cheese sandwich will prevent it being dry, and will also add interest and colour. A slice of cheese can be added to an egg and mayonnaise sandwich to prevent it being too moist.

Basic Preparation of Sandwiches

There are a number of important factors to consider when preparing a selection of sandwiches.

1. You will require a large chopping board and sufficient butter/margarine (at room temperature). Butter that is too hard will tear the bread when spreading. Butter that is too runny will result in soggy bread. It is extremely important that butter/margarine maintains the correct consistency. Butter can be softened in a microwave oven but this requires careful and constant observation. Ideally, it should be left out for an hour or two prior to use.

2. Prepare the bread by removing it from its packaging and storing it under a damp tea towel until required.

3. Pre-prepare all fillings and store them in the refrigerator.

General Rules for Sandwich Making

1. Stack sliced bread to the right of the chopping board together with soft butter.

NOTE: For made-to-order service, pre-butter bread and stack ready for fillings.

2. Place containers of fillings at the far side of the board.

3. Place sliced bread on the board creating two rows and add butter, taking care to cover each slice to its edge.

4. Place the filling on the bottom row and any sauces, mustards, etc on the top row.

5. Stack the sandwiches in content groups and cover with a damp tea towel.

6. Cut into the required size and wrap or place on a tray.

FILLING COMPATABILITY CHART

	Bacon	Burger	Cheese soft & hard	Chicken	Corned Beef	Egg	Fish Smoked	Fish Tinned	Ham	Ox Tongue	Pate	Roast Beef	Roast Lamb	Roast Pork	Sausage & Salami	Shellfish
Apple			✓	✓												
Asparagus	✓	✓	✓	✓	✓	✓	✓	✓	✓	✓	✓	✓	✓	✓		✓
Bacon		✓	✓	✓		✓		✓								
Beetroot	✓	✓	✓	✓	✓	✓		✓	✓	✓	✓	✓	✓	✓		✓
Capers		✓	✓	✓	✓	✓	✓	✓	✓	✓	✓	✓	✓	✓	✓	✓
Capsicum	✓	✓	✓	✓	✓	✓		✓	✓	✓	✓	✓	✓	✓	✓	✓
Carrot		✓	✓	✓	✓	✓		✓	✓	✓		✓	✓	✓		✓
Celery		✓	✓	✓	✓	✓		✓	✓	✓		✓	✓	✓		✓
Cheese	✓	✓		✓	✓	✓		✓	✓	✓		✓	✓	✓	✓	
Coleslaw	✓	✓	✓	✓	✓	✓		✓	✓	✓		✓	✓	✓		✓
Corn		✓	✓	✓	✓	✓			✓			✓	✓	✓		
Cucumber		✓	✓	✓	✓	✓	✓	✓	✓	✓		✓	✓	✓		✓
Egg	✓	✓	✓	✓	✓				✓	✓		✓	✓	✓		
Gherkin		✓	✓	✓	✓	✓			✓	✓		✓	✓	✓	✓	
Ham			✓	✓		✓										
Lettuce	✓	✓	✓	✓	✓	✓	✓	✓	✓	✓		✓	✓	✓		✓
Mushrooms	✓	✓	✓	✓	✓	✓		✓	✓	✓		✓	✓	✓		
Nuts																
Olives		✓	✓	✓	✓	✓		✓		✓	✓	✓	✓	✓	✓	
Onion	✓	✓	✓	✓	✓	✓	✓	✓	✓	✓	✓	✓	✓	✓	✓	✓
Orange			✓													
Pineapple	✓	✓	✓	✓												
Toasted	✓	✓	✓	✓	✓	✓		✓	✓	✓	✓	✓	✓	✓		
Tomato	✓	✓	✓	✓	✓	✓		✓	✓	✓	✓	✓	✓	✓	✓	✓
Sauces																
Barbecue	✓	✓		✓	✓	✓			✓	✓		✓	✓	✓		
Chilli		✓		✓												
English Mustard	✓	✓		✓	✓				✓	✓		✓	✓	✓	✓	
French Mustard	✓	✓		✓	✓				✓	✓		✓	✓	✓	✓	
Mayonnaise	✓	✓		✓	✓	✓			✓	✓		✓	✓	✓	✓	✓
Pickles	✓	✓	✓	✓	✓				✓	✓		✓	✓	✓	✓	
Tomato	✓	✓		✓					✓	✓					✓	

Recipes

- Breakfasts
- Stocks and Sauces
- Soups
- Beef Dishes
- Veal Dishes
- Lamb Dishes
- Pork Dishes
- Poultry Dishes
- Fish and Seafood Dishes
- Vegetarian and Rice Dishes
- Salads
- Salad Dressings and Marinades
- Vegetable Dishes
- Potato Dishes
- Dessert Dishes
- Accompaniments
- Garnishes

Breakfasts

Recipes are not given for some of the breakfast items on the menu cycles because they are now considered convenience foods, and are usually bought in from suppliers and rarely prepared on site. These items include breads, danish pastries, waffles, fruit loaf and crumpets, etc, from the bakers, and baked beans, spaghetti, jams, cereals, fruits and fruit juices, etc, from the dry stores supplier.

Fried Eggs

	25	50	100
Eggs	25	50	100
Oil	**as required**		

1. Place enough oil into a large frypan to approximately 1 cm depth.
2. Place over a moderate heat and heat oil until a light haze can be seen above it.
3. Break eggs gently into pan at regular intervals making sure they do not touch.
4. Cook steadily until whites are firm.
5. Assist cooking by gently agitating fat over eggs.
6. Remove eggs from pan using a fish slice and allow fat to drain off egg before serving.

NOTE: Egg rings are an excellent way to fry eggs because they keep the eggs in a uniform shape and also allow larger batches to be cooked at one time.

REMEMBER: When cooking a large amount of eggs, always allow fat to regain correct temperature before adding the next batch, and also remove any particles that are left over in the fat as they may burn and impart a burnt taste to the oil.

Poached Eggs

	25	50	100
Eggs	25	50	100
Water	as required		
Vinegar	30 mL	60 mL	120 mL
Salt	1 teaspoon	2 teaspoons	4 teaspoons

1. Place into a suitable pan (a deep-sided frypan is ideal) approximately 4 cm of water, vinegar and salt.
2. Bring to a slow simmer.
3. Gently break eggs into liquid at regular intervals.
4. Allow to cook until whites are firm.
5. Using a slotted vegetable server, gently remove eggs, draining off any excess liquid.
6. Serve as required.

Scrambled Eggs

	25	50	100
Eggs	30	60	120
Milk	750 mL	1.5 L	3 L
Butter	150 g	300 g	600 g
Salt and pepper	to taste		

1. Beat eggs, milk and seasoning together.
2. Melt butter in a double saucepan or steam pan.
3. Add egg mixture and cook with lid on until egg is firm but moist, stirring occasionally.
4. Serve as required.

Savoury Scrambled Eggs

As for scrambled eggs with the addition of:

	25	50	100
Basil, chopped	5 g	10 g	20 g
Chives, chopped	5 g	10 g	20 g

Add herbs just before serving, mixing in well.

Scrambled Eggs with Cheese

As for scrambled egg with the addition of:

	25	50	100
Cheddar cheese, grated	**200 g**	**400 g**	**800 g**

Add just before service folding in cheese lightly.

Parsley Scrambled Eggs

As for scrambled egg with the addition of:

	25	50	100
Parsley, chopped	**10 g**	**20 g**	**40 g**

Add parsley just before serving mixing in well.

Boiled Eggs

	25	50	100
Eggs	**25**	**50**	**100**
Water	**enough to immerse eggs**		

1. Place water into a large saucepan and bring to the boil.
2. Gently add eggs to water being careful not to crack shells.
3. Return water to the boil and cook eggs for approximately 5 minutes.
4. Drain water from eggs and serve with or without shell.

Omelette

	25	50	100
Eggs	**30**	**60**	**120**
Milk	**750 mL**	**1.5 L**	**3 L**
Butter	**150 g**	**300 g**	**600 g**
Salt and pepper	**to taste**		
Oil	**as required**		

1. Beat together eggs, milk, melted butter and seasoning.
2. Over a moderate heat in a suitable pan heat oil.
3. Add mixture so pan is evenly covered and cook for approximately 1 minute.
4. Using a small whisk or fork gently stir mixture.
5. Cook until all egg is firm (it can also be placed into a moderate oven until egg is firm or placed under a salamander).
6. Portion and serve as required.

Fillings

Filling for omelettes are usually pre-cooked and can be added to the beaten egg mixture before the cooking process. Fillings can be of your own choice. Some suggestions are:

1. Ham.
2. Ham and tomato.
3. Cheese.
4. Cheese and onion.
5. Cheese and tomato.
6. Cheese with chives.
7. Bacon.
8. Bacon and mushroom.
9. Mushroom.
10. Chicken.

Pancakes

	25	50	100
Eggs	25	50	100
Milk	5 L	10 L	20 L
Self-raising flour	3 kg	6 kg	12 kg
Salt	2 teaspoons	3 teaspoons	5 teaspoons
Sugar	750 g	1.5 kg	3 kg

1. Mix all ingredients together in industrial mixer until a smooth consistency is reached that will heavily coat the back of a spoon. If mixture is too thick, add small amounts of milk until required consistency is achieved. If mixture is too thin, add small amounts of flour and whisk further until the correct consistency is reached.

2. Either on a griddle or in a large frypan heat a little oil.

3. Using a ladle, add mixture in either small or large circles.

4. Cook until bubbles form on surface approximately 30–40 seconds.

5. Turn over and cook for a further 30–40 seconds or until pancake is cooked and golden brown.

6. Sprinkle with a little sugar and serve.

Lemon Pancakes

Add a little lemon essence to pancake batter to taste. Add lemon juice when serving.

Almond Pancakes

Add a little almond essence to pancake batter to taste.

Fruit-filled Pancakes

1. Prepare as for pancake recipe using plain flour instead of self-raising flour. Allow to cool.

2. Place a little cooked fruit or jam across the centre of pancake.
3. Roll pancake around filling.
4. Place onto a lightly greased tray.
5. Place into an oven preheated to 150°C and cook until heated through.
6. Serve with syrup or a little pureed fruit that has been mixed with a little water to a smooth consistency.

Bacon

	25	50	100
Bacon	**allow 2 rashers per person**		

1. Place bacon onto trays in rows.
2. Cook under preheated salamander for approximately 2 minutes on either side or until cooked.
3. Drain away any excess fat from tray.
4. Serve as required.

Sausages

	25	50	100
Sausages	**allow 1–2 per portion**		
Oil	**as required**		

1. Lightly grease suitably sized baking trays.
2. Place sausages onto trays in rows.
3. Place into an oven that has been preheated to a moderate setting and cook for approximately 10–15 minutes, or until cooked through depending on size.
4. Drain away any excess fat.
5. Serve as required.

Chipolata Sausage

As for sausages allowing 3–4 per portion and cooking for approximately 4–6 minutes or until cooked through.

Meat Patties

As for burger recipe (see p 137), making small burger shapes to the required size.

Bacon and Sausage Wraps

	25	50	100
Sausages	25	50	100
Bacon rashers	25	50	100

1. Wrap one bacon rasher around one sausage.
2. Place in rows onto lightly greased baking trays.
3. Place into an oven that has been preheated to a moderate setting and cook for approximately 10–15 minutes or until sausages are cooked through.
4. Drain away any excess fat.
5. Serve as required.

Grilled Ham Steaks / Grilled Gammon

	25	50	100
Gammon steaks	25	50	100

1. Place steaks onto a grill or on trays under a salamander.
2. Cook for approximately 2 minutes on either side, depending on size, or until cooked through.
3. Drain away any excess fat.
4. Serve as required.

Boiled Ham

This is ham that is usually bought in canned and is used on cold meat platters and sandwiches. It can be sliced thinly and rolled and is excellent when served with egg, or it can be sliced to a thickness of approximately 1 cm and cooked in an oven or on a griddle that has been preheated to a moderate setting until heated through.

Pressed Ham Steaks

As for boiled ham.

Hash Browns

Grated raw potato mixed with beaten egg, pepper and salt. Fry in pan in small amount of oil until golden brown.

Fried Potatoes

These are potatoes that have been blanched, sliced to a thickness of approximately ½ cm and deep-fried. See sautéed potatoes in potato section.

Fruit Fritters

See Dessert Dishes.

Fried Bread

	25	50	100
Bread, halved diagonally	25 slices	50 slices	100 slices
Oil	as required		

1. Heat a little oil over a moderate heat in a suitable frypan.
2. Add bread and cook on either side until golden brown.
3. Serve as required.

Tomatoes / Cheese Tomatoes

See Vegetable Dishes.

Ham and Cheese Croissants

	25	50	100
Croissants	25	50	100
Ham, boiled, thinly sliced	25	50	100
Cheese, thinly sliced	25	50	100
Parsley, chopped	5 g	10 g	20 g

1. Cut croissants in half horizontally.
2. On bottom half, place a slice of ham and a slice of cheese.
3. Sprinkle with a little chopped parsley.
4. Replace top of croissant.
5. Place onto baking trays and place into an oven that has been preheated to a moderate setting.
6. Bake until heated through and cheese has begun to melt.
7. Remove from oven and serve as required.

Cheese Potatoes

See Potato Dishes.

Corn Fritters

See sweet corn fritter recipe on p 169.

Stocks and Sauces

Basic stocks are the major ingredient and flavouring in many of the soups and sauces listed in this book.

When making stock, always use ingredients that are as fresh as possible, and any scum which forms on the surface of the stock should be removed regularly. Try not to bring stock to the boil, which will cause it to discolour, but simmer gently.

When a stock is to be stored in a refrigerator, it must always be left to cool beforehand, and when it is to be used again in a soup or sauce, it must always reach boiling point before being served.

Sauces are generally used to enhance the presentation and flavour of a dish. They should never overpower the dishes they are meant to complement.

Sauces should be of a smooth consistency which will coat the back of a spoon and be free from any lumps.

Basic (Brown) Beef Stock

Water	**18 L**
Bones (beef)	**7 kg**
Vegetables, roughly chopped	**2 kg**
Carrot	
Celery	
Onion	
Leek	
Tomato	
Parsley stalks	**50 g**
Thyme	**25 g**
Bay leaf	**4**

1. In an oven preheated to a moderate setting, brown bones and vegetables for approximately 45 minutes.

2. Add all ingredients together and simmer on a stove for 4–6 hours removing regularly any scum or fats that may rise to the surface.

3. Remove from heat and pass through a fine strainer. Allow to thoroughly cool before refrigerating.

4. Before use, remove any fat that has formed on the top of stock.

NOTE: This fat can be used for the roasting of potatoes to give an excellent flavouring.

White Beef Stock

As for basic brown stock without browning bones and vegetables.

Basic Chicken Stock

As for beef stock except:
Use same amount of chicken carcasses and bones in place of beef bones.

Fish Stock

Water	**18 L**
Fish bones and skin	**7 kg**

Vegetables, roughly chopped	2 kg
Carrot	
Celery	
Onion	
Leek	
Bay leaf	4
Parsley, stalks	75 g

1. Place all ingredients in a pan and bring to the boil.

2. Remove any scum or fat which may rise to the surface.

3. Simmer for 15–20 minutes. Do not cook for longer than this or the flavour will be impaired.

4. Remove from the heat and pass through a fine strainer. Allow to cool thoroughly before refrigerating.

Basic White Sauce / Bechamel

	25	50	100
Milk	1.5 L	3 L	6 L
Butter	125 g	250 g	500 g
Flour, plain	125 g	250 g	500 g
Salt and pepper	to taste		

1. Melt butter in a pan on a low heat and add flour gradually until a smooth paste is achieved. Do not allow flour to colour.

2. Slowly incorporate milk in small amounts making sure each addition has mixed with the flour and butter smoothly. Adjust consistency with the addition of a little extra milk. Add in small amounts.

3. When all milk has been added, add salt and pepper to taste.

NOTE: Margarine can be added in place of butter and will give a good finished product, but it is not recommended.

Court Bouillon

(Liquid for the cooking of fish, for example salmon)
To make 1 litre:

Water	1.2 L
Carrots, finely sliced	50 g
Onion, finely sliced	50 g
Peppercorns	4
Parsley, stalks	4
Vinegar	50 mL
Thyme, sprig	1
Bay leaves	2

1. Combine all ingredients and simmer for 30 minutes.

2. Refrigerate and use as required.

NOTE: Always allow to cool before refrigeration.

Preparation of Stock Using Powdered Stock Mix

Chicken and Beef Stock

1. To make 1 L of stock add 25 g stock powder to 1 L of boiling water and thoroughly whisk.
2. To make 3 L of stock add 75 g stock powder to 3 L of boiling water and thoroughly whisk.
3. To make 14 L of stock add 350 g stock powder to 14 L of boiling water and thoroughly whisk.

Fish/Seafood Stock

1. To make 1 L of stock add 35 g stock powder to 1 L of boiling water and thoroughly whisk.
2. To make 3 L of stock add 105 g stock powder to 3 L of boiling water and thoroughly whisk.
3. To make 14 L of stock add 490 g stock powder to 14 L of boiling water and thoroughly whisk.

NOTE: It is always a good idea to add a small amount of fresh vegetable and herbs to prepared stock. Allow to simmer gently for 30 minutes, then strain. It not only adds extra flavour, but also helps take away the very salty taste of powdered stock mixes.

Derivatives of White Sauce/Bechamel
Anchovy Sauce

To be served with any fish dish.

To white sauce add:

Anchovy essence	**to taste**

Basil Sauce

To be served with chicken and pasta dishes.

As for white sauce with the addition of:

	25	50	100
Garlic, chopped	**3**	**6**	**10**
Basil	**10 g**	**20 g**	**40 g**
Cream	**100 mL**	**200 mL**	**400 mL**

1. Add garlic and basil with butter cooking slowly for 2–3 minutes without browning before addition of flour.
2. Add cream just prior to service.

Cheese Sauce / Mornay Sauce

To be served with fish or vegetables.

To white sauce add:

	25	50	100
Grated cheese	**200 g**	**400 g**	**800 g**
Mustard, mild	**50 g**	**100 g**	**200 g**

Onion Sauce

To be served with lamb.

To white sauce add:

	25	50	100
Onion, cooked, finely diced	**150 g**	**300 g**	**600 g**

Onion and Mustard Sauce

As for onion sauce with the addition of:

Mustard, mild	**to taste**

Parsley Sauce

To be served with fish or vegetables.

To white sauce add:

	25	50	100
Parsley, chopped	**20 g**	**40 g**	**80 g**

Parsley and Lemon Sauce

To be served with fish and lightly spiced meat.

To parsley sauce add:

	25	50	100
Lemon juice	**50 mL**	**100 mL**	**200 mL**

Add lemon juice with seasoning.

Cream Sauce

To be served with fish or vegetables.

To white sauce add:

		25	50	100
Cream	approx	200 mL	400 mL	800 mL

Delete appropriate amount of milk in original recipe.

Cider and Cream Sauce

To be served with pork.

To cream sauce add:

		25	50	100
Cider	approx	125 mL	250 mL	500 mL

Add cider to taste, just prior to service.

Mustard Sauce

To be served with fish, beef and lamb.

To white sauce add:

Mustard, mild	to taste

Dijon Mustard Sauce

To be served with beef or lamb.

To white sauce add:

Dijon mustard	to taste

Velouté

	25	50	100
Stock, chicken, veal, fish	1.5 L	3 L	6 L
Butter	125 g	250 g	500 g
Flour, plain	125 g	250 g	500 g
Salt	to taste		
Pepper	to taste		
Cream	as required		

1. Melt butter in a pan on a low heat, add flour gradually until a smooth paste is achieved and cook until paste has turned a sandy colour.
2. Slowly incorporate stock in small amounts making sure that each addition has mixed with the flour and butter smoothly.
3. When all stock has been added, add salt and pepper to taste.
4. Bring to the boil and simmer for 30–40 minutes.
5. Pass through a fine strainer and add cream if necessary.

Derivatives of Velouté
Mushroom Sauce

To be served with chicken and fish.

To velouté add:

	25	50	100
Mushrooms, sliced, cooked	**100 g**	**200 g**	**400 g**

Sauté mushrooms until soft, add to velouté and simmer for a further 5–6 minutes.

Mushroom and Parmesan Cheese Sauce

As for mushroom sauce with addition of:

	25	50	100
Parmesan cheese, grated	**100 g**	**200 g**	**400 g**

Add at step 3 of velouté recipe.

Supreme Sauce

To be served with chicken and fish.

To velouté add:

	25	50	100
Mushrooms, sliced, cooked	**75 g**	**150 g**	**300 g**
Cream	**100 mL**	**200 mL**	**400 mL**
Juice of lemon	**½**	**1**	**2**

1. Sauté mushrooms until soft, add to velouté and simmer for a further 5–6 minutes.
2. Add cream and lemon juice just prior to service.

Basic Brown Gravy

	25	50	100
Margarine	50 g	100 g	200 g
Flour, plain	75 g	150 g	300 g
Stock, brown beef	1.5 L	3 L	6 L
Tomato puree	50 g	100 g	200 g
Salt	to taste		
Pepper	to taste		

1. Melt margarine on a low heat and stir in flour and tomato puree to a smooth paste.
2. Add stock slowly, stirring continuously until it has all been incorporated.
3. Bring to the boil and simmer. Add seasoning.
4. Simmer for approximately 1–1½ hours. Sauce can be thinned down by the addition of a little stock or thickened by the addition of small but equal amounts of flour and water mixed together and whisked in thoroughly.

Derivatives of Basic Brown Sauce
Brown Mushroom Sauce

To be served with beef.

To brown gravy add:

	25	50	100
Mushrooms, sliced, cooked	150 g	300 g	600 g

Sauté mushrooms until soft and add in last 5 minutes of cooking time.

Chasseur Sauce

To be served with chicken, beef or pork.

To brown gravy add:

	25	50	100
Onion, finely diced	100 g	200 g	400 g
Tomato, finely diced	100 g	200 g	400 g
Wine, red	100 mL	200 mL	400 mL
Tarragon, chopped	25 g	50 g	100 g

1. Add onion, tomato and tarragon with tomato puree.
2. Add wine for last 5 minutes of cooking time.

Cranberry Gravy

	25	50	100
Gravy sauce	1.3 L	2.6 L	5.2 L
Cranberry sauce	200 mL	400 mL	800 mL

Thoroughly whisk two sauces together and serve hot.

Lemon and Rosemary Sauce

To be served with lamb.

To brown gravy add:

	25	50	100
Rosemary	20 g	40 g	80 g
Lemon juice	50 mL	100 mL	200 mL

Add rosemary and lemon with tomato puree.

Mint Sauce

To be served with lamb.

To brown gravy add:

	25	50	100
Mint, chopped	30 g	60 g	120 g

Add mint with tomato puree.

Onion Gravy

To be served with beef, pork and sausages.

To brown gravy add:

	25	50	100
Onion, finely sliced	200 g	400 g	800 g

Add onions with margarine and cook out slowly without colour for 2–3 minutes until soft before addition of flour.

Pepper Sauce

To be served with grilled meats.

To brown gravy add:

Peppercorns, crushed or tinned	**to taste**
Cream	**to taste**

1. Add peppercorns with margarine and cook out slowly for 2–3 minutes.
2. Add cream just before serving, incorporating thoroughly.

Barbecue Sauce

To be served with all grilled and barbecued meats and poultry.

	25	50	100
Oil, olive	for frying		
Garlic, crushed	3	6	10
Onion, finely chopped	300 g	600 g	1.2 kg
Honey	250 mL	500 mL	1 L
Vinegar	100 mL	200 mL	400 mL
Tomato puree	750 g	1.5 kg	3 kg
Mustard, mild	50 g	100 g	200 g
Worcester sauce	125 mL	250 mL	500 mL
Sugar	50 g	100 g	200 g
Mint, chopped	15 g	30 g	60 g
Thyme	15 g	30 g	60 g
Stock, chicken or beef	1.5 L	3 L	6 L
Smoke essence	to taste		

1. Fry onions and garlic in oil over low heat for approximately 2–3 minutes.
2. Add all other ingredients and mix well.
3. Bring to the boil and simmer until correct consistency is reached.

Spicy Tomato Sauce

To be served with meatloaf and Italian dishes.

	25	50	100
Tomatoes	1 kg	2 kg	4 kg
Onion, chopped	250 g	500 g	1 kg
Butter	50 g	100 g	200 g
Garlic cloves, chopped	4	8	12
Chilli, chopped	20 g	40 g	80 g
Tomato paste	150 g	300 g	600 g

	25	50	100
Tomato juice	**250 mL**	**500 mL**	**1 L**
Worcester sauce	**1 L**	**2 L**	**4 L**
Basil	**10 g**	**20 g**	**40 g**
Oregano	**10 g**	**20 g**	**40 g**
Salt	**to taste**		
Pepper	**to taste**		

1. Remove stalks from tomatoes and prick tomato with a knife point.
2. Plunge tomatoes into boiling water until skin starts to peel.
3. Place into cold water and remove skins.
4. Seed and chop tomatoes.
5. Fry onions, garlic and chilli in butter for 4–5 minutes without colour.
6. Add all other ingredients and mix well.
7. Simmer gently for 30–40 minutes and serve.

Cranberry Sauce

To be served with poultry:

	25	50	100
Water	**325 mL**	**650 mL**	**1.3 L**
Sugar	**200 g**	**400 g**	**800 g**
Cranberries	**1.5 kg**	**3 kg**	**6 kg**

1. Place all ingredients into a pan and simmer gently until soft and of a thick consistency.
2. Chill before service.

Apple Sauce

To be served with pork.

	25	50	100
Water	**50 mL**	**100 mL**	**200 mL**
Apples, peeled and cored	**2 kg**	**4 kg**	**8 kg**
Sugar	**125 g**	**250 g**	**500 g**
Margarine	**50 g**	**100 g**	**200 g**

Put all ingredients into a pan with a lid and simmer, stirring often until apples have pureed.

Apple and Cinnamon Sauce

To be served with pork.

To apple sauce add:

	25	50	100
Cinnamon powder	**1 tablespoon**	**2 tablespoons**	**4 tablespoons**

Bread Sauce

To be served with poultry.

	25	50	100
Milk	**600 mL**	**1.2 L**	**2.4 L**
Butter	**50 g**	**100 g**	**200 g**
Breadcrumbs approx	**250 g**	**500 g**	**1 kg**
Onion, whole, peeled	**1**	**2**	**4**
Cloves	**8**	**16**	**32**
Salt	**to taste**		
Pepper	**to taste**		

1. Stud onion with cloves.
2. Place milk in saucepan with onion and bring to the boil.
3. Remove pan from heat and discard onion.
4. Place butter into milk and allow to melt.
5. Add breadcrumbs, mixing constantly until a thick consistency is reached. To thin down, add a little milk.
6. Place pan over a low heat and add salt and pepper.
7. Heat through and serve.

Minted Lemon Yoghurt

To be served with lightly spiced meats and meats cooked in an Asian style.

	25	50	100
Natural yoghurt	**750 mL**	**1.5 L**	**3 L**
Mint, preferably fresh,			
chopped	**50 g**	**100 g**	**200 g**
Lemon juice	**75 mL**	**150 mL**	**300 mL**
Caster sugar	**100 g**	**200 g**	**400 g**

1. Place all ingredients in a blender and bring to a smooth consistency. If blender is not available, whisk ingredients together.
2. Refrigerate for 2 hours before service.

Lemon and Garlic Yoghurt Sauce

To be served with lightly spiced meats and meats cooked in an Asian style.
As for minted lemon yoghurt omitting mint and adding:

	25	50	100
Garlic cloves, chopped	3	6	12

Diane Sauce

	25	50	100
Margarine	175 g	350 g	700 g
Onions, finely chopped	750 g	1.5 kg	3 kg
Garlic clove, chopped	4	6	8
Flour	175 g	350 g	700 g
Stock, beef	2 L	4 L	8 L
Mustard, French	200 g	400 g	800 g
Worcester sauce	100 mL	200 mL	400 mL
Salt and pepper	to taste		

1. Melt margarine in a suitably sized thick-bottomed pan over moderate heat.
2. Add onions and garlic and cook until onions are soft.
3. Reduce heat, add flour and incorporate thoroughly.
4. Add stock slowly, stirring continuously.
5. Bring to the boil.
6. Simmer gently.
7. Mix in mustard and Worcester sauce.
8. Simmer for 20 minutes.
9. Correct consistency and seasoning if required.
10. Serve as required.

Tomato, Parmesan and Garlic Sauce

	25	50	100
Margarine	100 g	200 g	400 g
Garlic cloves, chopped	4	7	12
Flour	100 g	200 g	400 g
Tomato puree	250 g	500 g	1 kg
Stock, chicken	1.5 L	3 L	6 L
Parmesan cheese, grated	100 g	200 g	400 g
Salt and pepper	to taste		

1. Melt margarine in a suitably sized pan over moderate heat.
2. Add garlic and cook for approximately 2 minutes.
3. Reduce heat and add flour, mixing thoroughly.
4. Add tomato puree and mix well.
5. Gradually add stock, mixing continuously until a smooth consistency is achieved.
6. Bring sauce to the boil and add parmesan cheese.
7. Simmer gently for 30 minutes.
8. Adjust consistency if too thick with the addition of a little more stock.
9. Season to taste.
10. Serve as required.

Provençal Sauce

	25	50	100
Onions, finely chopped	1 kg	2 kg	4 kg
Garlic cloves, chopped	4	6	8
Basil, chopped	20 g	40 g	80 g
Tomatoes, tinned	3 kg	6 kg	12 kg
Salt and pepper	to taste		
Oil	as required		

1. In a suitably sized thick-bottomed pan heat a little oil over moderate heat.
2. Add onions and garlic and cook until onions are soft.
3. Add basil and reduce heat.
4. Crush tinned tomatoes if whole, add to pan and mix thoroughly.
5. Simmer gently for 15 minutes and allow to reduce to required consistency.
6. Season to taste.
7. Serve as required.

Hollandaise Sauce

	25	50	100
Vinegar, white	**100 mL**	**200 mL**	**400 mL**
Black pepper, ground	**to taste**		
Butter	**1 kg**	**2 kg**	**4 kg**
Egg yolks	**4**	**8**	**16**

1. Place vinegar and pepper to taste in a pan over moderate heat, reduce by two-thirds and remove from heat.
2. Melt butter in a separate pan, remove from heat and allow to cool slightly.
3. Place egg yolks into suitably sized bowl.
4. Add vinegar reduction to egg yolks and whisk for several minutes.
5. While still whisking, gradually incorporate melted butter until thoroughly combined.
6. Correct seasoning.
7. Serve as required.

NOTE: Do not reheat because this will curdle sauce. If sauce should curdle, add a tablespoon of boiled water and rewhisk. If this fails to reconstitute sauce, repeat process with one egg yolk, whisking continually in a clean bowl, gradually adding curdled sauce.

Bearnaise Sauce

As for Hollandaise sauce with the addition of:

	25	50	100
Tarragon, dried	**10 g**	**20 g**	**40 g**

Add at step 1.

Tartare Sauce

To mayonnaise add:

	25	50	100
Parsley, chopped	**10 g**	**20 g**	**40 g**
Gherkin, finely chopped	**3**	**6**	**12**
Capers, chopped	**3**	**6**	**12**
Lemon juice	**50 mL**	**100 mL**	**200 mL**
Vinegar	**25 mL**	**50 mL**	**100 mL**

Seafood Sauce

To mayonnaise add:

	25	50	100
Tomato sauce	75 mL	150 mL	300 mL
Lemon juice	50 mL	100 mL	200 mL
Anchovy essence approx	1 tablespoon	2 tablespoons	4 tablespoons
Tabasco, drops approx	3	6	12
Worcester sauce	50 mL	100 mL	200 mL

——————— ◇ ———————

Soups

Basic Soup Recipe

	25	50	100
Named vegetable, diced or sliced	1.5 kg	3 kg	6 kg
Stock, chicken	7 L	14 L	28 L
Onions, sliced	250 g	500 g	1 kg
Celery, sliced	250 g	500 g	1 kg
Flour	125 g	250 g	500 g
Margarine	125 g	250 g	500 g
Bay leaf	4	8	12
Salt and pepper	to taste		

1. Fry onions in a little oil over a moderate heat in an adequately sized pan until tender, 2–3 minutes.
2. Add named vegetable and celery and fry gently for a further 3–5 minutes.
3. Add flour, mix well.
4. Slowly add stock, stirring continuously.
5. Add bay leaf and seasoning. Bring to the boil.
6. Simmer gently for 45 minutes to 1 hour.
7. Correct seasoning and serve.

Chinese Noodle Soup

Garnish: Thin julienne of capsicum.

As for basic soup recipe with addition of:

	25	50	100
Ginger, grated	10 g	20 g	40 g
Curry powder	30 g	60 g	120 g
Five spice powder	20 g	40 g	80 g
Noodles, dried	200 g	400 g	800 g
Lemon juice	100 mL	200 mL	400 mL

1. Add ginger, curry powder and five spice powder at step 5.
2. Add noodles broken into small pieces and lemon juice 5–10 minutes before cooking time elapses.

Vegetable Soup

Garnish: Parsley sprig.

As for basic soup recipe except for:

	25	50	100
Carrots, diced	600 g	1.2 kg	2.4 kg
Peas	200 g	400 g	800 g
Potato, diced	400 g	800 g	1.6 kg
Green beans, sliced	400 g	800 g	1.6 kg

Add at step 4.

Chunky Vegetable Soup

Garnish: Grated carrot.
As for vegetable soup with vegetables cut into 2 cm pieces.

Cream of Vegetable Soup

Garnish: Chives cut into 3 cm strips.
As for vegetable soup with the addition of:

	25	50	100
Cream	**400 mL**	**800 mL**	**1.6 L**

Add in the last 5 minutes of cooking time.
NOTE: This soup can be pureed if desired.

Potato Soup

Garnish: Croutons and crushed peppercorns.
As for basic soup recipe with the addition of:

	25	50	100
Potatoes, finely diced	**1.5 kg**	**3 kg**	**6 kg**

Add at step 4.
NOTE: This soup can be pureed if desired.

Potato and Chive Soup

Garnish: Chopped chives.
As for potato soup with the addition of:

	25	50	100
Chives, chopped	**30 g**	**60 g**	**120 g**

Add at step 4.
NOTE: This soup can be pureed if desired.

Potato and Leek Soup

Garnish: Sliced sautéed leek.

As for potato soup with the addition of:

	25	50	100
Leeks	**300 g**	**600 g**	**1.2 kg**

Add at step 2.

NOTE: This soup can be pureed if desired.

Potato and Watercress Soup

Garnish: Watercress sprig.

As for potato and chive soup, omitting chives and adding:

	25	50	100
Watercress, blanched and chopped	**150 g**	**300 g**	**600 g**

Add at step 5.

NOTE: This soup can be pureed if desired.

Chunky Celery Soup

Garnish: Diced tomato.

As for cream of celery soup, omitting sliced celery and adding diced celery (1–1.5 cm squared).

Cream of Celery Soup

Garnish: Sour cream, chives, paprika.

	25	50	100
Sliced celery	1.25 kg	2.5 kg	5 kg
Flour, plain	300 g	600 g	1.2 kg
Onions	400 g	800 g	1.6 kg
Leek	400 g	800 g	1.6 kg
Stock, chicken	7 L	14 L	28 L
Margarine	300 g	600 g	1.2 kg
Garlic cloves, chopped	2	4	7
Cream/milk	500 mL	1 L	2 L

1. Melt margarine in a thick-bottomed pan over moderate heat and add garlic.
2. Add all vegetables and cook out for approximately 5 minutes.
3. Add flour and stir. Cook for a further 2 minutes without colour.
4. Slowly add stock, stirring constantly.
5. Bring to the boil and season.
6. Simmer for another 45 minutes, then add the milk or cream.
7. Simmer for 15 minutes and serve.

NOTE: This soup can be pureed if desired.

Cream of Asparagus Soup

Garnish: Swirl of cream.

As for basic cream of celery soup, omitting celery and leek and adding:

	25	50	100
Asparagus, tinned	**600 g**	**1.2 kg**	**2.4 kg**

Add at step 5.

NOTE: This soup can be pureed if desired.

Cream of Broccoli Soup

Garnish: Blanched small broccoli florets.

As for basic cream of celery soup but replace half celery with small broccoli (florets).

Add at step 5.

NOTE: This soup can be pureed if desired.

Cream of Cauliflower Soup

Garnish: Blanched small cauliflower florets.

As for basic cream of celery soup but replace half celery with small cauliflower (florets).

Add at step 5.

NOTE: This soup can be pureed if desired.

Cream of Carrot Soup

Garnish: Thinly sliced radish and dill sprig.

As for basic cream of celery soup but replace half celery with carrot (finely diced).
Add at step 2.

NOTE: This soup can be pureed if desired.

Cream of Leek Soup

Garnish: Sliced sautéed leek.

As for basic cream of celery soup omitting half celery and adding:

	25	50	100
Leeks, finely sliced	**600 g**	**1.2 kg**	**2.4 kg**

Add tailed, washed and finely sliced leeks at step 2.

NOTE: This soup can be pureed if desired.

Leek and Chive Soup

Garnish: Grated cheese.

As for cream of leek soup with the addition of:

	25	50	100
Chives, chopped	**30 g**	**60 g**	**120 g**

Add chives 10 minutes before cooking time elapses.

NOTE: This soup can be pureed if desired.

Cream of Mushroom and Cheddar Soup

Garnish: Garlic croutons.

	25	50	100
Cheddar, grated	400 g	800 g	1.6 kg
Mushrooms sliced	1 kg	2 kg	4 kg
Onion, sliced	400 g	800 g	1.6 kg
Leek, sliced	200 g	400 g	800 g
Celery, sliced	400 g	800 g	1.6 kg
Stock, chicken	6.5 L	13 L	26 L
Cream	1 L	2 L	4 L
Flour	500 g	1 kg	2 kg
Margarine	500 g	1 kg	2 kg
Seasoning	as required		

1. Melt margarine in a thick-bottomed pan on moderate heat and add mushrooms, onion, leek and celery. Cook out, stirring occasionally for approximately 3 minutes.
2. Add flour and mix well.
3. Slowly add stock, stirring constantly.
4. Bring to the boil, season and simmer for 45 minutes.
5. Add cream and cheddar, simmer for a further 15 minutes and serve.

Cream of Mushroom Soup

Garnish: Turned mushroom.

As for cream of mushroom and cheddar soup omitting grated cheddar.

NOTE: This soup can be pureed if desired.

Garlic and Mushroom Soup

Garnish: Turned mushroom.

As for cream of mushroom soup with the addition of:

	25	50	100
Garlic cloves, chopped approx	**4**	**8**	**16**

Mushroom, Bacon and Parsley Soup

Garnish: Cooked and chopped bacon.

As for cream of mushroom soup with the addition of:

	25	50	100
Bacon, cooked, finely chopped	**250 g**	**500 g**	**1 kg**
Parsley, chopped	**25 g**	**50 g**	**100 g**

1. Add bacon at step 2.
2. Add parsley prior to service.

NOTE: This soup can be pureed if desired.

Creamy Spinach Soup

Garnish: Basil leaves.

	25	50	100
Spinach	2 kg	4 kg	8 kg
Onions, finely sliced	750 g	1.5 kg	3 kg
Margarine	175 g	350 g	700 g
Flour	175 g	350 g	700 g
Stock, chicken	3.5 L	7 L	14 L
Milk	3 L	6 L	12 L
Cream	500 mL	1 L	2 L
Salt and pepper	to taste		

1. Wash spinach thoroughly and remove stalks.
2. Finely slice spinach leaves.
3. Melt margarine over moderate heat in a suitably sized thick-bottomed pan.
4. Add onions and cook until soft.
5. Add spinach and cook until soft.
6. Reduce heat, add flour and incorporate thoroughly.
7. Gradually add stock, stirring continuously.
8. Add milk, stirring continuously, and bring to the boil.
9. Simmer gently for approximately 45 minutes
10. Season to taste and add cream.
11. Serve as required.

NOTE: This soup can be pureed if desired.

Cream of Sweet Corn Soup

Garnish: Finely sliced chives.
As for basic cream of celery soup omitting half celery and adding:

	25	50	100
Sweet corn niblets	600 g	1.2 kg	2.4 kg

NOTE: This soup can be pureed if desired.

Pumpkin and Orange Soup

Garnish: Sour cream, chopped coriander.

	25	50	100
Pumpkin, finely diced	2 kg	4 kg	8 kg
Onion, sliced	500 g	1 kg	2 kg

	25	50	100
Celery, sliced	500 g	1 kg	2 kg
Chicken stock	7 L	14 L	28 L
Margarine	400 g	800 g	1.6 kg
Flour	400 g	800 g	1.6 kg
Cream/milk	1 L	2 L	4 L
Garlic clove, chopped	1	2	4
Oranges, juice	2	4	8
Parsley, chopped	10 g	20 g	40 g
Coriander, chopped	10 g	20 g	40 g
Seasoning	as required		

1. Melt margarine in a thick-bottomed pan over moderate heat and add onion, celery and garlic. Cook out without colour for 3 minutes.

2. Add flour and cook out for a further 2 minutes.

3. Add stock slowly, stirring continuously.

4. Add diced pumpkin and seasoning, bring to the boil and simmer for 45 minutes.

5. Add cream/milk, orange juice, parsley and coriander, simmer for a further 15 minutes, correct seasoning and serve.

NOTE: All pumpkin soups may be pureed if required at step 5.

Pumpkin Soup

As for pumpkin and orange soup omitting orange.

Pumpkin and Sweet Potato Soup

Garnish: Slice of lemon.

As for pumpkin soup omitting half pumpkin and replacing with peeled, finely diced sweet potato.

Pumpkin and Coriander Soup

Garnish: Coriander sprig.

As for pumpkin soup with the addition of:

	25	50	100
Coriander, chopped	30 g	60 g	120 g

Add at step 2.

Pumpkin and Nutmeg Soup

Garnish: Orange segments.

As for pumpkin soup with the addition of:

	25	50	100
Nutmeg, ground	**10 g**	**20 g**	**40 g**

Add at step 2.

Pumpkin, Almond and Sour Cream Soup

Garnish: Toasted almonds.

As for pumpkin soup with the addition of:

	25	50	100
Almonds, ground	**200 g**	**400 g**	**800 g**
Sour cream	**200 mL**	**400 mL**	**800 mL**

1. Add almonds at step 2.
2. Add sour cream 5 minutes prior to service.

Chicken Broth

	25	50	100
Onion, finely sliced	**350 g**	**700 g**	**1.4 kg**
Celery, finely sliced	**350 g**	**700 g**	**1.4 kg**
Chicken, cooked and finely diced	**400 g**	**800 g**	**1.6 kg**
Margarine	**200 g**	**400 g**	**800 g**
Flour	**200 g**	**400 g**	**800 g**
Stock, chicken	**7 L**	**14 L**	**28 L**
Salt and pepper	**to taste**		
Bay leaves	**2**	**4**	**8**

1. Melt margarine in suitable pan over moderate heat.
2. Add celery, onions and bay leaves and cook for 3–4 minutes without colour until soft.
3. Add flour and mix well. Cook for further 2–3 minutes.
4. Reduce heat and add stock, stirring continuously.
5. Add chicken and salt and pepper.
6. Bring to the boil and simmer gently for 45 minutes to 1 hour.

Creamy Chicken Soup

Garnish: Rosemary sprig.
As for chicken broth except:

	25	50	100
Omit			
Stock, chicken	**1 L**	**2 L**	**4 L**
Add			
Milk/cream	**1 L**	**2 L**	**4 L**

Add milk or cream at step 6.

Chicken and Coriander Soup

Garnish: Grated carrot.
As for creamy chicken soup with the addition of:

	25	50	100
Coriander, chopped	**25 g**	**50 g**	**100 g**

Add at step 2.

Cream of Chicken and Sage Soup

Garnish: Diced chicken (white meat).
As for creamy chicken soup with the addition of:

	25	50	100
Sage, dried, chopped	**5 g**	**10 g**	**20 g**

Add at step 2.

Herb and Chicken Broth

As for chicken broth with the addition of:

	25	50	100
Parsley, chopped	**5 g**	**10 g**	**20 g**
Garlic cloves, chopped	**2**	**4**	**8**
Tarragon, chopped	**5 g**	**10 g**	**20 g**
Thyme, chopped	**5 g**	**10 g**	**20 g**
Rosemary, chopped	**5 g**	**10 g**	**20 g**

Add all ingredients at step 2.

Chicken and Sweet Corn Soup

Garnish: Chopped coriander.
As for chicken broth with the addition of:

	25	50	100
Sweet corn niblets	**200 g**	**400 g**	**800 g**

Add at step 5.

Chicken and Rice Soup

Garnish: Saffron rice.
As for chicken broth or creamy chicken soup with the addition of:

	25	50	100
Rice, long grain, cooked	**75 g**	**150 g**	**300 g**

Add 5 minutes prior to service.

Curried Chicken Soup

Garnish: Spun shallot.
As for chicken broth or creamy chicken soup with the addition of:

	25	50	100
Curry powder	50 g	100 g	200 g
Garlic cloves, chopped	2	4	8

Add all ingredients at step 2.

Chicken and Coconut Soup

Garnish: Lemon slice and chopped coriander.
As for chicken broth or creamy chicken soup with the addition of:

	25	50	100
Coconut, desiccated	**75 g**	**150 g**	**300 g**

Add at step 5.

Thai Style Chicken Soup

Garnish: Coriander sprig.

As for chicken broth or creamy chicken soup with the addition of:

	25	50	100
Coriander, chopped	20 g	40 g	80 g
Coconut, desiccated	30 g	60 g	120 g
Coconut milk	500 mL	1 L	2 L
Sugar	50 g	100 g	200 g
Curry powder	20 g	40 g	80 g
Peanuts, ground	50 g	100 g	200 g

1. Add curry powder at step 2.
2. Add all other ingredients at step 5.
3. Substitute coconut milk for that amount of chicken stock.

Chicken and Mushroom Soup

Garnish: Diced red capsicum.

As for chicken broth or creamy chicken soup except for:

	25	50	100
Omit			
Onion	175 g	350 g	700 g
Celery	175 g	350 g	700 g
Add			
Mushrooms, finely sliced	350 g	700 g	1.4 kg

Add at step 2.

Minestrone Soup

Garnish: Grated parmesan cheese and chopped parsley.

	25	50	100
Carrot, finely diced	300 g	600 g	1.2 kg
Onion, finely diced	300 g	600 g	1.2 kg
Celery, finely diced	300 g	600 g	1.2 kg
Capsicum, finely diced	300 g	600 g	1.2 kg
Garlic cloves, chopped	3	6	12
Spaghetti, uncooked	150 g	300 g	600 g
Stock, chicken	7 L	14 L	28 L
Margarine	150 g	300 g	600 g
Flour	150 g	300 g	600 g
Salt and pepper	to taste		
Basil, chopped	10 g	20 g	40 g

1. Melt margarine in suitable pan over moderate heat.
2. Add onions, garlic and basil and cook for 2–3 minutes or until soft.
3. Add all other vegetables and cook for a further 3–4 minutes.
4. Add flour, mix well and cook for further 2 minutes without colour.
5. Slowly add stock, stirring continuously.
6. Add spaghetti broken into 2 cm pieces.
7. Bring to the boil, add salt and pepper and simmer gently for 45 minutes to 1 hour.
8. Reseason and serve as required.

Mulligatawny

	25	50	100
Onions, small diced pieces	600 g	1.2 kg	2.4 kg
Celery, small diced pieces	200 g	400 g	800 g
Apple, peeled, cored, diced	300 g	600 g	1.2 kg
Margarine	175 g	350 g	700 g
Flour	175 g	350 g	700 g
Tomato puree	100 g	200 g	400 g
Minced beef	200 g	400 g	800 g
Rice, long grain, cooked	50 g	100 g	200 g
Stock, chicken	6 L	12 L	24 L
Curry powder	30 g	60 g	120 g
Milk/cream	1.5 L	3 L	6 L
Sultanas	50 g	100 g	200 g
Sugar	30 g	60 g	120 g
Salt and pepper	to taste		

1. Melt margarine in suitable pan over high heat.
2. Add onion, celery and minced beef and cook until beef turns a light brown.
3. Reduce heat, add flour, tomato puree, curry powder, salt and pepper and mix well cooking for a further 3–4 minutes without colour.
4. Add stock slowly, stirring continuously.
5. Bring to the boil and simmer gently.
6. Add apple and sultanas and simmer for 20 minutes.
7. Add milk/cream, rice and sugar.
8. Simmer for further 15 minutes and serve.

NOTE: More curry powder may be added if required to give a fuller flavoured curry taste but care should be taken not to produce too spicy a soup.

Pea and Ham Soup

Garnish: Croutons.

	25	50	100
Ham hocks	1	2	4
Water	7 L	14 L	28 L
Peas, split, pre-soaked	1 kg	2 kg	4 kg
Onions, finely chopped	200 g	400 g	800 g
Carrots, finely chopped	200 g	400 g	800 g
Celery, finely chopped	200 g	400 g	800 g
Margarine	100 g	200 g	400 g
Flour	100 g	200 g	400 g
Milk/cream	1 L	2 L	4 L
Parsley, chopped	25 g	50 g	100 g
Bay leaves	2	4	8
Salt and pepper	to taste		

1. Fill large pan with water and ham hocks, bring to the boil and simmer for 1 hour.
2. Remove ham hocks and leave to cool retaining stock that has been made up to 6 L, 13 L, 27 L respectively.
3. Melt margarine in suitable pan and fry onions, celery and carrots for 2–3 minutes.
4. Mix in flour and cook for further 2–3 minutes.
5. Slowly add stock, stirring continuously, and bring to the boil.
6. Add ham (removed from the bone and with excess fat cut away), bay leaves, split peas, salt, pepper, parsley and simmer for 45 minutes to 1 hour.
7. Add milk/cream 5 minutes prior to service.

NOTE: This soup can be pureed if desired.

Lentil Soup

As for pea and ham soup omitting split peas and replacing with desired pre-soaked lentils.

NOTE: Dried lentils should be thoroughly rinsed and soaked for 24 hours in cold water before being used in any dish.

Vichyssoise

Garnish: Chopped parsley, paprika.

	25	50	100
Margarine	125 g	250 g	500 g
Flour	125 g	250 g	500 g
Leek, white of, finely sliced	250 g	500 g	1 kg
Onion, finely chopped	350 g	700 g	1.4 kg
Stock, chicken	5 L	10 L	20 L
Milk/cream	2 L	4 L	8 L
Chives, chopped	20 g	40 g	80 g
Potato, peeled, finely diced	2 kg	4 kg	8 kg
Salt and pepper	to taste		

1. Melt margarine in suitable pan over moderate heat.
2. Add leeks and onions and cook for 2–3 minutes or until soft.
3. Add flour and mix well.
4. Slowly add stock, stirring continuously.
5. Add potato and chives, bring to the boil and simmer for 45 minutes to 1 hour.
6. Add cream 10 minutes prior to service.

NOTE: All vichyssoise recipes may be pureed if desired.

Sweet Potato and Chive Soup

Garnish: Mint leaves.
As for vichyssoise omitting potato and adding peeled, finely diced sweet potato.

Pumpkin Vichyssoise

As for vichyssoise omitting potato and adding peeled, seeded finely diced pumpkin.

Pumpkin and Coriander Vichyssoise

As for pumpkin vichyssoise omitting chives and adding finely chopped coriander.

Tomato Soup

Garnish: Croutons.

	25	50	100
Margarine	175 g	350 g	700 g
Flour	175 g	350 g	700 g
Tomato paste	325 g	650 g	1.3 kg
Garlic cloves, chopped	3	6	12
Onions, finely chopped	175 g	350 g	700 g
Stock, chicken	5 L	10 L	20 L
Milk	2 L	4 L	8 L
Sugar	50 g	100 g	200 g
Parsley, chopped	10 g	20 g	40 g
Salt and pepper	to taste		

1. Melt margarine in suitable pan and fry onions and garlic over a moderate heat until onions are soft.
2. Add flour and mix well cooking for 2–3 minutes without colour.
3. Add tomato paste and cook for further 1 minute.
4. Add stock slowly, stirring continuously.
5. Bring to the boil and simmer.
6. Add sugar, salt and pepper and simmer for 45 minutes to 1 hour.
7. Ten minutes prior to service, add milk and parsley.

Cream of Tomato Soup

Garnish: Chopped basil.

As for tomato soup substituting same amounts of cream for milk.

Tomato and Basil Soup

As for tomato soup with the addition of:

	25	50	100
Basil, chopped	25 g	50 g	100 g

Add at step 1.

Tomato and Chive Soup

As for tomato soup with the addition of:

	25	50	100
Chives, chopped	**30 g**	**60 g**	**120 g**

Add at step 5.

Tomato and Coriander Soup

As for tomato soup with the addition of:

	25	50	100
Coriander, chopped	**30 g**	**60 g**	**120 g**

Add at step 5.

Tomato and Rice Soup

As for tomato soup with the addition of:

	25	50	100
Rice, long grain, cooked	**125 g**	**250 g**	**500 g**

Add at step 5.

Tomato and Cucumber Soup

As for tomato soup with the addition of:

	25	50	100
Cucumber, peeled, seeded, finely diced	**150 g**	**300 g**	**600 g**

Add at step 5.

French Onion Soup

Garnish: Croutons.

	25	50	100
Margarine	**50 g**	**100 g**	**200 g**
Onions, sliced	**2 kg**	**4 kg**	**8 kg**
Garlic cloves, chopped	**3**	**6**	**12**
Stock, beef	**7 L**	**14 L**	**28 L**

1. Melt margarine in suitable pan over moderate heat and cook onions and garlic until brown.

2. Add stock, bring to the boil and simmer gently for 45 minutes to 1 hour.

NOTE: During cooking time remove any scum or fat that may rise to the surface.

White Onion Soup

Garnish: Croutons.

As for cream of celery soup except:

	25	50	100
Omit			
Celery	**750 g**	**1.5 kg**	**3 kg**
Add			
Onions, finely sliced	**1.5 kg**	**3 kg**	**6 kg**

Add at step 2.

Chilled Gazpacho Soup

Garnish: Dill sprig.

	25	50	100
Tomatoes, tinned, liquidised	**7 L**	**14 L**	**28 L**
Cucumbers, peeled, seeded, finely diced	**250 g**	**500 g**	**1 kg**
Onions, finely diced	**500 g**	**1 kg**	**2 kg**
Capsicum, seeded, diced	**500 g**	**1 kg**	**2 kg**
Garlic clove, chopped	**4**	**8**	**16**
Lemon, juice	**2**	**4**	**6**
Sugar	**50 g**	**100 g**	**200 g**
Vinegar, white	**75 mL**	**150 mL**	**300 mL**
Salt and pepper	**to taste**		

1. Mix all ingredients together and season to taste.

2. Chill for 4 hours in refrigerator before serving.

Crecy Soup

Garnish: Boiled rice.

As for cream of celery soup omitting celery and adding peeled grated carrot.
Add at step 2.

Brown Celery Soup

Garnish: Julienne of celery.

As for french onion soup omitting onion and adding finely diced celery.
Add at step 1.

Crab Chowder

Garnish: Chopped chives.

	25	50	100
Crab meat, chopped	500 g	1 kg	2 kg
Fish stock	6.5 L	13 L	26 L
Onion, finely chopped	500 g	1 kg	2 kg
Garlic cloves, crushed	2	4	8
Butter	300 g	600 g	1.2 kg
Flour	300 g	600 g	1.2 kg
Cream/milk	500 mL	1 L	2 L
Seasoning	as required		

1. Melt butter in thick-bottomed pan on high heat, add onion and garlic and cook until soft.
2. Reduce heat to low, add flour and mix in thoroughly.
3. Add warmed fish stock.
4. Add crab meat and seasoning.
5. Bring to the boil and simmer gently for 1 hour.
6. Pass through a fine strainer and add cream.
7. Reheat and correct seasoning.

James Island Soup

Garnish: Cooked prawns.

As for crab chowder omitting crab and half fish stock, and adding:

	25	50	100
Prawns, small, cooked, shelled and roughly chopped	500 g	1 kg	2 kg
White fish, cooked and crumbled	1 kg	2 kg	4 kg
Brandy	25 mL	50 mL	100 mL
Parsley, chopped	10 g	20 g	40 g
Milk	3.5 L	7 L	14 L

1. Add milk at step 3.
2. Add other ingredients at step 4.

Sweet Corn and Crab Chowder

Garnish: Chervil sprigs and lemon segments.
As for crab chowder with the addition of:

	25	50	100
Sweet corn niblets	**500 g**	**1 kg**	**2 kg**

Add at step 4.

Seafood and Dill Chowder

Garnish: Dill sprigs.
As for crab chowder omitting half crab meat and adding:

	25	50	100
Prawns, cooked, shelled and chopped	**250 g**	**500 g**	**1 kg**
White fish, cooked and crumbled	**500 g**	**1 kg**	**2 kg**
Dill, chopped	**20 g**	**40 g**	**80 g**

1. Add dill at step 1.
2. Add prawns and fish at step 4.

Beef Dishes

Roasted Beef

Garnish: Watercress.

This method of cookery applies to such joints of beef as topside, sirloin, rump, prime rib and fillet.

1. Preheat oven to 150–180°C (moderate).

2. Trim excess fat and any visible sinew from meat.

3. Place meat on trellis in suitable roasting tray (see Chapter 1), coat with oil, season and place in oven.

4. Baste joint with any juices that appear in the bottom of the roasting tray every 15–20 minutes.

5. See 'Cooking times for meat', Chapter 1, p 3.

6. Test to see if cooked by piercing meat with a meat fork and observing the colour of the juices released. If juices are clear, meat is cooked through; if blood appears, meat has been cooked to a rarer degree.

7. Once meat is cooked, it should be allowed to stand in a cool place for 15–20 minutes to help carving (do not place warm meat in refrigerator).

Probe Temperature for Beef

Rare:	**60°C**
Medium:	**70°C**
Well Done:	**75°C**

Grilled Steak

Garnish: Grilled tomato, watercress.

Steak, required cut	**25 x 100–150 g**	**50 x 100–150 g**	**100 x 100–150 g**
Salt	**as required**		
Pepper	**as required**		
Oil	**as required**		

1. Preheat grill or frypan.
2. Brush steaks with a little oil and lightly season.
3. Seal both sides quickly to minimise loss of juices and reduce heat.
4. Cook on either side slowly until required degree of cooking is reached.

Garlic Steak

Garnish: Garlic and herb butter.

As for grilled steak with the addition of:

	25	50	100
Garlic cloves, finely chopped	**8**	**16**	**32**
Oil	**150 mL**	**300 mL**	**600 mL**
Salt and pepper	**to taste**		

1. Combine all ingredients and mix.
2. Use as oil in grilled steak recipe.

Pepper Steak

Garnish: Chopped parsley.

As for garlic steak. Serve coated in pepper sauce (see Stocks and Sauces section).

Steak Diane

Garnish: Sliced shallots.

As for garlic steak with the addition of:

	25	50	100
Mustard, french	**100 g**	**200 g**	**400 g**
Worcester sauce	**100 mL**	**200 mL**	**400 mL**
Tomato sauce	**100 mL**	**200 mL**	**400 mL**
Lemon juice	**150 mL**	**300 mL**	**600 mL**
Parsley	**20 g**	**40 g**	**80 g**

1. Combine all ingredients.
2. Preheat grill or frypan.
3. Brush steaks with a little sauce.
4. Seal both sides and continue to baste with sauce until steaks are cooked and ready to serve.

Steak Diane Casserole

Garnish: Chopped parsley.

	25	50	100
Beef, chuck, diced	**5 kg**	**10 kg**	**20 kg**

1. Seal meat quickly on both sides.
2. Place into deep-sided baking tray.
3. Pour over sauce (see Diane Sauce, p 105).
4. Cover and cook in oven preheated to a moderate setting for approximately 1½–2 hours or until meat is tender.
5. Serve with a little of the sauce.

Mixed Grill

Garnish: Parsley sprigs.

	25	50	100
Steak, required cut	**13 x 100–150 g**	**25 x 100–150 g**	**50 x 100–150 g**
Lamb cutlets	**25**	**50**	**100**
Sausages	**25**	**50**	**100**
Tomatoes	**13**	**25**	**50**
Oil	**as required**		
Salt	**as required**		
Pepper	**as required**		

1. Cut steak and tomatoes in half.
2. Place sausages and halved tomatoes onto two lightly greased baking trays and place in preheated oven at a moderate setting for 15–25 minutes or until cooked.
3. Cook steak and lamb as for grilled steak.

English Mixed Grill

As for mixed grill with the addition of a piece of grilled liver.

Beef Madras Curry

Garnish: sliced roasted almonds served on a bed of cooked rice.

As for lamb curry replacing lamb with same amount of finely diced beef (chuck).

Basic Savoury Mince

Garnish: Tomato, finely diced mixed with a little chopped parsley.

	25	50	100
Minced beef	2.75 kg	5.5 kg	11 kg
Onions	500 g	1 kg	2 kg
Garlic, crushed	6	12	24
Tomato paste	200 mL	400 mL	800 mL
Tomatoes, tinned	1 kg	2 kg	4 kg
Worcester sauce	75 mL	150 mL	300 mL
Beef stock	750 mL	1.5 L	3 L
Flour	100 g	200 g	400 g
Salt and pepper	to taste		
Thyme	15 g	30 g	60 g

1. Fry onions, garlic and thyme in a little oil without colour until soft.
2. Add meat and cook until meat turns a light brown.
3. Reduce heat and add tomato paste, mixing well.
4. Add flour and mix well.
5. Add pureed tinned tomatoes, stock, salt and pepper and mix well.
6. Bring to the boil, skim, and simmer for approximately 30–40 minutes.
7. Correct seasoning before service.

Spiced Beef

Garnish: Chilli flowers.

As for savoury mince with the addition of:

	25	50	100
Chillies, finely chopped	**200 g**	**400 g**	**800 g**
Basil, chopped	**10 g**	**20 g**	**40 g**
Garlic cloves, chopped	**3**	**6**	**12**

Add chilli sparingly, as strength can vary from quite mild to extremely hot. Add more or less to taste. Add at step 3.

Cottage Pie

Garnish: Chopped parsley.

As for basic savoury mince with the addition of:

	25	50	100
Potato, creamed	**7 kg** **see Potato Dishes**	**14 kg**	**28 kg**
Eggs	**1**	**2**	**4**
Milk	**100 mL**	**200 mL**	**400 mL**

1. Place required amount of savoury mince evenly in the bottom of a deep-sided baking dish.
2. Top neatly with creamed potato and brush liberally with mixture of beaten eggs and milk.
3. Bake in moderate oven for approximately 30 minutes or until cooked and golden brown.
4. Portion and serve.

NOTE: Leftover roasted meat may be minced and used for minced beef dishes such as savoury mince and cottage pies.

Mexican Spiced Tacos

Garnish: Sour cream, guacamole, finely diced tomato, grated cheddar cheese, shredded lettuce.

As for basic savoury mince omitting beef stock and thyme, and adding:

	25	50	100
Tomatoes, tinned, **pureed**	**1 kg**	**2 kg**	**4 kg**
Chilli powder, mild	**100 g**	**200 g**	**400 g**

Add chilli powder at step 2.

NOTES:

1. Mexican style mince is used to fill taco shells which are commercially available and need only to be warmed and filled with a little mince and a little of the above garnishes.

2. Serve two filled taco shells per portion.

Curried Mince Beef

Garnish: Diced capsicum.

As for basic savoury mince with the addition of:

	25	50	100
Curry powder	**75 g**	**150 g**	**300 g**
Apple, peeled, diced	**250 g**	**500 g**	**1 kg**
Sultanas	**100 g**	**200 g**	**400 g**
Coconut, desiccated	**50 g**	**100 g**	**200 g**
Lemon juice	**75 mL**	**150 mL**	**300 mL**

1. Add curry powder at step 2.
2. Add all other ingredients at step 5.
3. Simmer for approximately 1 hour.

Bolognaise Sauce

Garnish: Chopped sprigs of basil.

As for basic savoury mince with the addition of:

	25	50	100
Red wine	**150 mL**	**300 mL**	**600 mL**
Basil	**15 g**	**30 g**	**60 g**
Oregano	**15 g**	**30 g**	**60 g**
Bay leaves	**4**	**8**	**12**

Add all ingredients at step 1.

Spaghetti Bolognaise

Garnish: Basil sprigs.

	25	50	100
Spaghetti	1 kg	2 kg	4 kg
Water			
Oil	50 mL	100 mL	200 mL
Bay leaves	4	8	12
Salt and pepper	to taste		

1. Boil enough water to thoroughly immerse spaghetti in large pan.

2. Add oil, salt and bay leaves, then spaghetti, making sure it does not lie in the pan uniformly because this will make pasta stick. Separate with a wooden spoon by mixing gently.

3. Simmer for approximately 15–20 minutes or until spaghetti is soft.

4. Remove from heat and strain. Wash with hot water if being served immediately or cold if being served at a later stage.

5. Reheat by running boiling water through spaghetti.

6. When ready for service, place a good amount of spaghetti onto a plate pushing slightly to the sides. Place a ladle full of bolognaise sauce (see p 135) in the centre and serve.

Italian Lasagne

Garnish: Finely sliced tomato, grated parmesan cheese.

As for bolognaise sauce omitting half stock, doubling the flour, and adding:

	25	50	100
Tomatoes, tinned	1 kg	2 kg	4 kg
Lasagne sheets	750 g	1.5 kg	3 kg
Cheddar cheese, grated	350 g	700 g	1.4 kg
Parmesan cheese, grated	100 g	200 g	400 g
Basic white sauce	1.5 L	3 L	6 L
	see Stocks and Sauces		

1. Add tomatoes at step 5 (if whole, crush or puree before adding).

2. If lasagne sheets need to be soaked or cooked prior to making lasagne, follow manufacturer's instructions. It is best purchased fresh.

3. Grease suitable deep-sided baking dish with a little oil and place a thin layer of bolognaise sauce on base of tin.

4. Top with a layer of lasagne sheets and continue process until desired depth is reached.

5. Top with approximately 1 cm of white sauce.

6. Sprinkle cheddar and parmesan cheese that has been mixed together.

7. Bake in moderate oven for approximately 30–40 minutes until cooked and light brown in colour.

8. Allow to stand for 5 minutes prior to service.

NOTE: It is often a good idea to pre-portion lasagne before serving.

Chilli Con Carne

Garnish: Sour cream, corn chips.

As for basic savoury mince with the addition of:

	25	50	100
Chilli powder, mild	**150 g**	**300 g**	**600 g**
Kidney beans, cooked, drained	**500 g**	**1 kg**	**2 kg**

1. Add chilli powder at step 2.
2. Add kidney beans at step 5.

NOTE: Extra chilli may be added if desired for a hotter dish.

Gourmet Burgers

Garnish: Side salad garnish.

	25	50	100
Minced beef	**2.5 kg**	**5 kg**	**10 kg**
Breadcrumbs	**500 g**	**1 kg**	**2 kg**
Onions, finely chopped	**500 g**	**1 kg**	**2 kg**
Eggs	**4**	**8**	**16**
Garlic	**4**	**8**	**16**
Worcester sauce	**50 mL**	**100 mL**	**200 mL**
Tomato sauce	**125 mL**	**250 mL**	**500 mL**
Mustard, mild	**75 g**	**150 g**	**300 g**
Barbecue sauce	**100 mL**	**200 mL**	**400 mL**
Oregano	**10 g**	**20 g**	**40 g**
Basil	**10 g**	**20 g**	**40 g**
Salt and pepper	**to taste**		

1. Cook onion, garlic and herbs until soft.
2. Put all other ingredients in commercial mixer and add cooked ingredients.
3. Mix thoroughly until all ingredients are combined.
4. If mixture is too moist, add extra breadcrumbs in small amounts. If too dry, add small amounts of tomato sauce.
5. Empty mixture onto lightly floured surface and mould into required size burgers.
6. In frypan with a little oil, fry burgers gently until golden brown.
7. Remove from pan, drain any excess oil and place in suitable sized baking tray.
8. Bake in oven preheated to a moderate setting for approximately 20–30 minutes.
9. Serve with choice of grilled bacon, pineapple, Swiss cheese, guacamole, fried onions etc in a toasted hamburger bun.

Garlic Burgers

Garnish: Side salad garnish.

As for gourmet burgers omitting Worcester sauce and barbecue sauce, and adding:

	25	50	100
Garlic	double original recipe		
Tomato puree	100 mL	200 mL	400 mL
Onions	double original recipe		

Thai Burgers

Garnish: Side salad garnish.

As for gourmet burgers omitting Worcester sauce and barbecue sauce and adding:

	25	50	100
Lemon juice	50 mL	100 mL	200 mL
Coconut, desiccated	50 g	100 g	200 g
Coriander, chopped	20 g	40 g	80 g
Peanut butter	100 g	200 g	400 g
Sugar	75 g	150 g	300 g

Steak and Onion Pie

Garnish: Spun shallot.

	25	50	100
Steak, chuck, small diced	3.5 kg	7 kg	14 kg
Onions, sliced	1.5 kg	3 kg	6 kg
Stock, beef	1.5 L	3 L	6 L
Flour, plain	125 g	250 g	500 g
Tomato puree	200 g	400 g	800 g
Thyme	5 g	10 g	20 g
Parsley	10 g	20 g	40 g
Short crust pastry	1.5 kg	3 kg	6 kg
Eggs	2	4	8
Milk	100 mL	200 mL	400 mL

1. Fry onions in a little oil until cooked.
2. Add steak, herbs and seasoning and cook until light brown.
3. Add flour and mix well.
4. Add tomato puree and mix well.

5. Add stock slowly, stirring constantly.

6. Simmer gently for 1 hour or until meat is tender and required consistency is reached. Skim top to remove any fat that may have risen to the surface. To thicken, if necessary, add equal amounts of flour and water which have been mixed. Incorporate thoroughly.

7. Fill pie dishes with meat mixture to required depth and allow to cool for 15–20 minutes.

8. On floured board, roll out pastry to a size larger than the dishes to a thickness of approximately ½ cm.

9. Cover pie dish with pastry, trim and crimp edges.

10. Brush with egg mixture of beaten eggs and milk.

11. Make approximately 4–6 one inch incisions along the centre of the pastry at regular intervals (depending on size of dish).

12. Bake in oven preheated to a moderate setting for approximately 25–40 minutes or until pastry is cooked and golden brown.

13. Portion and serve.

NOTE: A little red wine may be added at step 5 for extra flavour if desired.

Curried Beef Pie

Garnish: Spun shallot.

As for steak and onion pie with the addition of:

	25	50	100
Curry powder approximately depending on strength	75 g	150 g	300 g

Add curry powder at step 2.

Beef and Vegetable Pie

Garnish: Cucumber twist.

As for steak and onion pie with the addition of:

	25	50	100
Carrots, finely diced	500 g	1 kg	2 kg
Celery, finely sliced	250 g	500 g	1 kg
Mushrooms, sliced	150 g	300 g	600 g
Potatoes, finely diced	100 g	200 g	400 g

Omit

	25	50	100
Onions, *reduce by*	1 kg	2 kg	4 kg

Add prepared vegetables at step 2.

Steak and Mushroom Pie

Garnish: Turned, cooked mushrooms.

As for steak and onion pie except:

	25	50	100
Replace			
Onions	750 g	1.5 kg	3 kg
with			
Mushrooms, sliced	750 g	1.5 kg	3 kg

Add mushrooms at step 2.

Italian Meatballs

Garnish: Chopped basil.

As for gourmet burgers omitting tomato sauce and barbecue sauce and adding:

	25	50	100
Garlic	double original recipe		
Tomato puree	250 mL	500 mL	1 L
Oregano, dried	double original recipe		
Basil, dried	double original recipe		
Mint	10 g	20 g	40 g

1. Mould mixture into size of golf balls.

2. Fry in a little oil until light brown.

3. Remove from pan and drain any excess oil.

4. Place on roasting tray and place in oven preheated to a moderate setting for approximately 20 minutes, or until cooked to required degree.

Beef Satay

Garnish: Coriander leaves, capsicum rings, finely sliced chillies.

	25	50	100
Beef, rump, finely diced	4 kg	8 kg	16 kg
Tomato, finely diced	3 kg	6 kg	12 kg
Capsicum, finely diced	1 kg	2 kg	4 kg
Marinade			
Mild mustard	50 g	100 g	200 g
Five spice powder	20 g	40 g	80 g
Salt	to taste		
Mint, finely chopped	10 g	20 g	40 g
Coriander, finely chopped	25 g	50 g	100 g
Dry sherry	200 mL	400 mL	800 mL
Vinegar	50 mL	100 mL	200 mL
Soy sauce	50 mL	100 mL	200 mL
Sauce			
Margarine	100 g	200 g	400 g
Onion, chopped	500 g	1 kg	2 kg
Curry powder	40 g	80 g	160 g
Flour	100 g	200 g	400 g
Chicken stock	1 L	2 L	4 L
Tomato paste	500 mL	1 L	2 L
Lemon juice	1 lemon	2 lemons	4 lemons
Sugar	50 g	100 g	200 g
Peanut butter	150 g	300 g	600 g
Coriander, chopped	30 g	60 g	120 g

1. Using kebab sticks, place a piece of beef followed by a piece of tomato followed by a square of capsicum on stick until three-quarters full. Leave a small gap at either end of stick.

2. Blend marinade ingredients together and coat kebabs.

3. Place in refrigerator and leave overnight making sure kebabs are turned and recoated with marinade whenever possible.

4. Melt margarine in pan with the oil and gently fry onions.

5. Add curry powder and sugar.

6. Add flour and cook out for 3 minutes.

7. Add stock slowly, continuously stirring.

8. Add tomato paste, lemon juice, peanut butter and coriander and simmer for 15 minutes. Season with salt and pepper to taste.

9. Adjust consistency by the addition of a little tomato paste or chicken stock.

10. Place kebabs on tray under salamander or cook off on grill turning frequently. Cooking times will vary depending on the thickness of the meat. Serve on a bed of rice with a little sauce poured over the top.

Braised Steak and Onions

Garnish: Chopped parsley.

	25	50	100
Steak, chuck, finely diced	3 kg	6 kg	12 kg
Onions, finely sliced	1.5 kg	3 kg	6 kg
Flour, plain	150 g	300 g	600 g
Stock, beef	1. 75 L	3.5 L	7 L
Salt and pepper	to taste		

1. Trim steaks of any excess fat and cut into required portion sizes 100–150 g.

2. Combine flour, salt and pepper and coat steaks in seasoned flour.

3. Cook and seal steaks using a little oil for approximately 1 minute each side over high heat.

4. Drain excess juices from steaks and alternate layers of steak and onions in deep-sided baking dish.

5. Add stock to dish so steaks are just covered.

6. Cover dish with aluminium foil and bake in a moderate oven for approximately 2 hours or until steaks are tender.

7. Serve steaks with a little of the thickened stock.

NOTE: There are many variations to this classic dish. Other flavourings such as seeded mustard, garlic and creamed horseradish may be added to taste at steps 4–5.

New York Style Meatloaf

Garnishing: Finely sliced tomatoes, grated cheese.

	25	50	100
Minced beef	**3 kg**	**6 kg**	**12 kg**
Onions, finely diced	**500 g**	**1 kg**	**2 kg**
Eggs	**5**	**10**	**20**
Breadcrumbs	**500 g**	**1 kg**	**2 kg**
Tomato sauce	**100 g**	**200 g**	**400 g**
Barbecue sauce	**100 g**	**200 g**	**400 g**
Tabasco sauce	**1 teaspoon**	**2 teaspoons**	**4 teaspoons**
Oregano, chopped	**25 g**	**50 g**	**100 g**
Garlic clove, chopped	**2**	**4**	**8**
Basil, chopped	**25 g**	**50 g**	**100 g**
Oil	**as required**		

1. Over high heat, cook onions and garlic without colour in a little oil.

2. Add oregano, basil and garlic. Cook for further 2 minutes and remove from heat.

3. Place minced beef (raw) into large mixer with paddle attached.

4. Add cooked ingredients and all other ingredients and mix thoroughly.

5. Lightly grease aluminium foil and place meat in cylindrical shapes approximately 30 cm x 12 cm x 15 cm on foil.

6. Fold foil around mixture until totally enclosed.

7. Place on oiled baking tray and place in oven preheated to a moderate setting for approximately 45 minutes.

8. Remove from oven and gently remove foil.

9. Still on baking tray, garnish by laying thinly sliced tomatoes along meatloaf and then sprinkling generously with grated cheese.

10. Return to oven for further 10–15 minutes or until cooked through and cheese is melted and golden brown.

Braised Steak in Ale or Red Wine

Garnish: Tomato sails.

As for braised steak and onions except:

	25	50	100
Add			
Ale, beer	**½ L**	**1 L**	**2 L**
Wine, red	**½ L**	**1 L**	**2 L**
Omit			
Stock	**½ L**	**1 L**	**2 L**

Beef Casserole

Garnish: Grated carrot.

	25	50	100
Beef, chuck, finely diced	3 kg	6 kg	12 kg
Onions, finely sliced	500 g	1 kg	2 kg
Leeks, finely sliced	700 g	1.4 kg	2.8 kg
Celery, finely sliced	700 g	1.4 kg	2.8 kg
Carrots, finely sliced	500 g	1 kg	2 kg
Garlic, chopped	4	8	12
Tomato paste	100 g	200 g	400 g
Flour	125 g	250 g	500 g
Margarine	125 g	250 g	500 g
Stock, beef	1.75 L	3.5 L	7 L
Salt and pepper	to taste		

1. Fry garlic and onions in a little oil over a moderate heat until soft.
2. Add beef and cook until light brown.
3. Add vegetables and cook for 4–6 minutes.
4. Add flour, tomato paste and seasoning and mix well.
5. Slowly incorporate stock, stirring continuously.
6. Bring to the boil and simmer gently covering with a lid.
7. Cook for approximately 1½–2 hours, stiring regularly, or until meat is tender.
8. Serve as required.

Beef Spare Ribs in a Smokey Barbecue Sauce

Garnish: Coriander sprigs, coleslaw.

	25	50	100
Beef, ribs	12.5 kg	25 kg	50 kg
Tomato sauce	2.25 L	4.5 L	9 L
Worcester sauce	250 mL	500 mL	1 L
Mustard, hot English	125 g	250 g	500 g
Brown sugar, soft	500 g	1 kg	2 kg
Smoke essence	to taste		

1. Cut ribs into required size — in this case 500 g per person.
2. Preheat oven to a moderate setting and dry roast ribs for 30–45 minutes.
3. Remove from oven, drain all fat and combine all other ingredients in a saucepan over a low heat until thoroughly incorporated.
4. In clean roasting tray, combine half the sauces with the ribs and return to oven.
5. Every 15 minutes, mix contents of tray, cooking for 1 hour.
6. Serve ribs with a little warm reserved sauce as required.

Cornish Pasties

Garnish: Parsley sprigs.

	25	50	100
Beef, minced	2 kg	4 kg	8 kg
Onions, finely diced	500 g	1 kg	2 kg
Carrots, finely diced	300 g	600 g	1.2 kg
Potatoes, finely diced	300 g	600 g	1.2 kg
Salt and pepper	to taste		
Parsley, chopped	5 g	10 g	20 g
Oil	as required		
Flour	150 g	300 g	600 g
Tomato puree	200 g	400 g	800 g
Stock, beef	200 mL	400 mL	800 mL
Short crust pastry	2 kg	4 kg	8 kg

Egg mix

Eggs	4	8	16
Milk	100 mL	200 mL	400 mL

(make up a little more egg mix if required)

1. Heat a little oil in large pan over moderate heat.
2. Add onions and cook until soft.
3. Add carrot, potato and parsley and cook for a further 5 minutes.
4. Add beef and mix thoroughly.
5. Cook until beef is light brown and carrots and potatoes are soft.
6. Add flour and mix in thoroughly.
7. Add puree and mix in thoroughly.
8. Add stock and mix in.
9. Cook for 2 minutes until ingredients are lightly bound together.
10. Add salt and pepper, remove from heat and allow to cool.
11. On lightly floured work surface, roll out pastry to ½ cm.
12. Using a small plate (for example a side plate), cut as many circular pieces of pastry as possible. Leave them on work surface.
13. Place a little mixture into the centre of each circle.
14. Egg mix outside of each circle and fold over filling so a semicircular shape is achieved.
15. Press edges firmly together with fingers and place onto lightly greased baking tray.
16. Repeat steps 10–14 until required amount of cornish pasties is reached, making sure to use all pastry trimmings.
17. Brush each pastie with a little egg mix.
18. Place pasties into oven preheated to a moderate setting until pastry turns golden brown.
19. Serve as required, usually one per portion.

Mexican Chilli Con Carne

Garnish: Corn chips, sour cream, guacamole.

	25	50	100
Minced beef	2.75 kg	5.5 kg	11 kg
Onions, sliced	500 g	1 kg	2 kg
Tomato paste	600 g	1.2 kg	2.4 kg
Kidney beans	500 g	1 kg	2 kg
Stock, chicken	500 mL	1 L	2 L
Margarine	200 g	400 g	800 g
Flour	300 g	600 g	1.2 kg
Chillies, crushed	50 g	100 g	200 g
Garlic clove, chopped	2	4	8
Bay leaves	2	4	8
Seasoning	as required		

1. Heat oil on moderate heat and cook out chillies, garlic and onions without colour for approximately 3 minutes or until soft.
2. Add minced steak and cook out, stirring constantly.
3. Add flour and mix in thoroughly.
4. Add stock, tomato paste, kidney beans and bay leaves.
5. Add seasoning and simmer gently for 15–20 minutes, stirring regularly.
6. Correct seasoning and serve on a bed of plain boiled rice.

NOTE: More chilli and a little finely diced capsicum may be added if desired at step 1.

Stir Fried Beef with Cashew Nuts

Garnish: Finely sliced shallots.

As for stir fried chicken with cashew nuts substituting beef (rump, topside) that has been cut into strips approximately 1 cm x 3 cm, for same amount of chicken.

Steak and Kidney Pie

Garnish: Tomato sails.

As for steak and onion pie replacing one-quarter of steak with kidney.

NOTE: Kidneys should be thoroughly washed before being trimmed and chopped into ½ cm pieces and added at step 2.

Greek Moussaka

Garnish: Chopped parsley.

As for Italian lasagne using thinly sliced (½ cm) eggplant in place of pasta sheets.
Prepare eggplant as for eggplant recipe: see Vegetable Dishes, Aubergine.

―――――――― ◇ ――――――――

Veal Dishes

Swiss Style Veal Casserole

Garnish: Finely diced red capsicum.

	25	50	100
Veal, chuck, finely diced	3.5 kg	7 kg	14 kg
Onions, finely diced	1 kg	2 kg	4 kg
Garlic clove, chopped	2	4	8
Flour	150 g	300 g	600 g
Stock, chicken	1.5 L	3 L	6 L
Cream	500 mL	1 L	2 L
Salt and pepper	to taste		
Oil	as required		

1. Heat oil over moderate heat in suitable pan.
2. Add onion and garlic and cook until onions are soft.
3. Add diced veal and seal on all sides.
4. Reduce heat and stir in flour thoroughly.
5. Add stock, stirring continuously.
6. Bring to the boil and simmer gently for approximately 1 hour or until meat is tender.
7. Add cream and season to taste.
8. Serve as required.

NOTE: Other vegetables such as sliced mushrooms and finely diced capsicum may be added in place of equal amounts of onion if desired.

Veal Cordon Bleu

Garnish: Sprinkle of paprika.

	25	50	100
Veal schnitzel steaks	1 per portion		
Ham, pressed, thinly sliced	1 per portion		
Cheese, cheddar, thinly sliced	1 per portion		
Flour	750 g	1.5 kg	3 kg
Eggs	4	8	16
Milk	100 mL	200 mL	400 mL
Breadcrumbs	750 g	1.5 kg	3 kg
Salt and pepper	to taste		

1. Place one piece of cheese and one piece of ham onto one half of a schnitzel steak that has been laid out flat on lightly floured work surface. Repeat until required portions are completed.

2. Fold steaks in half so ham and cheese are completely enclosed by veal.

3. Add a little salt and pepper to flour and place into a clean bowl.

4. Whisk eggs and milk together and place into a clean bowl.

5. Place breadcrumbs into a clean bowl.

6. Carefully pass veal envelopes through flour until completely coated, gently tapping off any excess flour.

7. Pass envelopes through egg and milk mixture until completely coated. Allow any excess liquid to drip free.

8. Pass envelopes through breadcrumbs so veal is evenly coated.

9. Place veal onto lightly greased baking tray.

10. Place into oven preheated to a moderate setting for approximately 20 minutes or until veal is cooked through and golden brown.

11. Serve as required.

Seasoned Veal Schnitzel

Garnish: Sprinkle of chopped parsley.

	25	50	100
Schnitzel steaks, required size	25	50	100
Flour	750 g	1.5 kg	3 kg
Salt and pepper	to taste		
Paprika	5 g	10 g	20 g
Garlic, flakes, dried	5 g	10 g	20 g
Basil, chopped	10 g	20 g	40 g
Eggs	4	8	16
Milk	100 mL	200 mL	400 mL
Breadcrumbs	750 g	1.5 kg	3 kg
Oil	as required		

1. Mix paprika, garlic, basil, salt and pepper with eggs and whisk thoroughly with milk.

2. Pass steaks through flour to coat.

3. Pass steaks through seasoned egg and milk that has been whisked together.

4. Pass steaks through breadcrumbs covering whole of steak.

5. Heat a little oil in suitable sized pan over moderate heat.

6. Add steaks and cook for approximately 2–3 minutes each side. Remove from heat and drain off any excess oil.

7. Drain away excess oil and place onto baking tray.

8. Place into oven preheated to a moderate setting for approximately 5–10 minutes until steaks are cooked through and golden brown.

9. Serve as required.

Veal Parmigiana

Garnish: Basil sprigs.

As for seasoned veal schnitzel except:

	25	50	100
Veal schnitzels	25	50	100
Onions, finely chopped	1 kg	2 kg	4 kg
Garlic cloves, finely chopped	3	6	12
Tomatoes, tinned, roughly chopped	1.5 kg	3 kg	6 kg
Tomato puree	100 g	200 g	400 g
Cheese, grated	1 kg	2 kg	4 kg
Parmesan cheese, grated	100 g	200 g	400 g
Oil	as required		
Salt and pepper	to taste		

1. Heat a little oil in suitable pan over moderate heat, add onions and garlic and cook until onions are soft.

2. Add drained tomatoes and allow sauce to simmer gently for a further 2–3 minutes.

3. Add tomato puree, mix, remove from heat and season to taste.

4. Place semi-cooked schnitzels on lightly greased tray and spoon over a little of the sauce.

5. Sprinkle a little grated cheese and parmesan cheese over each schnitzel.

6. Place into oven preheated to a moderate setting for approximately 5 minutes or until cheese turns light golden brown.

7. Serve as required.

Minute Steak Schnitzel / Parmigiana

As for seasoned veal schnitzel/veal parmigiana using minute steaks.

Veal Olives

Garnish: Chopped parsley.

	25	50	100
Veal schnitzel, sliced very thinly	25	50	100
Stuffing, thyme and basil	see Accompaniments		
Flour	150 g	300 g	600 g
Stock, beef	see Stocks and Sauces		
Parsley, chopped	10 g	20 g	40 g
Salt and pepper	to taste		

1. Place a little stuffing in the middle of each slice of veal.

2. Roll tightly, insert a cocktail stick to hold olive together, season flour and carefully coat olives in a little flour. Cook and seal olives using a little oil over moderate heat.

3. Place onto deep-sided baking tray.

4. Pour over sufficient stock and cover with aluminium foil.

5. Place into oven preheated to a moderate setting and cook for approximately 1 hour or until olives are cooked through and tender.

6. Serve as required with a little thickened stock and sprinkled with a little chopped parsley.

NOTE: This dish can be experimented with adding a little white wine, finely chopped garlic or dijon mustard at step 4.

Lamb Dishes

Roasted Lamb

Garnish: Mint leaves, rosemary sprigs.

Prepare lamb joints as for roasted beef.

This method of cookery is suitable for cuts of lamb such as shoulder, leg, fillet and loin.

Optional seasonings for cuts of lamb to be roasted are lemon juice, rosemary and garlic.

Probe Temperature: 75°C (slightly less if lamb required to be pink in the middle).

Grilled Lamb Cutlets / Chops

Garnish: Rosemary and mint sprigs.

As for grilled steak except during cooking sprinkle chops with a little fresh or dried chopped mint/rosemary.

Lamb and Apricot Kebabs

Garnish: Minted lemon yoghurt.

	25	50	100
Lamb, leg, finely diced	5 kg	10 kg	20 kg
Apricots, dried	500 g	1 kg	2 kg
Capsicum, 3–4 cm squares			
red	3	6	12
green	3	6	12
Onions, 3–4 cm large cubes	3	6	12
Lemon and mint marinade	see Salad Dressings and Marinades		

1. On kebab skewers place alternate lamb, apricot, onion and capsicum.
2. Place kebabs in deep-sided dish and cover with marinade, making sure all kebabs have been coated. Refrigerate for 4–6 hours or preferably overnight.
3. Drain marinade into separate pan.
4. Brush kebabs with a little oil.
5. Heat large frypan or grill, and quickly seal sides of kebabs. Kebabs will turn light brown.
6. Place kebabs on suitable roasting tray, brush with remaining marinade mixture and place in oven preheated to a moderate setting. Cook for a further 20 minutes or until cooked.

Lamb and Mushroom Kebabs

Garnish: Lemon and garlic yoghurt.

As for lamb and apricot kebabs omitting apricots and capsicum and adding:

	25	50	100
Mushrooms, whole	750 g	1.5 kg	3 kg

Substitute honey and soy marinade for lemon and mint marinade.

Sweet Lamb Curry

Garnish: Mint, chopped and sprigs.

	25	50	100
Lamb leg, diced	**3 kg**	**6 kg**	**12 kg**
Flour, plain	**150 g**	**300 g**	**600 g**
Onions, sliced	**1 kg**	**2 kg**	**4 kg**
Apple, peeled, diced	**300 g**	**600 g**	**1.2 kg**
Curry powder, mild	**100 g**	**200 g**	**400 g**
Sultanas	**100 g**	**200 g**	**400 g**
Coconut, desiccated	**50 g**	**100 g**	**200 g**
Orange juice	**75 mL**	**150 mL**	**300 mL**
Stock, lamb or chicken	**1.5 L**	**3 L**	**6 L**
Sugar	**75 g**	**150 g**	**300 g**
Salt and pepper	**to taste**		

1. In large pan cook onions in a little oil until tender.
2. Increase heat, add meat and cook until all meat is light brown.
3. Reduce heat, add curry powder and flour, mix well and cook for a further 2–3 minutes.
4. Add sugar, coconut, sultanas and orange juice and mix well.
5. Slowly add stock, stirring continuously.
6. Add apple, season and simmer gently for 30–40 minutes stirring occasionally until lamb is tender.
7. Correct seasoning. Correct consistency by addition of equal amounts of flour and water mixed well in small quantities to thicken, or add small amounts of stock to thin down.

Lamb Curry

Garnish: Mint, chopped and sprigs.

As for sweet lamb curry omitting sultanas, coconut, orange juice and sugar, and adding:

	25	50	100
Carrot, finely diced	**400 g**	**800 g**	**1.6 kg**
Coriander, chopped (optional)	**15 g**	**30 g**	**60 g**

Lamb and Fresh Vegetable Casserole

Garnish: Watercress sprigs.

	25	50	100
Lamb, leg, finely diced	3.5 kg	7 kg	14 kg
Onions, sliced	750 g	1.5 kg	3 kg
Carrots, diced finely	350 g	700 g	1.4 kg
Celery, finely diced	250 g	500 g	1 kg
Mushrooms, sliced or quartered	100 g	200 g	400 g
Mint	5 g	10 g	20 g
Basil	5 g	10 g	20 g
Rosemary	5 g	10 g	20 g
Flour	150 g	300 g	600 g
Stock, lamb or beef	1.5 L	3 L	6 L
Salt and pepper	to taste		

1. In large pan cook onions in a little oil until tender.
2. Increase heat, add meat and cook until all meat is light brown.
3. Reduce heat and add flour mixing well.
4. Add herbs and mix.
5. Slowly add stock, stirring continuously.
6. Add salt, pepper, carrots, celery and mushrooms.
7. Place all ingredients into suitable deep-sided casserole dish or deep-sided baking tray and cover with a lid or aluminium foil.
8. Place in oven preheated to a moderate setting for approximately 1–1¼ hours or until meat is tender and sauce is rich and thickened.

Navarin of Lamb

Garnish: Rosemary sprigs.

	25	50	100
Lamb, leg, finely diced	3.5 kg	7 kg	14 kg
Flour	125 g	250 g	500 g
Stock, beef or lamb	1.5 L	3 L	6 L
Onions, sliced	500 g	1 kg	2 kg
Carrots, finely diced	250 g	500 g	1 kg
Garlic cloves, crushed	4	8	16
Tomato puree	75 g	150 g	300 g
Rosemary	5 g	10 g	20 g
Sage	5 g	10 g	20 g
Salt and pepper	to taste		

1. In large pan cook onions, garlic and herbs in a little oil until tender.
2. Increase heat, add lamb and cook until all lamb is light brown.
3. Add flour and tomato puree and mix well.
4. Slowly add stock, stirring continuously.
5. Add carrots, bring to the boil and skim.
6. Cover with a lid or aluminium foil and simmer gently for approximately 1–2 hours or until meat is tender and sauce is rich and thickened.

NOTE: A little red wine may be added at step 4 if desired.

Braised Lamb's Liver and Bacon

Garnish: Chopped parsley.

	25	50	100
Lamb's liver	3.75 kg	7.5 kg	15 kg
Flour, plain	1 kg	2 kg	4 kg
Bacon, diced, excess fat removed	1 kg	2 kg	4 kg
Onions, sliced	1 kg	2 kg	4 kg
Stock, beef	2 L	4 L	8 L
Salt and pepper	to taste		

1. Wash lamb's liver under cold running water and allow to drain.
2. Cut's lamb's liver into 3 x 7 cm pieces.
3. Season flour.
4. Place heavy-bottomed sauté pan over moderate heat with 1 cm deep of oil and allow to heat.
5. Pass liver through seasoned flour and add to oil.

6. Seal liver on both sides and cook until light brown.

7. Repeat process until all liver is cooked.

8. Layer liver, onion and bacon in deep-sided baking tray.

9. Pour stock over liver.

10. Cover with aluminium foil.

11. Place into oven preheated to a moderate to hot setting and cook for approximately 1–1½ hours or until liver is tender.

12. Serve as required with a little thickened stock.

Irish Stew

Garnish: Finely diced tomato.

	25	50	100
Lamb, leg, finely diced	3 kg	6 kg	12 kg
Onions, sliced	1 kg	2 kg	4 kg
Carrots, diced	700 g	1.4 kg	2.8 kg
Stock, chicken	4 L	8 L	16 L
Potatoes, peeled, roughly chopped	4 kg	8 kg	16 kg
Salt and pepper	to taste		

1. Place all ingredients into large pan, bring to the boil, and cover with lid.

2. Simmer gently until meat and all vegetables are cooked and tender — approximately 1–1½ hours.

3. Potatoes should thicken stock as cooking time elapses or add small amounts of equal quantities of flour and water that have been whisked together. Incorporate thoroughly.

NOTE: Extra water or stock can be added during cooking if sauce is too thick.

Blanquette of Lamb

Garnish: Paprika.

	25	50	100
Lamb, stewing, small diced	3 kg	6 kg	12 kg
Stock, chicken	2.5 L	5 L	10 L
Flour	125 g	250 g	500 g
Margarine	125 g	250 g	500 g
Onions, roughly chopped	400 g	800 g	1.6 kg
Carrots, roughly chopped	300 g	600 g	1.2 kg
Bay leaves	2	4	8
Thyme, chopped	15 g	30 g	60 g
Parsley, chopped	10 g	20 g	40 g
Salt and pepper	to taste		

1. Place lamb in saucepan and cover with water.

2. Bring to the boil and refresh lamb under cold running water.

3. Add stock and lamb to a clean pan with onion, carrot, bay leaves and thyme.

4. Bring to the boil and simmer for 30 minutes or until meat is tender.

5. Using another pan, melt margarine over moderate heat and mix in flour thoroughly.

6. Remove carrot, onion and bay leaves from stock.

7. Strain liquid from meat and gradually add stock to roux, stirring continuously.

8. When all stock has been incorporated, add lamb and simmer for a further 10 minutes.

9. Correct seasoning and serve as required, sprinkled with a little chopped parsley and paprika.

Pork Dishes

Roasted Pork

Garnish: Apple sauce, crispy crackling.

This method of cookery applies to joints such as leg, shoulder and loin.

Prepare pork as for roasted beef. Refer to cooking times for meats.

Options

Extra salt can be rubbed into the pork skin, which will result in a crisper crackling to be served as an accompaniment.

Probe Temperature: 85°C.

Stuffings for pork are listed in the Accompaniments section.

Honey Glazed Ham

Garnish: Glacé cherries, pineapple rings.

	25	50	100
Ham, whole leg cooked	**75–100 g per portion. Order as required.**		
Cloves	as required		
Honey	150 mL	300 mL	600 mL
Brown sugar	150 g	300 g	600 g
Orange juice	150 mL	300 mL	600 mL

Optional

Glacé cherries	as required		
Pineapple rings	as required		

1. Remove excess fat from ham making sure to retain a small covering to help in the cooking process and presentation.

2. Score skin into 2 cm squares.

3. Place in roasting tray.

4. Stud meat at regular intervals with the cloves, 2–3 cm apart over the whole surface of the meat.

5. If required, pierce half a glacé cherry inside a pineapple ring with a toothpick and attach to the meat in bands, approximately 4–5 cm apart.

6. Pour honey over meat and lightly coat with brown sugar.

7. Pour orange juice into base of roasting tray.

8. Place in oven preheated to a moderate setting for approximately 1–1½ hours.

9. Baste regularly every 15 minutes until cooked.

10. After removing cooked ham from oven, leave to stand for approximately 10 minutes before carving.

Pork Chops

Garnish: Sage butter.

As for grilled steak making sure pork chops are thoroughly cooked through before serving.

Optional

While pork chops are cooking sprinkle with a little brown sugar, orange juice and dried sage.

Hawaiian Ham and Pineapple

Garnish: Pineapple rings and glacé cherries.

	25	50	100
Ham steaks, uncooked, 80–100 g	25	50	100
Pineapple, tinned, rings	25	50	100
Glacé cherries	25	50	100
Pineapple juice, from tin	250 mL	500 mL	1 L
Orange juice	500 mL	1 L	2 L
Honey	125 mL	250 mL	500 mL
Brown sugar	250 g	500 g	1 kg

1. Place steaks on lightly greased tray and bake in oven preheated to a moderate setting for approximately 5 minutes.

2. While steaks are cooking, prepare sauce by mixing pineapple juice, orange juice and brown sugar in small pan over moderate heat stirring constantly for approximately 5–10 minutes or until sauce thickens slightly.

3. Remove steaks from oven and place one pineapple ring on each steak. In the centre of pineapple ring place a glacé cherry.

4. Brush steaks liberally with sauce and return to oven for a further 5–10 minutes or until cooked through.

5. Brush a little warmed sauce onto steaks before serving.

Pork, Apple and Cider Casserole

Garnish: Grated blanched apple.

	25	50	100
Pork, stewing, finely diced	3.5 kg	7 kg	14 kg
Apple, peeled, cored, finely diced	500 g	1 kg	2 kg
Onions, finely chopped	250 g	500 g	1 kg
Cream	250 mL	500 mL	1 L
Cider	250 mL	500 mL	1 L
Stock, chicken	1.25 L	2.5 L	5 L
Garlic, crushed	3	6	12
Sage	5 g	10 g	20 g
Mint	10 g	20 g	40 g
Flour, plain	150 g	300 g	600 g
Salt and pepper	to taste		

1. Cook onions, garlic and herbs in a little oil until tender.
2. Increase heat, add pork and cook until all pork is light brown.
3. Reduce heat, add flour and cook for a further 3–4 minutes.
4. Slowly add stock, stirring continuously.
5. Add apple, cider and salt and pepper.
6. Bring to the boil and gently simmer, covered with a lid or aluminium foil, for approximately 1 hour or until meat is tender and sauce is thickened and rich.
7. Immediately prior to service, mix in cream and serve.

Sweet and Sour Pork

Garnish: Chilli flowers.

	25	50	100
Pork, leg, finely diced	3 kg	6 kg	12 kg
Cornflour	as required		
Celery, finely diced	500 g	1 kg	2 kg
Capsicum, finely diced	500 g	1 kg	2 kg
Onions, finely diced	500 g	1 kg	2 kg
Garlic cloves, finely chopped	4	8	16
Ginger, ground	10 g	20 g	40 g
Vinegar	200 mL	400 mL	800 mL
Soy sauce	150 mL	300 mL	600 mL
Caster sugar	200 g	400 g	800 g
Pineapple, tinned, diced	750 g	1.5 kg	3 kg
Pineapple juice, from tin			
Tomato puree	250 mL	500 mL	1 L
Five spice powder	5 g	10 g	20 g
Water	500 mL	1 L	2 L
Salt and pepper	to taste		

1. Fry all vegetables in suitable pan in a little oil for 3–4 minutes or until soft.

2. To cornflour add salt and pepper and half five spice powder. Coat all pork with this mixture.

3. Add all other ingredients to vegetables and reduce liquid by half or until required consistency is reached.

4. Deep-fry meat in oil preheated to 175°C for 3–4 minutes or until cooked through and golden brown. Drain well.

5. Serve meat covered with a little of the sweet and sour sauce.

Pork Ribs in a Barbecue Sauce

Garnish: Chilli flowers.

As for barbecue beef substituting pork ribs for beef.

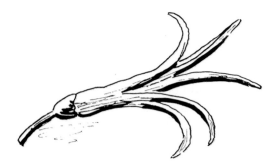

Bacon and Spinach Quiche

Garnish: Tomato sails.

	25	50	100
Short crust pastry	**1.25 kg** **see Dessert Dishes**	**2.5 kg**	**5 kg**

Spinach, stalk removed,
  shredded, washed,
  drained
	500 g	**1 kg**	**2 kg**

Bacon, diced	**500 g**	**1 kg**	**2 kg**
Onions, finely diced	**500 g**	**1 kg**	**2 kg**
Garlic clove, finely **chopped**	**2**	**4**	**8**
Cheese, cheddar, grated	**500 g**	**1 kg**	**2 kg**
Salt and pepper	**to taste**		
Milk	**1 L**	**2 L**	**4 L**
Eggs	**8**	**16**	**32**

1. Cook bacon, onions and garlic in a little oil until onions are tender.
2. Add spinach and cook for a further 2–4 minutes. Remove from heat and allow to cool.
3. Thoroughly beat eggs, milk and salt and pepper.
4. Roll out pastry to ½ cm thickness sufficient to fill baking trays.
5. Line greased baking tray with pastry, trim, add vegetable mix and spread evenly.
6. Pour milk and egg mixture to just below rim of tray.
7. Sprinkle with grated cheese and bake in oven preheated to a slow to moderate setting for approximately 45 minutes to an hour or until mixture is firm to touch.
8. Remove from oven and allow to stand for 30 minutes.
9. Portion to required sizes, refrigerate if serving cold or reheat if serving hot.

Bacon and Egg Quiche (also known as Quiche Lorraine)

As for bacon and spinach quiche omitting spinach.

Spinach and Fetta Cheese Quiche

As for bacon and spinach quiche with the addition of:

	25	50	100
Fetta cheese, small diced **cubes**	**250 g**	**500 g**	**1 kg**

NOTE: Bacon may be omitted if desired.

Fettuccine Carbonara

Garnish: Chopped basil, grated parmesan.

Carbonara Sauce

White sauce	**1.5 L**	**3 L**	**6 L**
	see Stocks and Sauces		
Bacon, finely chopped	500 g	1 kg	2 kg
Onions, finely chopped	500 g	1 kg	2 kg
Cream	250 mL	500 mL	1 L
Cheese, cheddar, grated	250 g	500 g	1 kg
Parmesan, grated	125 g	250 g	500 g
Paprika	5 g	10 g	20 g
Salt and pepper	to taste		
Garlic cloves, chopped	6	12	24
Fettuccine, uncooked	2 kg	4 kg	8 kg
Bay leaves	6	12	24
Oil	50 mL	100 mL	200 mL
Salt and pepper	to taste		

1. Cook fettuccine: see below.
2. Cook bacon, onions, bay leaves and garlic in a little oil until onion is tender.
3. Combine white sauce with bacon and onion mixture and add paprika, cream and salt and pepper.
4. Place fettuccine in suitable baking tray and cover with carbonara sauce.
5. Top with cheeses and place in oven preheated to a slow to moderate setting for 15-20 minutes or until cheese is golden brown. Serve as required.

To Cook Fettuccine

1. Add salt and oil to large pan and bring to the boil.
2. Add fettuccine and stir once.
3. Simmer for approximately 15-20 minutes or until fettuccine is tender.
4. Remove from heat and strain. If to be served immediately, run hot water through fettuccine and serve. If being used at a later stage, refresh fettuccine with cold water and run hot water through it when needed.

Bacon and Sweet Corn Puffs

Garnish: Sliced shallots.

		25	50	100
Puff pastry	approx	1.5 kg	3 kg	6 kg
		see Dessert Dishes		
White sauce	approx	250 mL	500 mL	1 L
		see Stocks and Sauces		
Bacon, chopped		500 g	1 kg	2 kg
Onions, chopped		500 g	1 kg	2 kg
Sweet corn niblets, cooked		500 g	1 kg	2 kg

	25	50	100
Garlic cloves, chopped	4	8	12
Salt and pepper	to taste		
Eggs	2	4	8
Milk	100 mL	200 mL	400 mL

1. Cook onions, bacon and garlic in a little oil until onions are tender.

2. Add white sauce to bacon mixture and cook slowly until correct consistency is reached. The sauce is meant to bind the other ingredients together and should not be runny.

3. Add corn niblets and mix.

4. Roll out puff pastry on lightly floured board to an approximate thickness of 4 mm and cut into 10 cm squares.

5. Place a little mixture in the centre of each square and brush the edges with a mixture of beaten eggs and milk.

6. Fold pastry over mixture and press edges firmly resulting in either rolls, triangles or pouches.

7. Place seafood puffs on lightly greased tray and brush with remaining egg mix.

8. Place in oven preheated to a moderate setting for approximately 15-20 minutes or until pastry is golden brown.

Bacon and Sweet Corn Vol-au-vents

Garnish: Parsley sprigs.

	25	50	100
Vol-au-vents (10 cm width)	25	50	100
Cheese sauce	1 L	2 L	4 L
	see Stocks and Sauces		
Bacon, cooked, chopped	500 g	1 kg	2 kg
Corn niblets, cooked	2 kg	4 kg	8 kg
Cheese, cheddar, grated	300 g	600 g	1.2 kg
Breadcrumbs	as required		
Salt and pepper	to taste		

1. Combine bacon and corn niblets with prepared cheese sauce.

2. Add breadcrumbs in small amounts until sauce is of a thick consistency.

3. Fill vol-au-vents with mixture.

4. Top with grated cheese and place onto lightly greased baking tray.

5. Bake in oven preheated to a moderate setting for approximately 20 minutes until cheese turns golden brown.

6. Serve as required.

Poultry Dishes

Roasted Chicken

Garnish: Watercress, game chips, lemon and thyme stuffing.

As for roast beef. Before cooking, fold wings tight against the chicken's body. Place in roasting tray breast side up. Place any excess bacon fat over bird prior to cooking to help basting process.

For cooking times refer to cooking times for meat chart, Chapter 1, p 3.

Probe Temperature: 90°C.

Probe should be inserted into thickest part of chicken thigh.

Poultry can be tested to see if cooked by gently prising away the leg from the rest of the bird to observe the colour of the juice. If blood is present, more cooking time is necessary. All poultry must be thoroughly cooked before serving.

Roasted Turkey

Garnish: Cranberry sauce, chestnut stuffing.

As for roasted chicken.

Southern Fried Chicken

Garnish: Chopped parsley, paprika.

	25	50	100
Chickens, whole	7	13	25
Cornflour approx	400 g	800 g	1.6 kg
Salt	10 g	20 g	40 g
Five spice powder	5 g	10 g	20 g
Paprika	5 g	10 g	20 g
Sugar, caster	5 g	10 g	20 g
Pepper	1 teaspoon	2 teaspoons	4 teaspoons
Mustard powder	1 teaspoon	2 teaspoons	4 teaspoons

Marinade

Sherry, worcester and garlic	**see Stocks and Sauces and Accompaniments**

1. Cut chicken into two legs and two breasts, then cut each piece into two further pieces.

2. Place chicken in deep-sided container and add marinade, mixing well. Refrigerate for 2 hours.

3. Combine all ingredients with cornflour.

4. Remove chickens and drain well.

5. Coat all chicken with cornflour mixture.

6. Deep-fry in oil preheated to 175°C for approximately 7–10 minutes or until chicken is cooked through and golden brown.

7. Drain well and serve two pieces per portion.

NOTE: Chicken carcass should be retained and used for chicken stock production.

Curry Crusted Chicken

Garnish: Minted yoghurt sauce.

		25	50	100
Oil for frying		**as required**		
Chicken breast, on the bone		**25**	**50**	**100**
Curry powder		**as needed**		
Salt	**approx**	**20 g**	**40 g**	**80 g**
Pepper		**5 g**	**10 g**	**20 g**

1. Cut chicken breasts in two removing any skin.

2. Mix curry powder, salt and pepper together and coat chickens thoroughly.

3. Heat a little oil in a frypan over high heat, add chicken pieces and keep moving all the time until seared on all sides.

4. Remove from frypan and drain excess oil.

5. Place in roasting tray and place in oven preheated to a moderate setting for approximately 20-30 minutes or until cooked through. Serve two pieces per portion.

NOTE: Chicken carcass should be retained and used for chicken stock production.

Almond Chicken

Garnish: Coriander leaves, lemon twist.

		25	50	100
Chickens, whole		**6 kg**	**12 kg**	**24 kg**
Almonds, crushed		**500 g**	**1 kg**	**2 kg**
Flour	**approx**	**500 g**	**1 kg**	**2 kg**
Salt, to taste		**20 g**	**40 g**	**80 g**
Pepper, to taste	**approx**	**5 g**	**10 g**	**20 g**
Lemon juice		**1 lemon**	**2 lemons**	**4 lemons**
Breadcrumbs		**as required**		
Eggs	**approx**	**8**	**16**	**32**

1. Cut chickens into eight pieces (two pieces each leg and breast).

2. Mix flour, salt and pepper and coat chicken pieces.

3. Blend eggs and lemon juice and coat floured chicken with mixture.

4. Mix breadcrumbs and crushed almonds and coat all chicken evenly.

5. Place chicken pieces into deep-fryer at 165°C for 10 minutes or until cooked through and golden brown.

NOTE: Chicken carcass should be retained and used for chicken stock production.

Chicken Maryland

Garnish: Sweet corn fritters, banana fritters.

		25	50	100
Chickens, whole		7	13	25
Bananas, medium		7	13	25
Flour		as required		
Salt and pepper		to taste		
Breadcrumbs		as required		
Eggs	approx	4	8	16
Milk	approx	300 mL	600 mL	1.2 L

Sweet Corn Fritters

	25	50	100
Sweet corn niblets, cooked	225 g	450 g	900 g
Flour	400 g	800 g	1.6 kg
Milk	1 L	2 L	4 L
Eggs	5	10	20
Salt	as required		
Pepper	as required		

1. Quarter chickens.

2. Coat with flour seasoned with a little salt and pepper.

3. Coat with eggs and milk which have been beaten together.

4. Coat with breadcrumbs.

5. Quarter bananas and proceed with steps 2–4.

6. Deep-fry chickens in oil preheated to 175°C for 8–10 minutes or until cooked through and golden brown.

7. Drain well and keep hot. (The cooking of the chicken pieces may be finished in a moderate oven if desired.)

8. Deep-fry bananas in oil at 175°C for 3–4 minutes or until golden brown.

9. Drain well and keep hot.

Sweet Corn Fritters

1. Beat flour, eggs, salt, pepper and milk until mixture thickly coats the back of a spoon.

2. Add cooked and drained sweet corn niblets and mix well.

3. Place a little oil in frypan on medium heat and add a little mixture to make approximately 6–8 cm circles. Repeat process until sufficient sweet corn fritters have been made.

4. Cook for 1 minute on each side.

5. Serve fritter with one piece of cooked chicken and a banana fritter.

NOTE: Chicken carcass should be retained and used for chicken stock production.

Chicken Kiev

Garnish: Sage butter.

	25	50	100
Chicken breasts	25	50	100
Butter	500 g	1 kg	2 kg
Garlic, chopped	8	16	24
Parsley, chopped	20 g	40 g	80 g
Breadcrumbs	as required		
Flour, plain	as required		
Salt and pepper	to taste		
Eggs	4	8	16
Milk	300 mL	600 mL	1.2 L

1. Make incision into side of chicken 3–4 cm deep.
2. Soften butter and mix with garlic and parsley.
3. Pipe a little mixture into incision and press firmly closed.
4. Coat chicken with flour.
5. Pass through mixture of beaten eggs and milk.
6. Cover completely with breadcrumbs.
7. Set in refrigerator for 1 hour before cooking.
8. Deep-fry in oil preheated to 175°C for approximately 4–6 minutes or until cooked and golden brown.
9. Drain well and serve.

Alternative Method

Place crumbed chicken on lightly greased roasting tray and bake in oven preheated to a moderate setting for approximately 25–30 minutes or until cooked through and golden brown.

Chicken à la King

Garnish: Finely sliced chives.

	25	50	100
Chicken, boiled, off bone, strips	4 kg	8 kg	16 kg
Mushrooms, sliced	750 g	1.5 kg	3 kg
Capsicum, strips	200 g	400 g	800 g
Onions, sliced	750 g	1.5 kg	3 kg
Garlic cloves, chopped	4	6	8
Chicken velouté	1.2 L	2.4 L	4.8 L
	see Stocks and Sauces		
Cream	250 mL	500 mL	1 L
Salt and pepper	to taste		

1. In a little oil, gently fry onions, garlic, capsicum and mushrooms until onions are tender.

2. Add chicken.

3. Drain any excess fat from pan and add velouté.

4. Bring to the boil and simmer. Adjust consistency as required by addition of a little flour and water (milk) in equal quantities if too thin, or by the addition of a little milk or chicken stock if too thick.

5. Add cream and salt and pepper to taste.

Tandoori Chicken

Garnish: Minted lemon yoghurt, fresh mint sprigs.

	25	50	100
Chicken, whole	7	13	25
Yoghurt, natural	1 L	2 L	4 L
Juice of lemon	3 lemons	6 lemons	12 lemons
Mint, finely chopped	50 g	100 g	200 g
Tandoori paste	250 g	500 g	1 kg

1. Cut chickens into eight pieces each (two pieces each leg and breast).

2. Combine all other ingredients.

3. Combine tandoori mixture with chickens and marinate for a minimum of 6 hours in a refrigerator. Turn mixture every 2 hours.

4. Place on roasting tray and place into oven preheated to a moderate setting for 30–40 minutes or until cooked through.

5. Serve with a little minted lemon yoghurt.

NOTES:

1. Tandoori paste is available from most suppliers.

2. Chicken carcass should be retained and used for chicken stock production.

Green Thai Chicken Curry

Garnish: Finely sliced chillies.

	25	50	100
Chicken, thigh fillets	3.75 kg	7.5 kg	15 kg
Green Thai curry paste	100 g	200 g	400 g
Coconut cream	1 L	2 L	4 L
Cream	250 mL	500 mL	1 L
Salt and pepper	to taste		

1. Cut each chicken thigh fillet into four even-sized pieces.

2. In a suitable saucepan over moderate heat, cook green curry paste for 1 minute stirring continuously.

3. Add coconut cream and cream and whisk thoroughly until a smooth consistency is reached. Remove from heat.

4. Using large sauté pan, place over moderate heat and brush with a little oil.

5. Gradually add chicken pieces in small batches and seal all sides.

6. Remove chicken pieces when sealed from sauté pan and place into deep-sided baking tray.

7. Repeat process until all chicken is in baking tray.

8. Pour over sauce.

9. Cover tray with aluminium foil, place into oven preheated to a moderate setting and cook for approximately 1 hour or until chicken is cooked and tender.

10. Serve as required.

NOTE: Green curry paste is available from most suppliers.

Paprika Chicken

Garnish: Finely sliced chives.

	25	50	100
Chicken, legs or thigh fillets	3.75 kg	7.5 kg	15 kg
Flour	750 g	1.5 kg	3 kg
Eggs	8	16	24
Milk	250 mL	500 mL	1 L
Breadcrumbs	750 g	1.5 kg	3 kg
Paprika	100 g	200 g	400 g
Salt and pepper	to taste		

1. Cut each chicken piece into two or three smaller pieces.

2. Season flour and place into container.

3. Whisk eggs and milk together and place into separate container.

4. Mix paprika and breadcrumbs together.

5. Pass chicken through flour making sure whole surface is coated.

6. Pass floured chicken through egg and milk mix coating chicken completely.

7. Coat chicken in breadcrumbs.

8. Place chicken pieces onto lightly greased baking tray one layer deep with small gap between each piece.

9. Roast in oven preheated to a moderate setting for approximately 45 minutes or until cooked through.

10. Serve as required.

Stir Fried Chicken with Cashew Nuts

Garnish: Coriander leaves, chopped parsley.

	25	50	100
Chickens, whole	4 x 1.5 kg	8 x 1.5 kg	16 x 1.5 kg
Cashew nuts	250 g	500 g	1 kg
Snow peas	1.25 kg	2.5 kg	5 kg
Ginger, grated	1 tablespoon	2 tablespoons	4 tablespoons
Capsicum, halved, seeded, finely sliced			
red	2	4	8
green	2	4	8
Garlic cloves	2	4	8
Stock, chicken	200 mL	400 mL	800 mL
Oil	as required		
Onion	500 g	1 kg	2 kg
Sugar	100 g	200 g	400 g
Soy sauce	50 mL	100 mL	200 mL
Cornflour	30 g	60 g	120 g
Parsley, chopped	10 g	20 g	40 g
Curry powder	50 g	100 g	200 g
Five spice powder	20 g	40 g	80 g
Salt and pepper	to taste		

1. Boil chickens until cooked through retaining stock. When chickens are cool remove meat from carcass, skin and dice.

2. Head and tail snow peas, crush garlic, and finely slice onions.

3. Heat oil and stir fry capsicum and onions.

4. Add ginger, garlic, cashew nuts, sugar, soy sauce, parsley, curry powder, five spice powder and salt and pepper, stirring continuously.

5. Add stock and cornflour that has been mixed with a little cold water.

6. Stir mix until juice adheres to vegetables.

7. Add diced chicken and snow peas.

8. Heat through and serve with boiled rice.

NOTE: Chicken carcass should be retained and used for chicken stock production.

Chicken Burgers

Garnish: Side salad garnish.

	25	50	100
Chicken mince	3 kg	6 kg	12 kg
Onions, finely chopped	1 kg	2 kg	4 kg
Worcester sauce	100 mL	200 mL	400 mL
Tomato sauce	150 mL	300 mL	600 mL
Eggs	3	6	12

1. Fry onions in a little oil over a moderate heat until soft and remove from heat.

2. In a large mixing bowl or commercial mixer add all ingredients and mix until thoroughly combined.

3. Gradually add breadcrumbs until desired texture is achieved.

4. Turn out onto lightly floured board.

5. Shape mixture into required size patties.

6. Seal patties in a sauté pan brushed with a little oil over moderate heat.

7. Place onto lightly greased roasting tray and place in oven preheated to a moderate setting. Cook for approximately 20 minutes or until cooked through.

8. Serve as required.

Chicken and Asparagus in Flaky Pastry

Garnish: Tomato sails.

	25	50	100
Puff pastry (see p 279)	1.5 kg	3 kg	6 kg
Chicken, cooked, shredded, boneless	2 kg	4 kg	8 kg
Asparagus, tinned	1 kg	2 kg	4 kg
Chicken velouté	2 L	4 L	8 L
Onions, sliced	1 kg	2 kg	4 kg
Salt and pepper	to taste		
Eggs	2	4	8
Milk	50 mL	100 mL	200 mL
Oil	as required		

1. Heat oil over moderate heat in suitable saucepan.

2. Add onions and cook in a little oil until soft.

3. Remove from heat and add prepared chicken, drained and roughly chopped asparagus and velouté, mixing together thoroughly.

4. Season to taste.

5. Place mix in suitable serving dish and top with pastry that has been rolled out to approximately ½ cm thickness.

6. Trim and crimp edges and brush pastry with beaten egg and milk.

7. Place into oven preheated to a moderate setting and cook until pastry turns golden brown.

8. Cut into required portion sizes.

9. Serve as required.

Chicken Satay

As for beef satay substituting chicken for beef.

Roasted Chicken Pieces / Wings

Garnish: Watercress and potato chips.

Follow rules for roasting and cooking times for meat. Different combinations of herbs can be used to flavour chicken, for example, curry powder, chinese five spice powder and chilli powder.

Fish and Seafood Dishes

Grilled Fish

Garnish: Lemon, wedges, slices or twists.

Whiting, cod, perch and most white fish can be used.

	25	50	100
Fish fillets, on or off bone	**2.5 kg**	**5 kg**	**10 kg**
Flour, plain	**as required**		
Salt and pepper	**to taste**		
Oil	**as required**		

1. Wash and drain fillets.
2. Coat with flour seasoned with a little salt and pepper.
3. Brush with a little oil.
4. Place on lightly greased tray under grill.
5. Cook for approximately 2 minutes on either side or until cooked.

NOTE: Fish is cooked when it flakes easily when a little pressure is applied to the flesh.

176

Shallow Fried Fish

Garnish: Deep-fried parsley, lemon wedges, slices or twists.

1. As for grilled fish, steps 1–2.

2. Shallow-fry in a little preheated oil over moderate heat in suitable frypan for 1–2 minutes on either side or until cooked through.

NOTE: Always place presentation side into oil first.

Deep Fried, Crumbed or Battered Fish

Garnish: Deep-fried parsley, lemon wedges, slices or twists.

1. As for grilled fish, steps 1–2.

2a. Place into deep fat fryer in oil preheated to 170°C for approximately 2 minutes or until cooked; OR

2b. Coat with egg mix and breadcrumbs and fry in oil preheated to 170°C for 2–3 minutes or until cooked; OR

2c. Coat with batter mix (see below) and cook in oil preheated to 175°C for 3–4 minutes or until cooked and golden brown.

3. Drain well and serve immediately.

NOTE: Fish being deep-fried will generally float to the surface once cooked through.

Beer Batter

	25	50	100
Flour, plain	1 kg	2 kg	4 kg
Beer	250 mL	500 mL	1 L
Water	500 mL	1 L	2 L
Vinegar, white	100 mL	200 mL	400 mL
Salt and pepper	to taste		

1. Mix all ingredients thoroughly until a smooth texture is achieved.

2. Refrigerate for 30 minutes.

3. Use as required.

NOTE: Beer batter gives a similar taste to that of yeast batter.

Poached Fish Fillets in Court Bouillon

Garnish: Lemon wedges.

	25	50	100
Fish fillets	2.5 kg	5 kg	10 kg
Water	enough to immerse fillets		
Juice of lemon	2	4	8
Bay leaves	3	6	12
Parsley, roughly chopped	5 g	10 g	20 g
White wine	100 mL	200 mL	400 mL
Salt	a little to taste		
Peppercorns	5	10	20

1. Wash and drain fillets.

2. Place all ingredients except fillets of fish into suitable pan and simmer.

3. Gently place fillets into liquid and cook for approximately 4–6 minutes or until cooked.

4. Carefully remove fillets and serve as required.

Lemon and Dill Stuffed Trout

Garnish: Dill, sprigs, lemon wedges, slices or twists.

	25	50	100
Trout	25	50	100
Breadcrumbs	1 kg	2 kg	4 kg
Onions, finely chopped	250 g	500 g	1 kg
Dill sprigs, finely chopped	20 g	40 g	80 g
Parsley, chopped	10 g	20 g	40 g
Juice of lemon	2	4	8
Butter	125 g	250 g	500 g
Eggs	3	6	12
Garlic, chopped	2	4	8
Oil	as required		

1. Cook onions, garlic, dill and parsley in butter until onions are tender and remove from heat.

2. Add breadcrumbs, lemon juice and eggs and mix well.

3. Gut and wash trout and allow to drain.

4. Fill cavity with a little mixture and brush trout with a little oil.

5. Place on lightly greased baking tray and place in oven preheated to a moderate setting for approximately 10–15 minutes or until cooked through.

Crab and Asparagus Vol-au-vents

Garnish: Diced tomato.

As for bacon and sweet corn vol-au-vents omitting bacon and sweet corn and adding:

	25	50	100
Crab meat, cooked	500 g	1 kg	2 kg
Asparagus, tinned, drained, roughly chopped	1.75 kg	3.5 kg	7 kg

Seafood Vol-au-vent Filling

Garnish: Deep-fried parsley, lemon wedges, slices or twists.

	25	50	100
White fish, cooked, flaked	1.5 kg	3 kg	6 kg
Prawns, cooked, peeled	500 g	1 kg	2 kg
Onions, finely chopped	250 g	500 g	1 kg
Garlic, chopped	2	4	8
Fish velouté	see Stocks and Sauces		
Cheese, grated	500 g	1 kg	2 kg
Vol-au-vents (10 cm width)	25	50	100

1. Cook onions and garlic in a little oil over a moderate heat until onions are tender.

2. Add seafood and bind together with the required amount of velouté to give a thick mixture.

3. Fill vol-au-vent cases with a little mixture and top with grated cheese.

4. Place on baking tray, place in oven preheated to a moderate setting and cook until cheese is golden brown.

Salmon and Dill Fish Cakes

Garnish: Dill sprigs, lemon wedges.

	25	50	100
Salmon, tinned	250 g	500 g	1 kg
White fish, cooked, flaked	1.5 kg	3 kg	6 kg
Potatoes, mashed	1 kg	2 kg	4 kg
Eggs	4	8	16
Parsley, chopped	10 g	20 g	40 g
Dill, chopped	25 g	50 g	100 g
Juice of lemon	1	2	4
Salt and pepper	to taste		
Eggs	4	8	16
Milk	300 mL	600 mL	1.2 L
Breadcrumbs	as required		
Flour, plain	as required		

1. In a large bowl mix together seafood, eggs, mashed potato, salt, pepper, lemon juice and parsley.

2. If mixture is too wet, add small amounts of breadcrumbs mixing well; if mixture is too dry, add small amounts of milk. Finished mixture must be of a texture that will mould.

3. Shape into required amount of patties, approximately 100–110 g each.

4. Coat each fishcake with flour and pass through mixture of beaten egg and milk.

5. Coat fishcakes with breadcrumbs patting gently.

6. Deep-fry in oil preheated to 175°C for approximately 4–5 minutes or until cooked and golden brown.

Spanish Paella

Garnish: Capsicum rings.

	25	50	100
White fish, cooked, flaked	500 g	1 kg	2 kg
Prawns, cooked, peeled	250 g	500 g	1 kg
Mussels, cooked, chopped	200 g	400 g	800 g
Calamari, cooked, sliced	200 g	400 g	800 g
Chicken, cooked, diced	500 g	1 kg	2 kg
Pork, cooked, diced	500 g	1 kg	2 kg
Capsicum, red, diced	200 g	400 g	800 g
Capsicum, green diced	100 g	200 g	400 g
Shallots, roughly chopped	100 g	200 g	400 g

	25	50	100
Garlic cloves, chopped	4	8	16
Peas	150 g	300 g	600 g
Chives, chopped	10 g	20 g	40 g
Oregano, dried	5 g	10 g	20 g
Parsley, chopped	10 g	20 g	40 g
Food colouring, yellow	1 tablespoons	2 tablespoons	4 tablespoons
Salt and pepper	to taste		
Rice, long grain	1.2 kg	2.4 kg	4.8 kg
Stock, chicken	3 L	6 L	12 L

1. Cook chicken, pork, garlic and shallots in a little oil over moderate heat for 1 minute.

2. Add vegetables and cook for a further 2–3 minutes.

3. Add rice and cook for a further 2–3 minutes.

4. Add stock, colouring, oregano, chives, parsley and salt and pepper, bring to the boil and simmer gently.

5. Add seafood and peas, cover with lightly greased greaseproof paper and place in oven preheated to a moderate heat for approximately 45 minutes or until rice is tender.

Baby Trout Poached in White Wine and Lemon Juice

Garnish: Sliced cucumber and parsley sprigs.

	25	50	100
Trout, whole, gutted (125 g)	25	50	100
Onions, finely chopped	1 kg	1.5 kg	2 kg
Garlic clove, finely chopped	3	6	12
Lemons, juice	3	6	10
White wine	1 L	2 L	4 L

1. Wash trout thoroughly under cold running water and allow to drain.

2. Combine onion, garlic, lemon juice and wine.

3. Place trout in deep-sided baking tray one deep.

4. Pour over poaching mix and seal tray with aluminium foil.

5. Place into oven preheated to a moderate setting for approximately 30–40 minutes or until trout is cooked.

6. Remove from oven.

7. Serve as required with a little poaching stock spooned over trout.

Baked Fish

Garnish: Dill sprigs.

	25	50	100
Fish, top and tailed,			
gutted (100–120 g)	**25**	**50**	**100**
Butter	**250 g**	**500 g**	**1 kg**
Salt and pepper	**to taste**		

1. Wash fish thoroughly under cold running water and leave to drain.
2. Lightly grease baking tray and place fish in rows onto tray.
3. Brush fish with melted butter and sprinkle with salt and pepper.
4. Place into oven preheated to a moderate setting for approximately 20–30 minutes. If fish starts to blacken early, depending on the oven you are using, adjust temperature so fish cooks evenly and gradually.)
5. Remove from oven when fish flakes when pierced with a fork.
6. Serve as required on its own or accompanied by a sauce of your choice.

Pasta Marinara

Garnish: Capsicum rings.

	25	50	100
Penne pasta, cooked	**2.5 kg**	**5 kg**	**10 kg**
	cook as for spaghetti: see p 136		
Onions, finely chopped	**1 kg**	**2 kg**	**4 kg**
Garlic cloves, finely			
chopped	**3**	**6**	**10**
Tomatoes, tinned	**3 kg**	**6 kg**	**12 kg**
Tomato puree	**150 g**	**300 g**	**600 g**
Basil, chopped	**5 g**	**10 g**	**20 g**
Prawns, cooked, shelled	**250 g**	**500 g**	**1 kg**
Calamari, cooked, sliced	**250 g**	**500 g**	**1 kg**
Mussels, cooked, shelled	**250 g**	**500 g**	**1 kg**
White fish fillets, cooked,			
flaked	**250 g**	**500 g**	**1 kg**
Cheese, cheddar, grated	**500 g**	**1 kg**	**2 kg**
Salt and pepper	**to taste**		
Oil	**as required**		

1. Heat a little oil in suitable pan, add onion and garlic and cook until onion is soft.
2. Add basil, tomatoes that have been drained and chopped, and tomato puree. Mix thoroughly and remove from heat.
3. Add seafood and mix thoroughly.
4. Add cooked pasta, combine all ingredients and season to taste.
5. Place all ingredients into roasting tray and sprinkle with grated cheese.
6. Place into oven preheated to a moderate setting and cook until cheese starts to turn golden brown.
7. Serve as required.

Seafood Crumble

Garnish: Lemon wedges, slices, twists.

	25	50	100
White sauce	2 L	4 L	8 L
White fish fillets, cooked, flaked	2 kg	4 kg	8 kg
Prawns, cooked, shelled	1 kg	2 kg	4 kg
Parsley, chopped	10 g	20 g	40 g
Lemon juice	1 lemon	2 lemons	4 lemons
Flour	1.5 kg	3 kg	6 kg
Margarine	500 g	1 kg	2 kg
Salt and pepper	to taste		

1. Mix together white fish, prawns, parsley, lemon juice and white sauce.

2. In large mixing bowl, rub flour and margarine (at room temperature) lightly between fingers until a sandy texture is achieved. Season with a little salt and pepper.

3. Place seafood sauce mix into suitable deep-sided container.

4. Place crumble mix evenly over seafood mix.

5. Place into oven preheated to a moderate setting and cook for approximately 25–35 minutes or until crumble mixture is golden brown and sauce is heated through.

6. Pre-portion and serve as required.

Vegetarian and Rice Dishes

Vegetable Lasagne

Garnish: Thinly sliced tomato and chopped basil.

As for Italian lasagne except use finely chopped prepared vegetables in place of meat.

Tomatoes
Onions, double weight of original recipe
Capsicums
Mushrooms
Zucchini
Eggplant
Celery

French Bread Pizzas

An ideal way to use any stale french bread or long crusty rolls.

French bread cut in half   1 piece per portion
then into approxi-
mately 15 cm pieces

Topping mixture

Tomato puree	700 g	1.4 kg	2.8 kg
Oregano, chopped	10 g	20 g	40 g
Basil, chopped	5 g	10 g	20 g
Garlic cloves, chopped	4	8	14
Salt and pepper	to taste		
Cheese, cheddar, grated	1 kg	2 kg	4 kg
Parsley, chopped	5 g	10 g	20 g

1. Mix all ingredients, except tomato puree for topping mixture together.
2. Place bread cut side up on baking tray.
3. Spread tomato puree generously over top of bread.
4. Sprinkle bread evenly with mixed herbs and grated cheese.
5. Place trays into oven preheated to a moderate setting until cheese has melted and pizzas are heated through.
6. Serve as required.

NOTE: French bread pizzas can be topped with any meat or vegetables which are compatible. This is an ideal menu item to use up any excess meats and certain vegetables.

Vegetable Stuffed Baked Capsicum

Garnish: Finely chopped fresh herbs.

	25	50	100
Capsicums, large, seeded	½ per portion		
Vegetable mix	as for vegetable roulade		
Rice, cooked	500 g	1 kg	2 kg
Tomato puree	200 g	400 g	800 g
Cheese, cheddar, grated	500 g	1 kg	2 kg

1. Cut capsicum in half lengthways removing seeds.
2. Mix rice with tomato puree and vegetable mix and combine thoroughly.
3. Fill capsicum with mixture.
4. Top with grated cheese and place on lightly greased baking tray.
5. Bake in oven preheated to a moderate setting for approximately 20–30 minutes.
6. Serve as required.

NOTE: Stuffing mix may be varied perhaps using some nuts or lentils, and rice weights may be increased depending on capsicum size.

Vegetable Kebabs

Garnish: Coriander sprigs.

Most vegetables can be used for kebabs and in almost any order. Vegetables for kebabs should be cut into pieces approximately 3 cm squared.

Prepare and cook as for lamb and apricot kebabs.

Brindisi Pasta

Garnish: Grated parmesan cheese and chopped basil.

	25	50	100
Pasta shells	1.2 kg	2.4 kg	4.8 kg
Tomato puree	500 g	1 kg	2 kg
Tomatoes, small pieces	300 kg	600 kg	1.2 kg
Onions, small pieces	500 g	1 kg	2 kg
Garlic cloves, chopped	4	6	10
Oregano, chopped	10 g	20 g	40 g
Basil, chopped	10 g	20 g	40 g
Cheese, grated	1 kg	2 kg	4 kg
Salt and pepper	to taste		
Parsley, chopped	10 g	20 g	40 g

1. Bring large saucepan of lightly salted water to the boil.

2. Add pasta, stir and bring back to the boil.

3. Cook pasta for approximately 12–15 minutes or until it is tender but still firm.

4. Strain in colander and return to clean pan.

5. Place pan over moderate heat and add all other ingredients using only half of cheese.

6. Heat all ingredients through, stirring constantly.

7. Place all ingredients into deep-sided baking tray and sprinkle with remaining cheese.

8. Place into oven preheated to a moderate setting until cheese has melted.

9. Serve as required sprinkled with chopped parsley.

Vegetable Moussaka

As for vegetable lasagne using sliced eggplant in place of pasta sheets.

Macaroni Cheese with Chives

Garnish: Whole chives.

	25	50	100
Macaroni	650 g	1.3 kg	2.6 kg
Grated cheese	500 g	1 kg	2 kg
White sauce, thin	1.5 L	3 L	6 L
	see Stocks and Sauces		
Mustard	40 g	80 g	160 g
Chives, chopped	15 g	30 g	60 g
Salt and pepper	to taste		
Parsley, chopped	10 g	20 g	40 g

1. Bring large pan of lightly salted water to the boil.

2. Add macaroni, stir and bring back to the boil.

3. Cook for approximately 12–15 minutes or until macaroni is tender but still firm.

4. Drain macaroni in colander.

5. Return to clean mixing bowl, add half cheese, white sauce, mustard, chives and salt and pepper and mix together thoroughly.

6. Place contents into deep-sided baking tray and sprinkle with remaining grated cheese and chopped parsley.

7. Place in oven preheated to a moderate setting until cheese starts to turn a golden brown.

8. Pre-portion and serve as required.

Stir Fried Vegetables with Cashews and Roasted Pine Nuts

	25	50	100
Onions, sliced	800 g	1.6 kg	3.2 kg
Garlic cloves, chopped	3	6	12
Carrots, small batons	800 g	1.6 kg	3.2 kg
Celery, small batons	800 g	1.6 kg	3.2 kg
Mushrooms, sliced	800 g	1.6 kg	3.2 kg
Capsicum, halved, seeded, sliced	800 g	1.6 kg	3.2 kg
Beansprouts	1 kg	2 kg	4 kg
Cashew nuts	250 g	500 g	1 kg
Pine nuts, roasted	250 g	500 g	1 kg
Sesame/olive oil	as required		
Soy sauce	200 mL	400 mL	800 mL
Curry powder	15 g	30 g	60 g
Honey	150 mL	300 mL	600 mL
Cornflour	100 g	200 g	400 g

1. Heat a little oil over a high heat in suitable pan.

2. Add onions and garlic and cook for 1 minute.

3. Add carrots and cook for a further minute. Repeat process with celery.

4. Add capsicum and mushrooms and cook for a further 3 minutes.

5. Add beansprouts, soy sauce, curry powder and honey and mix all ingredients thoroughly.

6. Mix cornflour with a little cold water and add in small amounts to vegetable mix until sauce adheres to vegetables.

7. Cook for a further 1 minute on a high heat.

8. Serve as required.

Vegetable Roulade

Garnish: Tomato sail.

	25	50	100
Puff pastry	3 kg see Dessert Dishes	6 kg	12 kg
Onions, finely chopped	400 g	800 g	1.6 kg
Garlic cloves, finely chopped	4	6	9
Celery, finely chopped	400 g	800 g	1.6 kg
Leeks, finely sliced	200 g	400 g	800 g
Capsicum, finely chopped	300 g	600 g	1.2 kg
Mushrooms, finely sliced	500 g	1 kg	2 kg

	25	50	100
Parsley, chopped	10 g	20 g	40 g
Tomato puree	250 g	500 g	1 kg
Salt and pepper	to taste		
Oil	as required		
Eggs	2	4	8
Milk	50 mL	100 mL	200 mL

1. Heat a little oil in suitable pan, add onions and garlic and cook until onions are soft.

2. Add washed and drained celery and leek, mix and cook for approximately 2 minutes.

3. Mix in capsicum and mushrooms, cook until all ingredients are tender and remove pan from heat.

4. Using a ladle, remove any excess liquid from mix.

5. Add tomato puree, chopped parsley and season to taste.

6. Roll out puff pastry on lightly floured work surface to width of approximately 35 cm and to length of approximately 50 cm keeping pastry 3–4 mm thick. Repeat process until required amount is achieved.

7. Divide mixture evenly between rolled puff pastry sheets and spread evenly over pastry leaving a gap of 5 cm from all edges. Using egg and milk that has been whisked together brush edges of pastry.

8. Carefully roll puff pastry tightly lengthways until cylindrical shaped roll is achieved.

9. Fold ends underneath roll.

10. Place onto lightly greased baking tray and brush with egg and milk mixture.

11. Place into oven preheated to a moderate setting and cook for approximately 45 minutes or until roulade is cooked through and golden brown.

12. Pre-portion and serve as required.

Boiled Rice

	25	50	100
Rice, long grain	625 g	1.25 kg	2.5 kg

1. Bring a large pan of lightly salted water to the boil (ratio of water to rice is 15:1).

2. Wash rice under cold running water in conical strainer, add to boiling water and stir.

3. Reduce heat so as to achieve a strong simmer.

4. Cook for approximately 15 minutes or until rice is tender.

5. Place rice in strainer until all excess liquid has drained away.

6. Serve as required.

NOTE: If rice is not to be served immediately, place into strainer and refresh with plenty of cold running water. Strain and store for future use. When required for service, place rice into strainer and pour over boiling water until heated through. Allow excess water to drain away, and serve as required.

Fried Rice

	25	50	100
Rice, long grain	as for boiled rice		
Soy sauce	100 mL	200 mL	400 mL
Curry powder	5 g	10 g	20 g
Chicken booster	10 g	20 g	40 g
Salt and pepper	to taste		
Oil	as required		

1. Cook rice as for boiled rice making sure it is well drained.
2. Spread rice evenly on tray and refrigerate for at least 2 hours.
3. Heat a little oil in suitable pan over high heat.
4. Add rice, stirring vigorously.
5. Add all other ingredients and mix.
6. When rice is heated through, remove from heat and keep covered with lightly greased greaseproof paper.
7. Serve as required.

Braised Rice

	25	50	100
Rice, long grain	as for boiled rice		
Stock, chicken	1.2 L	2.4 L	4.8 L
Onion, finely chopped	600 g	1.2 kg	2.4 kg
Butter	100 g	200 g	400 g
Pepper	to taste		

1. Place stock into suitable pan and bring to the boil.
2. Wash rice under cold running water in conical strainer.
3. Reduce stock to simmer and add rice stirring once to separate rice.
4. Add onion and butter and mix in.
5. Reduce heat to a slow simmer and cover pan with a tight fitting lid.
6. Cook very slowly for approximately 45 minutes on stove top, or in a moderately heated oven in a roasting tray sealed with aluminium foil, until all liquid is absorbed by rice and rice is tender.
7. Add a little water as required.
8. Add pepper to taste.
9. Serve as required.

NOTE: Rice can be cooked out in the oven after all ingredients have been added but it must still be covered and cooked slowly.

Saffron Rice

	25	50	100
Rice, long grain	as for boiled rice		
Yellow colouring	enough to turn water a mild yellow		

As for boiled rice with the addition of colouring (in moderation) just prior to adding rice.

NOTE: The spice saffron can be used, but because it is expensive it is usually outside a caterer's budget.

Prawn Rice

	25	50	100
Rice, long grain	as for boiled rice		
Prawns, cooked, shelled, finely diced	300 g	600 g	1.2 kg
Salt and pepper	to taste		

As for boiled rice adding cooked prawns and salt and pepper to strained rice just before serving.

Salads

Apple and Celery Salad

		25	50	100
Celery, finely diced		1 kg	2 kg	4 kg
Apples, red, cored, finely diced		1.5 kg	3 kg	6 kg
Mayonnaise, as binder	approx	250 mL	500 mL	1 L
		see Salad Dressings and Marinades		
Juice of lemon		½	1	2
Salt and pepper		to taste		

Combine all ingredients, adding mayonnaise in small amounts until all ingredients are bound together.

192

Waldorf Salad

As for apple and celery salad with the addition of:

	25	50	100
Walnuts, quartered	**200 g**	**400 g**	**800 g**

Apple and Sultana Salad

As for apple and celery salad with the addition of:

	25	50	100
Sultanas	**200 g**	**400 g**	**800 g**

Coriander and Peanut Salad

As for apple and celery salad with the addition of:

	25	50	100
Peanuts, roasted	**300 g**	**600 g**	**1.2 kg**
Coriander, roughly chopped	**20 g**	**40 g**	**80 g**

Apple and Mint Salad

As for apple and celery salad with the addition of:

	25	50	100
Mint, roughly chopped	**20 g**	**40 g**	**80 g**

Coleslaw Salad

	25	50	100
Carrots, grated	**500 g**	**1 kg**	**2 kg**
Cabbage, cored, finely sliced	**2 kg**	**4 kg**	**8 kg**
Onions, finely sliced	**250 g**	**500 g**	**1 kg**
Parsley, chopped	**5 g**	**10 g**	**20 g**
Mayonnaise, as binder approx	**250 mL**	**500 mL**	**1 L**
	see Salad Dressings and Marinades		
Salt	**to taste**		

Combine all ingredients, adding mayonnaise in small amounts until all ingredients have bound together.

NOTE: If coleslaw is to be made and stored, do not add onions until coleslaw is to be served; this will prolong its storage time.

Vegetable Salad

	25	50	100
Carrots, peeled, diced, cooked	750 g	1.5 kg	3 kg
Peas, cooked	750 g	1.5 kg	3 kg
Green beans, cooked	200 g	400 g	800 g
Capsicum, red, green, diced	300 g	600 g	1.2 kg
Corn niblets, cooked	250 g	500 g	1 kg
Celery, diced	250 g	500 g	1 kg
Mayonnaise as binder approx	200 mL	400 mL	800 mL
see Salad Dressings and Marinades			
Parsley, finely chopped	5 g	10 g	20 g
Basil, finely chopped	5 g	10 g	20 g
Salt and pepper	to taste		

Combine all ingredients, adding mayonnaise, in small amounts until all ingredients have bound together.

Dill and Cucumber Salad

	25	50	100
Cucumber, peeled, seeded, sliced	2.5 kg	5 kg	10 kg
Dill, chopped	30 g	60 g	120 g
Sour cream, as binder approx	200 g	400 g	800 g

Combine all ingredients, adding sour cream in small amounts until all ingredients have bound together.

Cucumber and Minted Yoghurt Salad

	25	50	100
Cucumber, peeled, seeded, finely diced	2.5 kg	5 kg	10 kg
Mint, chopped	20 g	40 g	80 g
Yoghurt, natural	200 mL	400 mL	800 mL

Combine all ingredients and use as required.

Tomato Salad

	25	50	100
Tomato, diced, seeded	2.5 kg	5 kg	10 kg
Onion, finely chopped	250 g	500 g	1 kg
Parsley, finely chopped	25 g	50 g	100 g
Garlic vinaigrette, as			
binder approx	100 mL	200 mL	400 mL
	see Salad Dressings and Marinades		
Coriander, chopped			
(optional)	15 g	30 g	60 g

Combine all ingredients, adding vinaigrette in small amounts until all ingredients have bound together.

Tomato and Black Olive Salad

As for tomato salad with the addition of:

	25	50	100
Olives, black, whole	200 g	400 g	800 g

NOTE: Olives may be stoned if desired.

Cherry Tomato Salad

As for tomato salad substituting cherry tomatoes whole or halved for tomatoes.

Tomato and Basil Salad

As for tomato salad with the addition of:

	25	50	100
Basil, chopped	30 g	60 g	120 g

Tomato and Oregano Salad

As for tomato and basil salad substituting chopped oregano for the same amount of basil.

Tomato, Basil and Pine Nut Salad

As for tomato and basil salad with the addition of:

	25	50	100
Pine nuts	50 g	100 g	200 g

Roast pine nuts in oven at 150°C until light golden brown. Allow to cool before use.

Cucumber, Tomato and Oregano Salad

	25	50	100
Cucumber, diced	1 kg	2 kg	4 kg
Tomatoes, diced	1.5 kg	3 kg	6 kg
Onions, finely chopped	250 g	500 g	1 kg
Oregano, chopped	15 g	30 g	60 g
English mustard vinaigrette, as binder	approx 100 mL	200 mL	400 mL
	see Salad Dressings and Marinades		

Combine all ingredients, adding vinaigrette in small amounts until all ingredients have bound together.

Tomato, Cucumber and Coriander Salad

As for cucumber, tomato and oregano salad omitting basil and adding:

	25	50	100
Coriander, chopped	15 g	30 g	60 g

Cucumber and Tomato Salad

As for cucumber, tomato and oregano salad omitting oregano.

Snow Pea and Beansprout Salad

	25	50	100
Snow peas, topped, tailed, blanched	2 kg	4 kg	8 kg
Beansprouts	500 g	1 kg	2 kg
Vinaigrette, as binder	sufficient to bind		
Sugar, caster	50 g	100 g	200 g

Combine all ingredients and use as required.

Niçoise Salad

	25	50	100
French beans, cooked, diced	1 kg	2 kg	4 kg
Capers	40 g	80 g	160 g
Anchovy fillets	60 g	120 g	240 g
Tomatoes, seeded, diced	400 g	800 g	1.6 kg
Olives, black	60 g	120 g	240 g
Potatoes, cooked, diced	400 g	800 g	1.6 kg
Salt and pepper	to taste		
Mayonnaise, as binder	sufficient to bind		

1. Mix together beans, tomatoes and potatoes, season and bind with mayonnaise.
2. Neatly arrange other ingredients over the top.
3. Serve as required.

Greek Salad

As for cucumber, tomato and oregano salad with the addition of:

	25	50	100
Fetta cheese, diced	200 g	400 g	800 g
Olives, black, whole	200 g	400 g	800 g

Italian Salad

	25	50	100
Pasta, penne, cooked	1.5 kg	3 kg	6 kg
Capsicum, red, diced	250 g	500 g	1 kg
Capsicum, green, diced	250 g	500 g	1 kg
Ham, cooked, diced	250 g	500 g	1 kg
Tomatoes, seeded, diced	250 g	500 g	1 kg
Basil, chopped	10 g	20 g	40 g
Oregano, chopped	10 g	20 g	40 g
Marjoram, chopped	5 g	10 g	20 g
Salt and pepper	to taste		
Garlic vinaigrette, as binder approx	100 mL	200 mL	400 mL
	see Salad Dressings and Marinades		

Combine all ingredients, adding vinaigrette in small amounts until all ingredients have bound together.

Potato Salad

	25	50	100
Potatoes, peeled, cooked, diced	2.5 kg	5 kg	10 kg
Onions, finely chopped	250 g	500 g	1 kg
Parsley, finely chopped	5 g	10 g	20 g
Salt and pepper	to taste		
Mayonnaise, as binder approx	200 mL	400 mL	800 mL
	see Salad Dressings and Marinades		

Combine all ingredients, adding mayonnaise in small amounts until all ingredients have bound together.

Potato and Chive Salad

As for potato salad with the addition of:

	25	50	100
Chives, finely sliced	15 g	30 g	60 g

Potato and Shallot Salad

As for potato salad with the addition of:

	25	50	100
Shallots, finely sliced	4	8	16

Italian Style Cauliflower and Caper Salad

	25	50	100
Cauliflower, florets	1.2 kg	2.4 kg	4.8 kg
Capers	200 g	400 g	800 g
Basil dressing	enough to bind		

1. Place cauliflower into boiling water and bring back to the boil.
2. Place into strainer and refresh under cold running water.
3. Place into clean bowl and mix in capers.
4. Add dressing and mix together.
5. Use as required.

Rice Salad

	25	50	100
Rice, long grain, cooked	2 kg	4 kg	8 kg
Celery, diced	250 g	500 g	1 kg
Peas, cooked	150 g	300 g	600 g
Capsicum, red, diced	250 g	500 g	1 kg
Parsley, chopped	10 g	20 g	40 g
Salt and pepper	to taste		
Vinaigrette, as binder approx	100 mL	200 mL	400 mL

Combine all ingredients, adding vinaigrette in small amounts until all ingredients are bound together.

Tuna, Olive and Rice Salad

As for rice salad omitting peas and adding:

	25	50	100
Olives, black, whole	150 g	300 g	600 g
Tuna, cooked, flaked	250 g	500 g	1 kg

Marinated Mushroom Salad

	25	50	100
Mushrooms, quartered	2.5 kg	5 kg	10 kg
Parsley, chopped	10 g	20 g	40 g
English mustard vinaigrette	as required to bind		

Combine all ingredients and refrigerate for a minimum of 2 hours before serving.

Marinated Mushroom and Celery Salad

As for marinated mushroom salad with the addition of:

	25	50	100
Celery, finely sliced	250 g	500 g	1 kg

Marinated Mushroom and Tomato Salad

As for marinated mushroom salad with the addition of:

	25	50	100
Tomatoes, seeded, diced	250 g	500 g	1 kg

Mixed Leaf Salad

**Lettuce, for example
mixture of cos, iceberg,
mignonette, coral etc**

1. Separate all leaves and tear into bite-size pieces. Discard any discoloured leaves.
2. Thoroughly wash leaves and leave to drain.
3. Serve accompanied by dressing of your choice.

NOTE: There are many varieties of lettuce available and it is a good idea to mix different coloured lettuces.

Green Leaf Salad

As for mixed leaf salad using only green lettuce.

Mix lettuce with large sprigs of parsley and serve with dressing of your choice.

NOTE: Sprigs of other fresh herbs may be added if desired, for example basil.

Side Salad Garnish

	25	50	100
Lettuce cups, iceberg	1½	3	6
Tomatoes, sliced	1.5 kg	3 kg	6 kg
Cucumber, sliced	500 g	1 kg	2 kg
Shallots, sliced	250 kg	500 kg	1 kg
Watercress, sprigs	as required		

1. Quarter lettuce and peel off individual leaves.
2. Neatly place two slices of tomato and two slices of cucumber inside each lettuce cup.
3. Sprinkle with sliced shallots and place sprig of watercress on each salad garnish.

Zucchini and Apple Salad

	25	50	100
Zucchinis, washed, topped and tailed, small diced	1.5 kg	3 kg	6 kg
Apples, cored, small diced	1 kg	2 kg	4 kg
Mayonnaise	sufficient to bind		
Lemon juice	½ lemon	1 lemon	2 lemons

Combine all ingredients and refrigerate until required.

Cauliflower Salad with Mayonnaise and Satay Dressing

	25	50	100
Cauliflower, florets	1.5 kg	3 kg	6 kg
Mayonnaise and satay dressing	enough to bind		
	see Salad Dressings and Marinades		

1. Place cauliflower into lightly salted boiling water and bring back to the boil.
2. Remove from heat immediately, place into strainer and refresh under cold running water.
3. Place into clean bowl and add enough dressing to coat cauliflower florets lightly.
4. Serve as required.

Carrot, Coconut and Sultana Salad

	25	50	100
Carrots, small batons	1.1 kg	2.2 kg	4.4 kg
Coconut, desiccated	200 g	400 g	800 g
Sultanas	200 g	400 g	800 g
Mayonnaise	enough to bind		
	see Salad Dressings and Marinades		

1. Place carrot batons into lightly salted boiling water, cook for 2 minutes and remove from heat.
2. Refresh immediately in a strainer under cold running water.
3. Drain all excess water from carrots.
4. Wash sultanas and leave to drain.
5. Place carrots into clean bowl and mix in coconut and sultanas.
6. Bind together with mayonnaise adding a little at a time.
7. Serve as required.

Salad Dressings and Marinades

Mayonnaise

Chill all mayonnaise products before service and store in refrigerator at all times.

	25	50	100
Oil, vegetable/olive	1 L	2 L	4 L
Vinegar	50 mL	100 mL	200 mL
Egg yolks	6	12	24
English mustard	25 g	50 g	100 g
Salt and pepper	to taste		

1. Place egg yolks, vinegar and seasoning in a bowl and whisk well.
2. Slowly add oil, whisking continuously until all oil has been incorporated.
3. Correct seasoning to taste.

NOTE: If mixture curdles, add one egg yolk and a dash of vinegar to a clean mixing bowl and add curdled mixture slowly whisking continuously.

Fresh Dill and Garlic Dressing

To mayonnaise add:

	25	50	100
Dill, finely chopped	15 g	30 g	60 g
Garlic cloves, finely chopped	3	6	12

Thousand Island Dressing

To mayonnaise add:

	25	50	100
Gherkins, finely chopped	6	12	24
Tomato sauce	50 mL	100 mL	200 mL
Parsley, chopped	10 g	20 g	40 g

Sour Cream with Chives

	25	50	100
Sour cream	300 g	600 g	1.2 kg
Chives, chopped	10 g	20 g	40 g

Combine ingredients and refrigerate. Use as required.

Light Curried Mayonnaise

	25	50	100
Mayonnaise	see Mayonnaise recipe		
Curry powder, mild	10 g	20 g	40 g
Lemon juice	1 tablespoon	2 tablespoons	4 tablespoons

Combine all ingredients and refrigerate. Use as required.

Lemon Mayonnaise

	25	50	100
Mayonnaise	see Mayonnaise recipe		
Lemon juice	1 tablespoon	2 tablespoons	4 tablespoons

Combine all ingredients and refrigerate. Use as required.

Mayonnaise and Satay Sauce

	25	50	100
Mayonnaise	200 g	400 g	800 g
	see Mayonnaise recipe		
Satay sauce, commercial	100 g	200 g	400 g
Lemon juice	1 tablespoon	2 tablespoons	4 tablespoons

Combine all ingredients and use as required. This sauce should be kept refrigerated.

Vinaigrette Dressing

	25	50	100
Oil, vegetable/olive	500 mL	1 L	2 L
Vinegar	200 mL	400 mL	800 mL
Salt and pepper	to taste		

Combine all ingredients and mix well.

Thick Vinaigrette

As for vinaigrette dressing with the addition of:

	25	50	100
Egg white	2	4	8

Beat egg whites until stiff and fold gently into vinaigrette dressing.

Creamy Vinaigrette

As for vinaigrette dressing with the addition of

	25	50	100
Cream	100 mL	200 mL	400 mL

English Mustard Vinaigrette / Dressing

As for vinaigrette/salad dressing with the addition of:

	25	50	100
English mustard	25 g	50 g	100 g
Sugar, caster	50 g	100 g	200 g

Basil Dressing

As for vinaigrette with the addition of:

	25	50	100
Basil, finely chopped	**10 g**	**20 g**	**40 g**

Garlic and Chive Dressing

As for vinaigrette/salad dressing with the addition of:

	25	50	100
Garlic cloves, chopped	**3**	**6**	**12**
Chives, finely sliced	**10 g**	**20 g**	**40 g**

Chive Dressing

As for garlic and chive dressing omitting garlic and adding extra:

	25	50	100
Chives, finely sliced	**15 g**	**30 g**	**60 g**

Lemon and Herb Dressing

As for vinaigrette/salad dressing with the addition of:

	25	50	100
Lemon juice	**50 mL**	**100 mL**	**200 mL**
Basil, chopped	**5 g**	**10 g**	**20 g**
Chives, finely sliced	**5 g**	**10 g**	**20 g**
Parsley, finely chopped	**5 g**	**10 g**	**20 g**

Lemon and Oregano Dressing

As for vinaigrette/salad dressing with the addition of:

	25	50	100
Lemon juice	**50 mL**	**100 mL**	**200 mL**
Oregano, dried	**10 g**	**20 g**	**40 g**

Parsley and Dill Dressing

As for vinaigrette/salad dressing with the addition of:

	25	50	100
Parsley, finely chopped	**5 g**	**10 g**	**20 g**
Dill, finely chopped	**5 g**	**10 g**	**20 g**

Herb Vinaigrette

	25	50	100
Vinaigrette	see Vinaigrette recipe		
Basil, finely chopped	5 g	10 g	20 g
Garlic cloves, finely chopped	1	1	2
Chives, finely sliced	5 g	10 g	20 g
Parsley, finely chopped	5 g	10 g	20 g

Combine all ingredients and refrigerate. Use as required.

Ginger and Garlic Vinaigrette

	25	50	100
Vinaigrette	see Vinaigrette recipe		
Ginger, grated	10 g	20 g	40 g
Garlic cloves, chopped	1	1	2

Combine ingredients and refrigerate. Use as required.

Basil and Peppercorn Vinaigrette

	25	50	100
Vinaigrette	see Vinaigrette recipe		
Basil, chopped	10 g	20 g	40 g
Peppercorns, ground	to taste		

Combine ingredients and refrigerate. Use as required.

Lemon Vinaigrette

	25	50	100
Vinaigrette	see Vinaigrette recipe		
Lemon juice	1 lemon	1½ lemons	2 lemons

Combine ingredients and refrigerate. Use as required.

Lemon and Chive Vinaigrette

	25	50	100
Vinaigrette	see Vinaigrette recipe		
Lemon juice	½ lemon	1 lemon	1½ lemons
Chives, finely sliced	10 g	15 g	20 g

Combine ingredients and refrigerate. Use as required.

Salad Dressing

	25	50	100
Margarine	100 g	200 g	400 g
Flour, plain	100 g	200 g	400 g
Milk	1.25 L	2.5 L	5 L
Sugar	100 g	200 g	400 g
Mustard	25 g	50 g	100 g
Salt	to taste		
Cayenne pepper	2 g	4 g	8 g
Vinegar	200 mL	400 mL	800 mL

1. Melt margarine over moderate heat, and stirring continuously, blend in flour until mixture is smooth (do not colour).

2. Add milk slowly, stirring continuously.

3. Bring to the boil and allow to simmer gently for 5 minutes.

4. Add sugar and stir.

5. Allow to cool.

6. Mix together mustard, vinegar, salt and cayenne pepper, and add to milk mixture.

7. Allow to cool and refrigerate. Use as needed.

Variations

As for vinaigrette variations using same amounts. Does not apply to thick vinaigrette or creamy vinaigrette.

Marinades

A marinade is a liquid flavoured with various amounts of wine, sauce and herbs. It has two purposes:

    (a) to impart into food a particular flavour; and
    (b) to tenderise foods prior to cooking.

A basic marinade can be made from one sauce or wine, for example soy sauce or white wine, or it can contain numerous amounts of liquids and herbs. In most cases, basic recipes are more than adequate. It is recommended, however, that marinades be experimented with.

The recipes below will make 3 litres of marinade. Adjust as required.

Basic Chinese Marinade

Soy sauce	2 L
Sherry, dry	1 L

Mix all ingredients together and use as required.

Soy, Lemon and Chilli Marinade

Oil	**2 L**
Soy sauce	**500 mL**
Lemon juice	**500 mL**
Garlic, chopped	**6**
Chillies, chopped	**4**
Sugar, caster	**100 g**

Mix all ingredients together and use as required.

Wine and Herb Marinade

Oil	**2 L**
Wine, white	**1 L**
Basil, chopped	**10 g**
Thyme, chopped	**10 g**
Parsley, chopped	**5 g**

Red Wine and Herb Marinade

As for wine and herb marinade, but use red wine instead of white.
Mix all ingredients together and use as required.

Lemon and Rosemary Marinade

As for red wine and herb marinade omitting herbs and adding:

	25	50	100
Lemon, juice, zest	**2**	**4**	**8**
Rosemary, chopped	**5 g**	**10 g**	**15 g**

Soy, Honey and Ginger Marinade

As for soy, lemon and chilli marinade omitting lemon and chillies and adding:

	25	50	100
Honey	**150 mL**	**300 mL**	**600 mL**
Ginger, grated	**10 g**	**20 g**	**40 g**

Asian Style Marinade

Oil	**1 L**
Soy sauce	**1 L**
Lemon juice	**500 mL**
Sesame oil	**250 mL**
Wine, white	**250 mL**
Five spice powder	**100 g**
Ginger	**50 g**
Garlic cloves, chopped	**5**

Mix all ingredients together and use as required.

Red Wine Marinade

Wine, red	**2.75 mL**
Garlic cloves, chopped	**5**
Worcester sauce	**250 mL**

Mix all ingredients together and use as required.

──────────── ◇ ────────────

Vegetable Dishes

Introduction

The most commonly used cuts of vegetables are as follows:

(a) brunoise: which is a very fine dice;

(b) julienne: fine strips of vegetables;

(c) jardinière: small vegetable batons;

(d) macédoine: large diced vegetables;

(e) sliced: to the required thickness; and

(f) diced: to the required size.

Methods of Preparation and Cookery of Vegetables

Refer to vegetable portion control table, pp 36–7, for portion sizes.

Times of year given stipulate only when an item is at its best, not necessarily its availability.

Compatibility is not meant to restrict the use of any vegetable; it points out proven options that can be used with the given vegetable.

All weights given are uncooked, unprepared weights and allow for average wastage during preparation and cooking.

Asparagus

Spring, Summer.

Method of cookery: Boiled, steamed.

Compatible with white sauces, butter sauces.

	25	50	100
Asparagus	**1.5 kg**	**3 kg**	**6 kg**

To Prepare

1. Trim asparagus 2 cm from base of stalks.
2. Using a potato peeler, gently scrape bottom half of the stem.
3. Wash thoroughly under cold running water.
4. Using a little string, tie asparagus into bunches of 10–14 pieces.

To Cook

1. Place bundles of asparagus into slightly salted boiling water.
2. Cook for approximately 2 minutes depending on size of asparagus stalks.
3. Asparagus is cooked when thickest part of stem gives way with a little pressure from fingers.
4. If not serving immediately, refresh under cold running water.

Asparagus with Mornay Sauce / Hollandaise Sauce

	25	50	100
Asparagus	as above		
Cheese sauce	750 mL	1.5 L	3 L
	OR		
Hollandaise sauce	500 mL	1 L	2 L

1. Prepare sauce according to recipe in Stocks and Sauces section.

2. Prepare and cook asparagus as above.

3. Lay portion of asparagus onto plate and spoon a little sauce over centre of asparagus.

NOTE: Once asparagus has been coated with a little cheese sauce it may be topped with a little grated cheese and placed under a heated grill until golden brown.

Aubergine (Eggplant)

All year.

Methods of cookery: Deep-fried, shallow-fried, grilled, braised.

Compatible with Asian dishes, Italian dishes.

	25	50	100
Aubergine	2 kg	4 kg	8 kg

To Prepare

1. Remove stalk and wash well under cold running water.

2. Either cut into halves for stuffing, or for the more common frying, cut into the required sized and shaped pieces.

To Cook

1. Lightly sprinkle aubergine with salt and allow to stand for 20 minutes while salt draws out bitter juices.

2. Wash well under cold running water.

3. Drain well until all excess water is removed.

4. Deep-fry in oil preheated to 175°C for approximately 2 minutes or until cooked.

OR

1. Salt as before and allow to stand for 20 minutes. Wash and drain well.

2. Pass pieces through lightly seasoned flour.

3. Deep-fry in oil preheated to approximately 175°C for approximately 2 minutes or until cooked.

4. Drain well before service.

To shallow-fry, apply step 1 and step 3.

Bamboo Shoots

Available fresh, though usually bought tinned.
Methods of cookery: Fried, boiled, braised, casserole.
Compatible with oriental dishes.

	25	50	100
Bamboo shoots	**1 kg**	**2 kg**	**4 kg**

Beans, Broad

Spring, Summer.
Methods of cookery: Boiled, steamed.
Compatible with cream, cream sauce.

	25	50	100
Beans, broad	**1.5 kg**	**3 kg**	**6 kg**

To Prepare

1. Wash beans thoroughly under cold running water.
2. Trim ends and remove string from either side of bean.
3. Cut into required size.

To Cook

1. Cook in lightly salted boiling water approximately 4–6 minutes or until tender.
2. If not serving immediately refresh under cold running water.

Beans, Snake / Green / French

All year.
Methods of cookery: Boiled, steamed, casserole, fried.
Compatible with almonds, cream, cream sauce.

	25	50	100
Beans	**1.5 kg**	**3 kg**	**6 kg**

1. Prepare as for broad beans.
2. Cook as for broad beans, for approximately 2–4 minutes or until cooked. Beans can be stir fried.

Crispy Green Beans

	25	50	100
Green beans	**1.5 kg**	**3 kg**	**6 kg**

To Prepare

1. Top and tail beans.
2. Wash thoroughly under cold running water.

To Cook

1. Place beans into lightly salted boiling water.
2. Cook for approximately 1 minute.
3. Drain and serve. If not serving immediately, refresh under cold running water.

Green Beans with Toasted Almonds

	25	50	100
Green beans	**1.5 kg**	**3 kg**	**6 kg**
Almonds, slivered	**150 g**	**300 g**	**600 g**
Butter	**100 g**	**200 g**	**400 g**

To Prepare

1. Top and tail beans.
2. Wash thoroughly under cold running water.

To Cook

1. Place beans into lightly salted boiling water and cook for 2–4 minutes or until cooked.
2. Place almonds onto a tray and place under heated salamander and grill until light brown.
3. Drain beans well in colander.
4. Place beans into a clean bowl with melted butter, gently mix in almonds and mix thoroughly.
5. Serve as required.

Sautéed French Beans

	25	50	100
French beans	**1.5 kg**	**3 kg**	**6 kg**
Butter	**150 g**	**300 g**	**600 g**
Salt and pepper	**to taste**		

To Prepare

1. Top and tail French beans.
2. Wash thoroughly under cold running water.

To Cook

1. Place French beans into boiling water and cook for approximately 2 minutes.
2. Drain well in colander.
3. Melt butter in a large frypan or pan on a moderate heat.
4. Place French beans into butter and turn up heat to high and cook for 1 minute.
5. Serve as required.

Broccoli

All year.

Methods of cookery: Boiled, steamed, baked.

Compatible with cheese sauce, hollandaise sauce.

	25	50	100
Broccoli	**1.75 kg**	**3.5 kg**	**7 kg**

To Prepare

1. Trim leaves and base of broccoli stalks.
2. Cut into required size florets.
3. Wash well under cold running water.
4. Any thick stalks should have a cross cut into them to help the cooking process.

To Cook

1. Add broccoli to lightly salted boiling water, bring water to the boil again and remove florets.
2. Florets are cooked when a knife can pierce the stalks with relative ease. Broccoli can be served crisp.
3. Refresh in cold running water if not serving immediately.

Broccoli can be steamed, but care should be taken not to overload steamer trays because the weight may damage broccoli that is on the bottom of the tray.

Broccoli and Cauliflower Medley

Prepare broccoli and cauliflower in accordance with relevant instructions. Substitute half broccoli florets for cauliflower florets and cook as for relevant vegetable.

Broccoli Mornay

1. Prepare and cook broccoli as above.
2. Place cooked broccoli onto a plate and coat generously with cheese sauce.

OR

1. Place cooked broccoli onto baking tray.
2. Coat with sauce.
3. Place in oven preheated to a moderate setting.
4. Cook for approximately 5–10 minutes or until sauce turns golden brown.

Broccoli Florets with Walnut and Apple

	25	50	100
Broccoli	1.5 kg	3 kg	6 kg
Walnuts, quartered	200 g	400 g	800 g
Apple, peeled, cored, finely diced	200 g	400 g	800 g
Butter	100 g	200 g	400 g
Salt and pepper	to taste		

To Prepare
1. Remove florets from broccoli stalk.
2. Wash thoroughly under cold running water.
3. Quarter walnuts and peel, core and dice apple into 1 cm pieces.

To Cook
1. Place broccoli florets into boiling water and cook for 1 minute.
2. Drain well in colander.
3. Melt butter in large frypan or pan over moderate heat.
4. Add walnuts and apple.
5. Cook for 1 minute.
6. Add broccoli florets and mix all ingredients together thoroughly.
7. Season to taste.
8. Serve as required.

Brussels Sprouts

All year.

Methods of cookery: Boiled, steamed.

Compatible with roast dishes.

	25	50	100
Brussels sprouts	**1.75 kg**	**3.5 kg**	**7 kg**

To Prepare

1. Remove outer leaves and trim back stalk.
2. Wash thoroughly under cold running water.
3. Cross the base of each with a sharp vegetable knife to aid the cooking process.

To Cook

1. Place into lightly salted boiling water.
2. Reduce heat to strong simmer.
3. Cook for approximately 4–6 minutes or until cooked, depending on size.
4. Drain well before serving.

Brussels sprouts can be steamed. See broccoli instructions.

Cabbage, Boiled

All year.

Methods of cookery: Boiled, steamed, braised, fried.

Compatible with onion, apple.

	25	50	100
Cabbage	**2.5 kg**	**5 kg**	**10 kg**

To Prepare

1. Remove outer leaves.
2. Cut in half, then into quarters.
3. Remove stalk using a knife.
4. Cut cabbage in required style.
5. Wash thoroughly under cold running water.

To Cook

1. Place cabbage into lightly salted boiling water.
2. Cook for approximately 1–2 minutes or to the required degree. Cabbage can be plunged into salted boiling water and removed immediately and refreshed under cold running water to give a crisp vegetable dish.
3. Drain well and serve.
4. If not to be served immediately, refresh under cold running water.

Braised Cabbage with Sultanas and Apple

	25	50	100
Cabbage	as above		
Margarine/butter	250 g	500 g	1 kg
Vinegar, preferably white	100 mL	200 mL	400 mL
Apple, peeled, cored, small pieces	½ kg	1 kg	2 kg
Sultanas	250 g	500 g	1 kg
Sugar	50 g	100 g	200 g

To Prepare

As for boiled cabbage.

To Cook

1. Melt margarine/butter in heavy-bottomed pan over moderate heat.

2. Add vinegar, apple, sultanas and cabbage and mix thoroughly.

3. Reduce heat to low, place lid on pan and allow to cook for approximately 45 minutes or until cabbage is tender, stirring every 10 minutes.

4. Season to taste and serve.

NOTE: Red cabbage is ideally suited to this dish.

Braised Cabbage

	25	50	100
Cabbage	2.5 kg	5 kg	10 kg
Onion, finely diced	200 g	400 g	800 g
Stock, chicken	200 mL	400 mL	800 mL
Water	as required		

To Prepare

As for boiled cabbage.

To Cook

1. Place cabbage, onion, stock and enough water to cover half cabbage into large saucepan.

2. Bring to the boil.

3. Simmer and cover with a tight fitting lid.

4. Cook for approximately 15–20 minutes.

5. Serve as required with a spoonful of stock.

Capsicum

All year.
Methods of cookery: Fried, boiled, baked.
Compatible with most meats and vegetables.

	25	50	100
Capsicum	**625 g**	**1.25 kg**	**2.5 kg**

To Prepare
1. Cut capsicum in half.
2. Remove stalk and seeds.
3. Using a knife cut away any white visible on inside of capsicum.
4. Cut into required size.

To Cook
Place into lightly salted boiling water for approximately 1 minute.
Capsicum can be eaten raw or served as a colourful garnish to a dish.

Sautéed Capsicum and Onion

	25	50	100
Capsicum, red, strips	**500 g**	**1 kg**	**2 kg**
Onions, ½ cm slices	**1 kg**	**2 kg**	**4 kg**
Margarine/butter	**150 g**	**300 g**	**600 g**
Parsley, chopped	**10 g**	**20 g**	**40 g**

To Prepare
Wash capsicum under cold running water.

To Cook
1. Melt butter over moderate heat in large saucepan.
2. Add capsicum and onion and fry for 1 minute.
3. Add parsley and mix well.
4. Serve as required.

Carrots

All year.
Methods of cookery: Boiled, steamed, roasted, braised.
Compatible with swede, turnip, honey.

	25	50	100
Carrots	**1.5 kg**	**3 kg**	**6 kg**

To Prepare
1. Peel a thin layer of skin from carrot.
2. Trim both ends.
3. Wash well under cold running water.
4. Cut into required size pieces.

To Cook
1. Place into lightly salted water with a little sugar.
2. Bring back to the boil.
3. Simmer for approximately 2–4 minutes or until tender.
4. If not serving immediately refresh under cold running water.

Whole Baby Carrots

	25	50	100
Whole baby carrots	**1.75 kg**	**3.5 kg**	**7 kg**
Sugar	**100 g**	**200 g**	**400 g**
Butter	**50 g**	**100 g**	**200 g**

To Prepare
1. Peel carrots.
2. Top and tail.
3. Wash thoroughly under cold running water.

To Cook
1. Place carrots into boiling water.
2. Cook until tender depending on size.
3. Drain well in colander.
4. Melt butter in clean pan over moderate heat.
5. Add carrots and sugar.
6. Cook until sugar has glazed carrots, approximately 30 seconds to 1 minute.
7. Serve as required.

Puree of Carrot

	25	50	100
Carrot, small pieces	as above		
Butter, melted	200 g	400 g	800 g
Cream	50 mL	100 mL	200 mL
Nutmeg	5 g	10 g	20 g

To Prepare

As above.

To Cook

1. Cover carrots with cold water in suitable pan.
2. Bring to the boil over moderate heat and cook until soft.
3. Drain all liquid from carrots.
4. Place in mixer or suitable food processor.
5. Add cream, nutmeg and melted butter.
6. Liquidise or beat until smooth consistency is achieved.
7. Season to taste and place in suitable ovenproof dish.
8. Place in oven preheated to a moderate setting and bake for approximately 20 minutes.
9. Serve as required.

Carrot and Swede

	25	50	100
Carrot	750 g	1.5 kg	3 kg
Swede	750 g	1.5 kg	3 kg
Butter	100 g	200 g	400 g

1. Prepare and cook vegetables according to instructions for boiling.
2. Mix together lightly with a little melted butter and serve.

Pureed Carrot and Swede

	25	50	100
Carrot	750 g	1.5 kg	3 kg
Swede	750 g	1.5 kg	3 kg
Butter	200 g	400 g	800 g

1. Prepare and cook vegetables according to instructions for puree of carrot.
2. Place in mixer or suitable food processor and puree.
3. When a smooth consistency has been achieved, season to taste and place in a suitable ovenproof dish.
4. Place in moderate oven and bake for approximately 20 minutes.
5. Serve as required.

Braised Carrots

	25	50	100
Carrots	1.5 kg	3 kg	6 kg
Stock, chicken	as required		
Butter	150 g	300 g	600 g

To Prepare

1. Peel carrots.
2. Top and tail.
3. Cut into single portion pieces.
4. Wash thoroughly under cold running water.

To Cook

1. Place carrots in roasting tray and half cover with stock.
2. Brush exposed carrot with melted butter.
3. Place into oven preheated to a moderate setting for approximately 1 hour or until cooked.
4. Drain away any stock that may be left.
5. Serve as required.

Lemon Carrots

	25	50	100
Carrots	1.5 kg	3 kg	6 kg
Lemon juice	50 mL	100 mL	200 mL
Sugar	50 g	100 g	200 g
Salt and pepper	to taste		

To Prepare

1. Peel and top and tail carrots.
2. Cut into required size.
3. Wash well under cold running water.

To Cook

1. Place carrots into boiling water and cook until just tender.
2. Drain and return to clean pan.
3. Add lemon juice, salt and pepper and sugar and cook over moderate heat for 1 minute.
4. Serve as required.

Cauliflower

All year.

Methods of cookery: Boiled, steamed, baked.

Compatible with broccoli, cheese sauce, cream, hollandaise sauce.

	25	50	100
Cauliflower	**1.75 kg**	**3.5 kg**	**7 kg**

Prepare and cook as for broccoli instructions.

Cauliflower Mornay

	25	50	100
Cauliflower	**as above**		
Cheese sauce	**see Stocks and Sauces**		
Cheese, grated	**150 g**	**300 g**	**600 g**

To Prepare

As above.

To Cook

1. Place cooked florets in deep-sided baking tray.

2. Coat florets with sauce.

3. Sprinkle with grated cheese.

4. Place in oven preheated to a moderate setting for approximately 15–20 minutes or until golden brown.

NOTE: All broccoli recipes apply to cauliflower.

Cauliflower Polonaise

	25	50	100
Cauliflower florets, cooked	**see above**		
Butter	**250 g**	**500 g**	**1 kg**
Eggs, hard boiled, finely chopped	**4**	**8**	**16**
Breadcrumbs	**200 g**	**400 g**	**800 g**
Parsley, chopped	**5 g**	**10 g**	**20 g**

1. Melt butter in suitable pan over moderate heat.

2. Add breadcrumbs, grated egg and parsley, mixing thoroughly, and remove from heat.

3. Sprinkle polonaise mix over cooked cauliflower florets, place under a heated grill and cook until golden brown.

4. Serve as required.

Celery

All year.
Methods of cookery: Boiled, braised, fried.
Compatible with salads, stir fries, casseroles.

	25	50	100
Celery	**1.5 kg**	**3 kg**	**6 kg**

To Prepare

1. Cut away 2–3 cm from base of celery and separate stalks.
2. Cut away leaves and trim ends.
3. Wash well under cold running water.
4. Cut into required size.

To Cook

1. Place into lightly salted boiling water.
2. Cook for approximately 4–6 minutes or until tender.
3. Drain and serve as required.

Braised Celery

	25	50	100
Celery, large dice	**as above**		
Stock, beef or chicken	**sufficient to cover celery**		

To Prepare

As above.

To Cook

1. Place celery in suitable baking tray.
2. Cover with stock and cover tray with aluminium foil.
3. Place in oven preheated to a moderate setting for approximately 1–1½ hours or until tender.
4. Serve as required.

Celery can be used raw with salads and as an accompaniment to dips. Celery can also be steamed.

NOTE: The remaining flavoured stock from braised vegetable dishes is an ideal base for soups and sauces.

Leeks

Winter.
Methods of cookery: Boiled, braised, fried.
Compatible with soups, casseroles.

	25	50	100
Leeks	**1.5 kg**	**3 kg**	**6 kg**

To Prepare
1. Trim ends and remove outer layer.
2. Cut in half lengthways.
3. Wash well under cold running water.
4. Cut into required size pieces.

To Cook
1. Add to lightly salted boiled water.
2. Cook for approximately 2 minutes or until tender.
3. Strain well.
4. If not serving immediately refresh under cold running water.

Leeks sautéed in Butter

	25	50	100
Leeks, finely sliced	**as above**		
Butter	**200 g**	**400 g**	**800 g**
Garlic clove, finely chopped	**2**	**4**	**8**

To Prepare
As above.

To Cook
1. Melt butter in heavy-bottomed pan over moderate heat.
2. Add garlic and cook for 1 minute.
3. Add leeks, turn up heat and cook for 3–5 minutes stirring continuously until tender.
4. Remove from pan and serve as required.

Braised Leeks

	25	50	100
Leeks, 3 cm pieces	**as above**		
Stock, chicken	**sufficient to cover leeks**		

To Prepare

As above.

To Cook

1. Place leeks in suitable baking tray.

2. Cover with stock and cover with aluminium foil.

3. Place in oven preheated to a moderate setting and cook for approximately 1–1½ hours or until tender.

4. Serve as required with a little of the flavoured stock.

NOTE: Stock that is left is suitable for a sauce or soup.

Mushrooms

All year.

Methods of cookery: Boiled, deep-fried, shallow-fried, grilled.

Compatible with most herbs, casseroles.

	25	50	100
Mushrooms	**1 kg**	**2 kg**	**4 kg**

To Prepare

1. Wash well under cold running water.

2. Stalks can be removed if required.

To Cook

1. Place in cold salted water.

2. Bring to the boil and simmer for 2 minutes.

3. Drain well.

4. If not serving immediately refresh under cold running water.

Mushrooms Tossed in Butter and Parsley

	25	50	100
Mushrooms	as above		
Butter	150 g	300 g	600 g
Parsley, chopped	50 g	100 g	200 g

To Prepare

As above, but mushrooms can be left whole, quartered or sliced.

To Cook

1. Melt butter in heavy-bottomed pan over moderate heat.
2. Add mushrooms and cook for 4–6 minutes, depending on size, until tender.
3. Add parsley and mix well.
4. Remove from heat and serve as required.

Garlic Mushrooms

	25	50	100
Mushrooms	as above		
Garlic cloves, chopped	4	8	16
Butter	150 g	300 g	600 g

To Prepare

As above.

To Cook

1. Melt butter in heavy-bottomed pan over moderate heat.
2. Add garlic and cook for 1 minute.
3. Add mushrooms and cook for 4–6 minutes, depending on size, until tender.
4. Remove from heat and serve as required.

Mushrooms with Garlic and Chives

	25	50	100
Mushrooms	as above		
Garlic, finely chopped	as above		
Butter	150 g	300 g	600 g
Chives, finely sliced	10 g	20 g	40 g

Prepare and cook as for garlic mushrooms. Add chives with mushrooms.

Braised Mushrooms

	25	50	100
Mushrooms	**1 kg**	**2 kg**	**4 kg**
Stock, chicken	**as required**		
Onions, finely diced	**100 g**	**200 g**	**400 g**

To Prepare

1. If mushrooms are very large, cut in half.
2. Wash thoroughly under cold running water.

To Cook

1. Place mushrooms into suitable pan.
2. Add enough stock so mushrooms do not float.
3. Add onions.
4. Place on moderate heat and simmer gently covered with a lid.
5. Cook for approximately 15 minutes.
6. Serve as required.

NOTE: Stock that is left is suitable for a sauce or soup.

Onions

Summer, Autumn.
Methods of cookery: Boiled, steamed, roasted, braised, fried.
Compatible with soups, casseroles. Very flexible vegetable.

	25	50	100
Onions	**1 kg**	**2 kg**	**4 kg**

To Prepare

1. Cut a fine slice from each end of onion.
2. Gently peel away one or two outer layers.

Fried Onions

	25	50	100
Onions, sliced	**as above**		
Margarine/butter	**100 g**	**200 g**	**400 g**

To Prepare

1. Cut onion in half lengthways.
2. Finely slice onion.

To Cook

1. Melt margarine in thick-bottomed pan over moderate heat.

2. Add onions and cook for 4–6 minutes or until golden brown.

3. Remove from heat and serve as required.

Roasted Onions

	25	50	100
Onions, quartered	**1.5 kg**	**3 kg**	**6 kg**
Oil	**50 mL**	**100 mL**	**200 mL**

To Prepare

As above but cut into quarters.

To Cook

1. Brush bottom of baking tray with a little oil.

2. Place onions onto baking tray side by side one layer deep only.

3. Brush onions with a little oil.

4. Place in oven preheated to a moderate setting for 45 minutes to 1 hour or until tender and golden brown.

5. Remove from oven and serve as required.

Braised Onions

	25	50	100
Onions	**as for Roasted Onions recipe**		
Stock, beef or chicken	**sufficient to cover onions**		

To Prepare

As for roasted onions recipe.

To Cook

1. Place onions into suitable baking tray.

2. Cover with stock and cover tray with aluminium foil.

3. Place in oven preheated to a moderate setting for 45 minutes to 1 hour or until tender.

4. Remove from oven and serve as required.

Sautéed Onion and Capsicum

See capsicum recipes.

Parsnips

All year.
Methods of cookery: Boiled, braised, roasted.
Compatible with carrots, casseroles, stews, roasts.

	25	50	100
Parsnips	**1.5 kg**	**3 kg**	**6 kg**

To Prepare
1. Peel and trim ends.
2. Cut into required size.

To Cook
1. Place parsnips into lightly salted boiling water.
2. Cook for 4–6 minutes or until tender.
3. Strain well.
4. Serve as required.

Roasted Parsnips

	25	50	100
Parsnips	**as above**		
Oil	**50 mL**	**100 mL**	**200 mL**

To Prepare
As above.

To Cook
1. Grease bottom of suitable baking tray.
2. Place parsnips into tray.
3. Add remaining oil and mix through with hands.
4. Place into oven preheated to a moderate setting and cook for approximately 1–1½ hours or until tender and golden brown.
5. Season to taste.
6. Remove from oven and serve as required.

Roasted Parsnip Chips

	25	50	100
Parsnips	**1.5 kg**	**3 kg**	**6 kg**
Oil	**as required**		
Salt and pepper	**to taste**		

To Prepare

1. Peel skin from parsnips.
2. Cut parsnips into 1½ cm slices.
3. Cut slices into 1½ cm strips.
4. Wash thoroughly under cold running water.

To Cook

1. Place parsnip into lightly greased roasting tray.
2. Pour on a little oil and mix in with your hands.
3. Add more oil as required to coat each parsnip chip.
4. Season.
5. Place into oven preheated to a moderate setting for approximately 1 hour or until tender.
6. Drain away any excess fat.
7. Serve as required.

Pureed Parsnip

	25	50	100
Parsnip	**as above**		
Butter	**200 g**	**400 g**	**800 g**
Cream	**50 mL**	**100 mL**	**200 mL**

Prepare as above, and cook as for pureed carrot recipe.

Peas

All year except winter.
Methods of cookery: Boiled, steamed.
Compatible with most vegetables, casseroles, stews, stir fries. Flexible use.

	25	50	100
Peas, removed from pod	**1.25 kg**	**2.5 kg**	**5 kg**

To Prepare

If fresh, remove from shell or pod and wash well under cold running water.

To Cook

1. Place peas into lightly salted boiling water.
2. Simmer for 3–5 minutes or until tender.
3. Strain well.
4. Serve as required.

Peas à la Creme

	25	50	100
Peas	1.25 kg	2.5 kg	5 kg
Cream, thickened	100 mL	200 mL	400 mL

To Prepare

As above.

To Cook

1. As above.
2. Once strained return peas to clean pan.
3. Add cream over moderate heat.
4. Cook for 2 minutes.
5. Serve as required.

Minted Peas

	25	50	100
Peas	1.25 kg	2.5 kg	5 kg
Mint, chopped	15 g	30 g	60 g
Butter	50 g	100 g	200 g

To Prepare

If fresh, remove from shell or pod and wash well under cold running water.

To Cook

1. Place peas into lightly salted boiling water and simmer for 3–5 minutes or until tender.
2. Drain peas in colander.
3. Melt butter in clean pan.
4. Add peas and mint and mix thoroughly.
5. Serve as required.

Mushy Peas

	25	50	100
Peas, dried	600 g	1.2 kg	2.4 kg
Salt	1 teaspoon	2 teaspoons	4 teaspoons
Green colouring, optional	3 drops	6 drops	12 drops
Sugar	50 g	100 g	200 g
Mint, chopped	10 g	20 g	40 g
Margarine	25 g	50 g	100 g

To Prepare
1. Wash peas thoroughly.
2. Cover with hot water and add the same amount of hot water on top of this.
3. Mix in colouring.
4. Leave to stand overnight covered with a clean cloth.

To Cook
1. Drain and wash in colander.
2. Place in suitable saucepan and cover with water.
3. Add sugar, margarine and mint.
4. Bring to the boil and simmer for 1–1½ hours until peas are tender and smooth consistency has been reached.
5. Add a little more water when needed.
6. Add salt 5 minutes before cooking is completed.
7. Drain off any cooking liquid that may be left.
8. Serve as required.

Petite Pois

As for peas.

Peas à la Francais

	25	50	100
Peas	**1.25 kg**	**2.5 kg**	**5 kg**
Shallots, peeled, roughly cut	**1/2 bunch**	**1 bunch**	**2 bunches**
Lettuce, small, shredded	**1/2**	**1**	**2**
Butter	**30 g**	**60 g**	**120 g**
Salt and pepper	**to taste**		
Flour	**30 g**	**60 g**	**120 g**
Sugar	**50 g**	**100 g**	**200 g**

To Prepare
1. Prepare as for peas.
2. Wash peas, shallots and lettuce separately under cold running water.

To Cook
1. Melt butter in suitable pan.
2. Add peas, salt and pepper, sugar, lettuce and onions.
3. Add enough water to just cover ingredients.
4. Bring to a simmer and cover with a tight fitting lid.
5. Cook until peas are tender.
6. Mix flour with a little cold water until smooth and pour onto peas, mixing gently until all is incorporated.
7. Serve as required.

Snow Peas (Mangetout)

Methods of cookery: Stir fry, boiled.
Compatible with Asian and oriental style dishes, meat, salads.

	25	50	100
Snow peas	**as above**		

To Prepare
1. Top and tail and remove any string.
2. Wash well under cold running water.

To Cook
1. Place snow peas into lightly salted boiling water.
2. Cook for 1 minute.
3. Strain.
4. If not serving immediately refresh under cold running water.
This vegetable is ideal for stir frying.
NOTE: A serving of snow peas is usually 6–8 per portion depending on size.

Sugar Snap Peas

	25	50	100
Sugar snap peas	**as above**		

To Prepare
1. Top and tail and remove any string.
2. Wash well under cold running water.

To Cook
1. Place into lightly salted boiling water.
2. Bring water back to the boil and strain immediately.
3. If not being served immediately refresh under cold running water.
This vegetable is ideal for stir frying.

Pumpkin

All year especially winter.
Methods of cookery: Boiled, steamed, roasted.
Compatible with nutmeg.

	25	50	100
Pumpkin	**1.5 kg**	**3 kg**	**6 kg**

To Prepare

1. Cut pumpkin into quarters.
2. Remove all skin and seeds.
3. Cut into required size.

To Cook

1. Place into steamer trays.
2. Cook until tender.

OR

1. Place into lightly salted boiling water.
2. Cook until tender.
3. Strain and serve as required (handle with care).

Roasted Pumpkin

	25	50	100
Pumpkin	**as above**		
Oil	**100 mL**	**200 mL**	**400 mL**
Nutmeg	**5 g**	**10 g**	**15 g**

To Prepare

As above.

To Cook

1. Brush a little oil onto bottom of baking tray.
2. Place pumpkin into lightly greased roasted tray.
3. Pour remaining oil over pumpkin and using hands mix thoroughly.
4. Sprinkle with nutmeg.
5. Place into oven preheated to a moderate setting for approximately 1 hour or until tender.
6. Remove from oven and tray and serve as required.

Pureed Pumpkin

	25	50	100
Pumpkin	**as above**		
Butter	**150 g**	**300 g**	**600 g**

To Prepare

As above.

To Cook

1. Boil or steam pumpkin until tender.
2. Place pumpkin and melted butter into mixer or blender.
3. Mix until desired smooth consistency is achieved.
4. Season to taste.
5. Place in ovenproof dish.
6. Place into oven preheated to a moderate setting and cook for 15-20 minutes.
7. Serve as required.

Spinach

All year.
Methods of cookery: Boiled, steamed.
Compatible with lamb dishes, stir frys.

	25	50	100
Spinach	**1.5 kg**	**3 kg**	**6 kg**
Butter	**50 g**	**100 g**	**200 g**

To Prepare

1. Separate leaves.
2. Cut out stems.
3. Wash thoroughly under cold running water.
4. Cut into required size or leave in leaf form.

To Cook

1. Place into pan of lightly salted boiling water.
2. Simmer for approximately 2-4 minutes.
3. Strain.
4. If not serving immediately refresh under cold running water.
5. Melt butter over moderate heat in suitable pan.
6. Add spinach and cook without colour for approximately 1 minute.

Squash (Marrow)

All year.
Methods of cookery: Boiled, steamed.
Compatible with cheese sauces.

	25	50	100
Squash	**1.5 kg**	**3 kg**	**6 kg**

To Prepare
1. Top and tail.
2. Wash thoroughly under cold running water.

To Cook
1. Place into pan of lightly salted boiling water.
2. Bring water to a simmer.
3. Cook for approximately 12–14 minutes or until tender.
4. If not serving immediately refresh under cold running water.

Swede

All year especially winter.
Methods of cookery: Boiled, steamed.
Compatible with casseroles, roast dishes.

	25	50	100
Swede	**1.5 kg**	**3 kg**	**6 kg**
Sugar	**30 g**	**60 g**	**120 g**

To Prepare
1. Cut swede in half.
2. Cut into slices of required thickness.
3. Peel skin from slices.
4. Cut into required size.
5. Wash under cold running water.

To Cook
1. To suitable pan add swede and barely cover with water.
2. Add a little salt and sugar.
3. Cover with a lid and bring to the boil.
4. Allow to boil until water has evaporated and swede is tender.

NOTE: Care should be taken not to overcook swede. It may be cooked before all water has evaporated.

Buttered Swede

	25	50	100
Swede	**1.5 kg**	**3 kg**	**6 kg**
Butter	**100 g**	**200 g**	**400 g**

To Prepare

As above.

To Cook

1-4. As above.

5. Melt butter in suitable pan over high heat.

6. Toss swede for approximately 1-2 minutes.

7. Serve.

Sweet Corn on the Cob

All year.

Methods of cookery: Boiled, steamed, barbecued in foil with butter.

Compatible with melted butter and grated parmesan cheese.

	25	50	100
Sweet corn	**one per portion or half if large**		

To Prepare

1. Cut off base of corn cob.

2. Trim all but the innermost husks.

3. Wash under cold running water.

To Cook

1. Place into lightly salted boiling water.

2. Cook for 13-15 minutes or until corn is tender.

3. Strain.

4. Trim away remaining husk.

5. Coat with melted butter.

6. Serve.

Tomatoes, Grilled

All year.

Methods of cookery: Grilled, baked, fried.

Compatible with fresh herbs, grilled foods. Complements most dishes.

	25	50	100
Tomatoes	**between half and one full tomato per portion depending on size**		
Oil	**as required**		

To Prepare

1. Wash tomatoes under cold running water.
2. Cut tomatoes in half across middle.

To Cook

1. Lightly grease baking tray.
2. Place tomatoes in rows on tray.
3. Lightly brush tomatoes with oil.
4. Sprinkle with salt and pepper.
5. Place in oven preheated to a moderate setting.
6. Cook for approximately 15 minutes or until tender.
7. Serve.

Herb and Cheese Tomatoes

	25	50	100
Tomatoes	**allow between half and one per portion**		
Cheese, grated	**300 g**	**600 g**	**1.2 kg**
Basil, chopped	**10 g**	**20 g**	**40 g**
Parsley, chopped	**10 g**	**20 g**	**40 g**
Mint, chopped	**10 g**	**20 g**	**40 g**
Salt and pepper	**to taste**		

To Prepare

As for grilled tomatoes.

To Cook

1. Lightly grease baking tray.
2. Place tomatoes cut in half onto tray in rows.
3. Sprinkle with herbs.
4. Sprinkle with salt and pepper.
5. Place a little grated cheese onto each tomato half.
6. Place into oven preheated to a moderate setting.
7. Cook for 15 minutes or until cheese turns light golden brown.

Turnips

All year.
Methods of cookery: Boiled, steamed.
Compatible with casseroles, roast dishes.
All recipes for swede apply to turnip.

Water Chestnuts

Rarely available fresh, usually bought tinned.
Compatible with stir frys, most Asian influenced dishes.

Yams

All year.
Methods of cookery: As for potato.
Compatible with roasted dishes, curried dishes, most hot dry dishes.

	25	50	100
Yams	**1.75 kg**	**3.5 kg**	**7 kg**

Prepare and cook as for potatoes. See Potato Dishes.

Zucchini (Courgette)

All year.
Methods of cookery: Boiled, braised, sautéed.
Compatible with most dishes.

	25	50	100
Zucchinis	**1.5 kg**	**3 kg**	**6 kg**

To Prepare
1. Wash zucchinis thoroughly under cold running water.
2. Top and tail zucchinis.
3. Cut into required size.

To Cook
1. Place into lightly salted boiling water.
2. Cook for 2–4 minutes until tender.
3. If not serving immediately refresh under cold running water.

Zucchini Sticks

	25	50	100
Zucchinis	**2.5 kg**	**5 kg**	**10 kg**

To Prepare

1. Wash zucchinis thoroughly under cold running water.
2. Top and tail.
3. Cut into 6 cm pieces.
4. Slice each piece into four equal pieces lengthways.
5. Cut each slice into 1 cm sticks.

To Cook

1. In a suitable pan bring enough water to cover zucchinis to the boil.
2. Add zucchini and allow to reboil.
3. Remove zucchini immediately.
4. Drain well.
5. Serve as required, or refresh under cold running water.

Sautéed Zucchini with Onions

	25	50	100
Zucchinis, sliced	**2 kg**	**4 kg**	**8 kg**
Onions, finely sliced	**500 g**	**1 kg**	**2 kg**
Butter	**100 g**	**200 g**	**400 g**
Oil	**as required**		
Salt and pepper	**to taste**		

1. Wash zucchini thoroughly under cold running water.
2. Melt butter in a suitable pan over moderate heat.
3. Add a little oil to the butter.
4. Add onions and cook until soft.
5. Add zucchinis and cook for approximately 5 minutes or until cooked through.
6. Season to taste.
7. Serve as required.

Braised Zucchini

	25	50	100
Zucchinis	**1.25 kg**	**2.5 kg**	**5 kg**
Stock, chicken or beef	**as required**		

1. Wash, top and tail, and slice in half lengthways.
2. Place cut side down onto suitable roasting tray.
3. Half cover with stock and cover roasting tray with aluminium foil.
4. Place into oven preheated to a moderate setting for approximately 20–30 minutes or until zucchini is soft and tender.
5. Serve as required with a little flavoured stock.

NOTE: Remaining flavoured stock may be used for soups and sauces if desired.

———————— ◇ ————————

Potato Dishes

Introduction

There are many different ways to prepare and serve potatoes. As well as their versatility, potatoes have become a necessity to the western world and many meals would seem incomplete without them. Potatoes are a tasty way of boosting the size of a dish and can be served boiled, roasted or fried. They are an asset when budget constraints apply. This does not mean it is acceptable to serve excessively large portions. It does mean, however, that a controlled serving will often provide satisfaction to the consumer.

As a general guide, the following amounts of potatoes will be sufficient for the recipes that follow. Weights refer to raw and unprepared potatoes.

Single serve	**150 g**		
Large-scale portions for	25	50	100
	3.75 kg	**7.5 kg**	**15 kg**

These weights can be increased or decreased at your discretion.

Boiled Potatoes

	25	50	100
Potatoes	**3.75 kg**	**7.5 kg**	**15 kg**
Margarine or butter	**300 g**	**600 g**	**1.2 kg**

1. Peel potatoes thinly and wash.

2. Cut into required size.

3. Place prepared potatoes in suitable pan and cover with sufficient water. Place over moderate heat and bring to a simmer.

4. Cook gently until tender.

5. Carefully strain water from potatoes taking care not to damage them.

6. Serve with a little margarine placed or brushed on top.

New Potatoes / Chatz Potatoes

	25	50	100
Potatoes	**3.75 kg**	**7.5 kg**	**15 kg**
Margarine or butter	**150 g**	**300 g**	**600 g**

1. Wash potatoes thoroughly under cold running water.

2. Boil enough water to completely immerse potatoes.

3. Add potatoes and a little salt and simmer for approximately 10–15 minutes or until tender.

4. Strain and serve with a little melted margarine or butter.

New Potatoes / Chatz Potatoes with Chives

	25	50	100
Potatoes	**3.75 kg**	**7.5 kg**	**15 kg**
Chives, chopped	**10 g**	**20 g**	**40 g**
Margarine or butter	**150 g**	**300 g**	**600 g**

1. Cook as for new potatoes/chatz potatoes.
2. Melt margarine or butter in large pan over moderate heat.
3. Add chives and cooked, drained potatoes and agitate pan for 1 minute or until potatoes are thoroughly coated.
4. Serve as required.

New Potatoes / Chatz Potatoes with Caramelised Onion

	25	50	100
Potatoes	3.75 kg	7.5 kg	15 kg
Onions, finely diced	150 g	300 g	600 g
Margarine or butter	150 g	300 g	600 g

1. Cook as for new potatoes/chatz potatoes.
2. Melt margarine or butter in large pan.
3. Add finely chopped onion and cook until onion starts to brown.
4. Add cooked, drained potatoes.
5. Agitate pan for 1 minute or until potatoes are thoroughly coated.
6. Serve as required.

Garlic and Onion Potatoes

	25	50	100
Potatoes	3.75 kg	7.5 kg	15 kg
Onions, finely diced	150 g	300 g	600 g
Garlic cloves, chopped	4	6	9
Margarine or butter	150 g	300 g	600 g

As for new potatoes with caramelised onion with the addition of garlic at step 3.

Parsley Potatoes

	25	50	100
Potatoes	3.75 kg	7.5 kg	15 kg
Margarine or butter	300 g	600 g	1.2 kg
Parsley, finely chopped	10 g	20 g	40 g

1. Prepare and cook as for boiled potatoes.
2. Before service, brush potatoes with a little melted margarine or butter.
3. Sprinkle with chopped parsley and serve.

Herbed Potatoes

	25	50	100
Potatoes	3.75 kg	7.5 kg	15 kg
Margarine or butter	300 g	600 g	1.2 kg
Basil, finely chopped	3 g	6 g	12 g
Mint, finely chopped	3 g	6 g	12 g
Parsley, finely chopped	3 g	6 g	12 g

1. Prepare and cook as for boiled potatoes.
2. Brush with melted margarine or butter, sprinkle with herbs and serve.

Creamed / Mashed Potatoes

	25	50	100
Potatoes	3.75 kg	7.5 kg	15 kg
Margarine or butter	150 g	300 g	600 g
Salt and pepper	to taste		
Cream or milk (optional)	100 mL	200 mL	400 mL

1. Prepare and cook as for boiled potatoes.
2. Place potatoes into large mixing bowl.
3. Add margarine or butter, seasoning and cream if desired.
4. Beat mixture until a smooth thick consistency, which is free of any lumps, is achieved.
5. Serve as required.

Potato and Onion Smash

	25	50	100
Potatoes	3.75 kg	7.5 kg	15 kg
Onions, finely diced	300 g	600 g	1.2 kg
Margarine or butter	150 g	300 g	600 g
Salt and pepper	to taste		
Cream or milk (optional)	100 mL	200 mL	400 mL
Parsley, chopped	10 g	20 g	40 g

As for creamed/mashed potatoes with the addition of onions which have been lightly fried without colour in a little oil. Add parsley at step 3.

Creamed Herbed Potatoes

	25	50	100
Potatoes	3.75 kg	7.5 kg	15 kg
Margarine or butter	150 g	300 g	600 g
Salt and pepper	to taste		
Cream or milk (optional)	100 mL	200 mL	400 mL
Parsley, finely chopped	3 g	6 g	12 g
Basil, finely chopped	3 g	6 g	12 g
Mint, finely chopped	3 g	6 g	12 g

As for creamed/mashed potatoes adding herbs at step 3.

Baked Cheese Potatoes

	25	50	100
Potatoes	3.75 kg	7.5 kg	15 kg
Margarine or butter	150 g	300 g	600 g
Salt and pepper	to taste		
Cream or milk (optional)	100 mL	200 mL	400 mL
Cheese, cheddar, grated	300 g	600 g	1.2 kg
Parsley, finely chopped	10 g	20 g	40 g

1. Prepare and cook as for mashed potatoes.
2. When mixed, place potato into lightly greased baking tray and smooth flat with pallet knife. Potato must be at least 4 cm deep.
3. Sprinkle grated cheese over potato.
4. Place into oven preheated to a moderate setting for approximately 15 minutes or until cheese has melted and turned golden brown.
5. Sprinkle with chopped parsley.
6. Serve as required.

Baked Cheese Potatoes with Herbs

	25	50	100
Potatoes	3.75 kg	7.5 kg	15 kg
Margarine or butter	150 g	300 g	600 g
Salt and pepper	to taste		
Cream or milk (optional)	100 mL	200 mL	400 mL
Parsley, finely chopped	3 g	6 g	12 g
Basil, finely chopped	3 g	6 g	12 g
Mint, finely chopped	3 g	6 g	12 g
Cheese, cheddar, grated	300 g	600 g	1.2 kg

1. Prepare, cook and blend as for creamed herbed potatoes.
2. Proceed as for baked cheese potatoes.
3. Add basil and mint at step 5.
4. Serve as required.

Duchess Potatoes

	25	50	100
Potatoes	3.75 kg	7.5 kg	15 kg
Margarine or butter	150 g	300 g	600 g
Salt and pepper	to taste		
Cream or milk (optional)	100 mL	200 mL	400 mL

1. Prepare and cook as for mashed potatoes.
2. Place mixture into piping bag.
3. Pipe potato onto greased baking tray in spirals (approximately 4–6 cm).
4. Place into oven preheated to a moderate setting for approximately 6–8 minutes or until outside of potato hardens slightly and turns golden brown.
5. Carefully remove potato using pallet knife and serve.

Croquette Potatoes

	25	50	100
Potatoes	3.75 kg	7.5 kg	15 kg
Margarine or butter	150 g	300 g	600 g
Salt and pepper	to taste		
Cream or milk (optional)	100 mL	200 mL	400 mL
Eggs, beaten	as required		
Flour	as required		
Breadcrumbs	as required		

1. Prepare and cook as for creamed/mashed potatoes.
2. With hands, mould potatoes into small cylindrical shapes.
3. Pass through flour, egg mix and breadcrumbs ensuring entire potato is covered.
4. Deep-fry in oil preheated to approximately 175°C.
5. Cook until golden brown.
6. Drain well and serve.

Almond Potatoes

As for croquette potatoes substituting ground almonds for breadcrumbs.

Steamed Potatoes

	25	50	100
Potatoes	**3.75 kg**	**7.5 kg**	**15 kg**

1. Prepare potatoes as for boiled potatoes.
2. Place potatoes into steamer on steamer trays.
3. Cook until tender.
4. Serve plain or with a little margarine or butter or sprinkled with chopped parsley.

Steamed Jacket Potatoes

	25	50	100
Potatoes	**3.75 kg**	**7.5 kg**	**15 kg**

1. Select small whole potatoes.
2. Using a scourer, rub surface clean and wash thoroughly.
3. Place into steamer on steamer trays.
4. Cook until tender.
5. Serve plain or with a little margarine or butter or sprinkle with chopped parsley.

Sautéed Potatoes

	25	50	100
Potatoes	**3.75 kg**	**7.5 kg**	**15 kg**
Salt and pepper	**to taste**		
Parsley, chopped	**10 g**	**20 g**	**40 g**

1. Peel evenly sized potatoes and wash well under cold running water.
2. Cut into ½ cm slices.
3. Place into salted boiling water and cook for a few minutes so potatoes are still under-cooked.
4. Carefully drain away water taking care not to damage potatoes.
5. When thoroughly drained place into deep-frying baskets.
6. Deep-fry in oil preheated to 175°C until golden brown.
7. Drain well and serve sprinkled with chopped parsley.

NOTE: See Chapter 1 for information about deep-frying.

Lyonnaise Potatoes

	25	50	100
Potatoes	**3.75 kg**	**7.5 kg**	**15 kg**
Onions, sliced	**400 g**	**800 g**	**1.6 kg**
Parsley, chopped	**10 g**	**20 g**	**40 g**

1. Prepare and cook potatoes as for sautéed potatoes.
2. When cooked, mix in with warm onions that have been fried in a little oil until tender.
3. Sprinkle with chopped parsley and serve.

French Fried Potatoes

	25	50	100
Potatoes	**3.75 kg**	**7.5 kg**	**15 kg**

1. Peel potatoes and wash well under cold running water.
2. Cut potatoes into 1 cm slices.
3. Cut slices into 1 cm batons.
4. Wash well under cold running water.
5. Drain potatoes well and pat dry with kitchen towel if necessary.
6. Deep-fry in baskets in oil preheated to 175°C until tender and golden brown.
7. Drain well and serve.

ALTERNATIVELY

Place prepared chipped potatoes into boiling water and cook for a few minutes before deep-frying, ensuring potatoes are well drained before placing them in oil.

NOTE: See Chapter 1 for information about frying.

Fondant Potatoes

	25	50	100
Potatoes	**3.75 kg**	**7.5 kg**	**15 kg**
Stock, chicken	**as required**		
Margarine or butter	**150 g**	**300 g**	**600 g**

1. Prepare potatoes as for boiled potatoes.
2. Place in roasting tray and half cover with stock.
3. Brush tops of potatoes with melted margarine or butter.
4. Place in oven preheated to a moderate setting and cook until tender and golden brown.

NOTE: When cooked, potatoes should have soaked up stock.

Rosemary Potatoes

	25	50	100
Potatoes	3.75 kg	7.5 kg	15 kg
Stock, chicken	as required		
Margarine or butter	150 g	300 g	600 g
Rosemary, dried	20 g	40 g	80 g

As for fondant potatoes with the addition of rosemary to stock before cooking.

Roast Potatoes

	25	50	100
Potatoes	3.75 kg	7.5 kg	15 kg
Oil	to coat potatoes		
Salt and pepper	to taste		

1. Prepare potatoes as for boiled potatoes.
2. Place into roasting tray.
3. Pour oil over and completely coat potatoes.
4. Place into oven preheated to a moderate setting and cook for approximately 1–1½ hours or until potatoes are tender and golden brown. Gently turn potatoes every 20 minutes during cooking.

Roast Sage and Thyme Potatoes

	25	50	100
Potatoes	3.75 kg	7.5 kg	15 kg
Oil	to coat potatoes		
Salt and pepper	to taste		
Sage, dried	10 g	20 g	40 g
Thyme, dried	10 g	20 g	40 g

As for roast potatoes with the addition of sage and thyme at step 4.

Roast Sage and Onion Potatoes

	25	50	100
Potatoes	3.75 kg	7.5 kg	15 kg
Oil	to coat potatoes		
Onions, finely diced	300 g	600 g	1.2 kg
Sage, dried	10 g	20 g	40 g

1. Prepare and cook potatoes as for roast sage and thyme potatoes using only sage.
2. In suitable pan over moderate heat cook onions in a little oil until they begin to brown.
3. When potatoes are cooked remove from tray and add onion.
4. Serve as required.

Noisette Potatoes

	25	50	100
Potatoes	**3.75 kg**	**7.5 kg**	**15 kg**
Parsley, chopped	**10 g**	**20 g**	**40 g**

1. Prepare potatoes as for boiled potatoes.
2. Using either Parisienne cutter, melon baller or small teaspoon, scoop out small balls of potato.
3. Wash potatoes thoroughly under cold running water.
4. Place potatoes into basket and deep-fry in oil preheated to 175°C until tender and golden brown.

NOTE: See Chapter 1 for information about deep-frying.

Parisienne Potatoes

	25	50	100
Potatoes	**3.75 kg**	**7.5 kg**	**15 kg**
Stock, beef	**100 mL**	**200 mL**	**400 mL**

1. As for noisette potatoes.
2. Add stock to large sauté pan and reduce over high heat by half.
3. Just before service, add cooked potato to sauté pan and glaze with reduced stock.
4. Serve immediately as required.

Baked Jacket Potatoes

	25	50	100
Potatoes, whole, required size	**25**	**50**	**100**

1. Scrub potatoes with scourer until clean and free from any soil.
2. Wrap each potato in aluminium foil so no part of potato is exposed.
3. Place on tray into oven preheated to a moderate setting and cook for approximately 1½–2 hours depending on size of potatoes.
4. Check to see whether cooked by piercing potato with thin bladed knife — if knife enters potato easily, potatoes are cooked.

NOTE: Jacket potatoes kept in aluminium foil will retain their heat for a long time.

Fillings for Baked Jacket Potatoes

1. Flaked fish in cheese sauce.
2. Mushrooms in cheese sauce.
3. Vegetables in cheese sauce. .
4. Cottage cheese with chives.
5. Bolognaise sauce.

6. Chicken pieces in curried sauce.
7. Tuna with lemon dressing.
8. Baked beans.
9. Prawns in white sauce.
10. Melted cheese with parsley.

Parmentier Potatoes

	25	50	100
Potatoes	**3.75 kg**	**7.5 kg**	**15 kg**

1. Peel and wash potatoes under cold running water.
2. Cut potatoes into 1 cm slices.
3. Cut slices into 1 cm strips.
4. Cut strips into 1 cm pieces.
5. Place potatoes into baskets and deep-fry in oil preheated to 175°C.
6. Cook until tender and golden brown.
7. Drain thoroughly and serve as required.

NOTE: See Chapter 1 for information about deep-frying.

Italian Potatoes

	25	50	100
Potatoes	**3.75 kg**	**7.5 kg**	**15 kg**
Onions, finely diced	**300 g**	**600 g**	**1.2 kg**
Oregano, chopped	**10 g**	**20 g**	**40 g**
Mint, chopped	**10 g**	**20 g**	**40 g**
Parmesan cheese, grated	**50 g**	**100 g**	**200 g**
Salt and pepper	**to taste**		
Tomatoes, seeded, small dice	**100 g**	**200 g**	**400 g**
Cheese, grated	**200 g**	**400 g**	**800 g**

1. Cook as for parmentier potatoes.

2. When cooked, combine all other ingredients, in large bowl and then place all ingredients into deep-sided baking tray to depth of approximately 4 cm.

3. Place into oven preheated to a moderate setting and bake for approximately 10 minutes.

4. Serve as required.

Hungarian Potatoes

	25	50	100
Potatoes	3.75 kg	7.5 kg	15 kg
Onions, finely diced	200 g	400 g	800 g
Paprika	10 g	20 g	40 g
Salt and pepper	to taste		
Parsley, chopped	10 g	20 g	40 g

1. Cook as for parmentier potatoes.
2. When cooked, combine all ingredients in large bowl and then place all ingredients in deep-sided baking tray to depth of approximately 4 cm.
3. Place into oven preheated to a moderate setting and bake for approximately 10 minutes.
4. Serve as required.

Cheese Potatoes with Chives

	25	50	100
Potatoes	3.75 kg	7.5 kg	15 kg
Cheese, grated	300 g	600 g	1.2 kg
Chives, chopped	20 g	40 g	80 g
Salt and pepper	to taste		

1. Cook as for parmentier potatoes.
2. Place parmentier potatoes into tray at depth of approximately 4 cm.
3. Season, sprinkle on chives and then grated cheese.
4. Place into oven preheated to a moderate setting and bake for approximately 10 minutes or until cheese has melted.
5. Serve as required.

Spiced Cheese Potatoes

As for cheese potatoes with chives omitting chives and adding:

	25	50	100
Chilli powder	15 g	30 g	60 g
Garlic cloves, chopped	2	4	8
Shallots, finely sliced	2	4	8

Mix with potatoes at step 2.

Chateau Potatoes

	25	50	100
Potatoes	3.75 kg	7.5 kg	15 kg
Oil	as required		
Salt and pepper	to taste		

1. Select similar sized potatoes.
2. With small vegetable knife or turning knife, cut potatoes into eight-sided barrel shapes to required size.
3. Wash potatoes thoroughly under cold running water.
4. Allow to drain in colander.
5. Place potatoes into roasting tray one potato deep.
6. Pour on a little oil and using your hands mix together until potatoes are lightly coated in oil.
7. Season to taste.
8. Place in oven preheated to a moderate setting for approximately 1–1¼ hours or until tender and golden brown.
9. Drain well and serve as required.

Deep-fried Potato Curls

	25	50	100
Potatoes	5 kg	10 kg	20 kg
Salt and pepper	to taste		

1. Wash whole potatoes thoroughly under cold running water and allow to dry.
2. Using small vegetable knife, peel potatoes in thick long strips.
3. Reserve leftover peeled potatoes in container covered with cold water for future alternative potato dishes.
4. Place dry potato skins into baskets and deep-fry in oil preheated to 175°C for approximately 2–4 minutes until crisp and golden brown.
5. Drain thoroughly.
6. Season to taste and serve as required.

Deep-fried Cheesy Potato Curls/Potato Skins

	25	50	100
Potatoes	**5 kg**	**10 kg**	**20 kg**
Cheese, grated	**300 g**	**600 g**	**1.2 kg**
Salt and pepper	**to taste**		
Paprika	**as required**		

1. As for deep-fried potato curls.

2. After removal from fryer and being thoroughly drained, place into baking tray or serving dish.

3. Season and sprinkle with grated cheese.

4. Place into oven preheated to a moderate setting and bake until cheese has turned golden brown.

5. Sprinkle with a little paprika.

6. Serve as required.

Cheesy Potato Curls with Chives

	25	50	100
Potatoes	**5 kg**	**10 kg**	**20 kg**
Cheese, grated	**300 g**	**600 g**	**1.2 kg**
Salt and pepper	**to taste**		
Chives, chopped	**15 g**	**30 g**	**60 g**
Paprika	**as required**		

As for deep-fried cheesy potato curls with the addition of a sprinkle of chives at step 5.

Boulangère Potatoes

	25	50	100
Potatoes	**3.75 kg**	**7.5 kg**	**15 kg**
Stock, beef	**1.5 L**	**3 L**	**6 L**
Onions, finely sliced	**600 g**	**1.2 kg**	**2.4 kg**
Salt and pepper	**to taste**		

1. Peel and wash potatoes under cold running water.

2. Cut potatoes into 1 cm slices.

3. Place one layer of potato into bottom of baking dish.

4. Cover with one layer of onion and a little salt and pepper.

5. Repeat process until all potato and onion is used.

6. Carefully pour over stock until potatoes are barely covered.

7. Cover with aluminium foil.

8. Place into oven preheated to a moderate setting for approximately 1–1½ hours or until potatoes are tender and stock has been absorbed.

9. Serve as required.

Dessert Dishes

Basic Sponge Mixture

	25	50	100
Margarine	**400 g**	**800 g**	**1.6 kg**
Sugar, caster	**400 g**	**800 g**	**1.6 kg**
Eggs	**8**	**16**	**32**
Flour, self-raising	**400 g**	**800 g**	**1.6 kg**
Baking powder	**1 teaspoon**	**2 teaspoons**	**4 teaspoons**

1. Sift flour and salt.
2. Cream margarine and sugar.
3. Beating well, add one egg at a time.
4. Add flour and mix until thoroughly incorporated.
5. Line baking trays with lightly greased greaseproof paper and fill three-quarters full.
6. Place in oven preheated to a moderate setting for approximately 1 hour depending on required thickness.
7. To taste whether sponge is cooked, pierce with skewer and see if any sponge mix sticks to skewer. If it does, further cooking is required.

NOTE: To steam. Totally cover with greaseproof paper and aluminium foil or place in lined steaming sleeve.

Apple Sponge

As for basic sponge mix with the addition of:

	25	50	100
Apples, peeled, cored, finely sliced	**500 g**	**1 kg**	**2 kg**

Add apples after step 4 and mix in lightly.

Banana Sponge

As for basic sponge mix with the addition of:

	25	50	100
Bananas, peeled, thinly sliced	**500 g**	**1 kg**	**2 kg**

Add bananas after step 4 and mix in lightly.

Sultana Sponge

As for basic sponge recipe with the addition of:

	25	50	100
Sultanas	**500 g**	**1 kg**	**2 kg**

Add at step 4.

Golden Syrup Sponge

As for basic sponge recipe with the addition of:

	25	50	100
Golden syrup	**400 mL**	**800 mL**	**1.6 L**

1. Add one-quarter syrup to mixture at step 4.
2. Pour remaining warmed syrup over sponge just prior to service.

Chocolate Sponge

As for basic sponge recipe with the addition of:

	25	50	100
Cocoa powder	**100 g**	**200 g**	**400 g**

Add at step 4.

Coconut and Orange Sponge

As for basic sponge recipe with the addition of:

	25	50	100
Coconut, desiccated	**110 g**	**220 g**	**440 g**
Orange, juice and grated zest	**2**	**4**	**8**

Add at step 4.

Caribbean Rum Sponge

As for basic sponge recipe with the addition of:

	25	50	100
Rum essence	**to taste (approximately 1 teaspoon per 25 portions)**		
Cinnamon	**2 teaspoons**	**4 teaspoons**	**8 teaspoons**

Add at step 4.

NOTE: Other variations to the basic sponge mix can be made using jams and marmalades placed in the bottom of the steaming trays before addition of sponge mix. Care must be taken when turning sponges out so they do not stick to the pan.

If essences are to be used in sponge mixes they should be used in extreme moderation. Place only a few drops at a time in the mix until the right taste is achieved.

Pineapple and Cherry Upside Down Cake

As for basic sponge recipe with the addition of:

	25	50	100
Pineapple rings	**sufficient to layer bottom of baking dish**		
Glacé cherries	**½ cherry for centre of pineapple ring**		
Sugar, brown	**as required**		

1. Line bottom of baking dish with well-greased greaseproof paper, place one layer of pineapple rings with cherry in centre of ring and sprinkle generously with brown sugar.
2. Pour sponge mixture carefully over pineapples without dislodging.
3. Cook as for sponge.
4. When cooked, turn out so pineapple and cherries are on top.
5. Portion and serve.

Banana Upside Down Cake

As for pineapple and cherry upside down cake omitting pineapple and cherries and adding:

	25	50	100
Bananas, peeled, sliced	**600 g**	**1.2 kg**	**2.4 kg**

Layer bottom of tray with sliced banana in place of pineapple and cherries.

Apple Pie

	25	50	100
Apples, peeled, cored, roughly chopped	2.75 kg	5.5 kg	11 kg
Sugar approx	400 g	800 g	1.6 kg
Water approx	100 mL	200 mL	400 mL
Pastry, short crust	see pastry		
Eggs	2	4	8
Milk	100 mL	200 mL	400 mL

1. Place apples in required sized baking dish or pie trays and add a little water.
2. Sprinkle apple with a thin layer of sugar.
3. Roll out pastry to a little larger than pie dish.
4. Cover pie dish with pastry making sure edges are firmly squeezed to side of dish overlapping slightly.
5. With a knife make a few incisions about 3 cm in length along the centre of the pie from side to side.
6. Brush pie liberally with egg mix (egg and milk beaten together).
7. Bake in oven preheated to a moderate setting for approximately 30 minutes or until pastry is golden brown.
8. Sprinkle with a little sugar, portion and serve.

Apple and Cinnamon Pie

As for apple pie with the addition of:

	25	50	100
Cinnamon	2 tablespoons	4 tablespoons	8 tablespoons

Add at step 2.

Apple and Sultana Pie

As for apple pie with the addition of:

	25	50	100
Sultanas, washed	100 g	200 g	400 g

Add at step 1 mixing well with apples.

Peach and Lemon Pie

As for apple pie omitting apple and adding:

	25	50	100
Peaches, peeled, sliced	**2.75 kg**	**5.5. kg**	**11 kg**
Zest of lemon	**2**	**4**	**8**

Add at step 1 mixing well with peaches.

Fruit Pies

Any required variation in fruit pies can be achieved by replacing the quantity of apple with that of the desired prepared fruit. When using two fruits to make a pie, the total weight of all fruit must not exceed original weight for apple.

The type of pie to be made will usually depend on what fruits are in season; this means that the fruit is not only at its freshest, it is also less costly.

NOTE: Fruits with a high water content, for example pears, melons etc, should be avoided because they break down to a liquid during cooking. They can be used, however, to enhance the flavour of a pie which contains a suitable fruit, but care should be taken and minimal amounts of these type of fruits should be used.

Lattice Pies

As for fruit pies except: When pastry is rolled out cut into strips approximately 1 cm wide and place across fruit from left to right approximately 3 cm apart. Make sure each strip overlaps dish and is firmly gripping the edge. Using egg mix brush strips liberally. Now using the same method place more strips from top to bottom to give a criss-cross effect. Brush with egg mix again and cook as for fruit pies.

Fruit Crumbles

All the instructions for making fruit pies apply, except omit pastry and top fruit with a crumble mix, making sure that crumble mix is spread evenly over fruit.

Basic Crumble

	25	50	100
Flour	**600 g**	**1.2 kg**	**2.4 kg**
Margarine	**325 g**	**650 g**	**1.3 kg**
Salt	**½ teaspoon**	**1 teaspoon**	**2 teaspoons**
Sugar, caster	**300 g**	**600 g**	**1.2 kg**

1. Sift flour and salt.
2. Incorporate softened margarine by lightly rubbing flour and margarine together with fingers until a sandy texture is reached.

3. Add sugar and mix.

4. Place crumble evenly over desired fruit and bake in preheated oven for approximately 30 minutes until golden brown.

NOTE: Brown sugar may be substituted for caster sugar and will give a darker crumble.

Coconut Crumble

As for basic crumble with the addition of:

	25	50	100
Coconut, desiccated	**150 g**	**300 g**	**600 g**

Add at step 3.

Flavoured Crumbles

These can be achieved by mixing a few drops of any essence (to taste) to margarine before incorporating with flour.

Lemon Meringue Pie

	25	50	100
Pastry, short crust	see p 278		
Lemon curd	**750 g**	**1.5 kg**	**3 kg**
Egg whites	**7**	**14**	**28**
Sugar, caster	**150 g**	**300 g**	**600 g**

1. Line required size dish with pastry and prick pastry every 6 cm with fork. Bake in oven preheated to a moderate setting for approximately 15–20 minutes.

2. Remove from oven and allow to cool.

3. In a mixer with beater attachment add egg whites and beat on high speed until eggs are firm and stiff.

4. Gently fold in sugar.

5. Evenly spread lemon curd onto pastry and top with beaten egg whites (meringue).

6. Place in oven until meringue mixture is light brown.

Fruit Meringue Pies

Meringues can be made with most fruit jams, which can be complemented with fine slices of the named fruit placed on top of the jam.

Baked Fruits
Baked Apples

	25	50	100
Apples, cored	25	50	100
Sugar, brown	500 g	1 kg	2 kg
Cloves	25	50	100
Water	as required		
Syrup, golden or maple	200 mL	400 mL	800 mL

1. Make a skin-deep incision around each apple and cut away a small slice from the bottom of the apple to give it a flat surface to stand on.
2. Pierce each apple with a clove.
3. Place apples in rows in deep-sided baking tray.
4. Pour in a little water to reach a depth of approximately 2 cm.
5. Place syrup in a small funnelled sauce bottle and pour a little on each apple.
6. Sprinkle with brown sugar.
7. Place in oven preheated to a moderate setting for approximately 45 minutes to 1 hour until apples are soft.
8. Can be served with any sweet sauce or a thickened reduction of cooking liquor.

Baked Stuffed Apples

As for baked apples omitting cloves and adding:

	25	50	100
Mixed nuts, roughly chopped	300 g	600 g	1.2 kg
Sultanas	100 g	200 g	400 g
Apricots, dried, chopped	200 g	400 g	800 g
Butter	50 g	100 g	200 g

1. Prepare apples as in step 1 and mix above ingredients together.
2. Spoon a little into the centre of each apple and proceed as above from step 3.

Baked Pears

	25	50	100
Pears	25	50	100
Sugar	200 g	400 g	800 g
Cinnamon	2 teaspoons	4 teaspoons	8 teaspoons
Water	as required		

1. Cut pears in half and scoop out centre.
2. Place pears in rows in deep-sided baking tray.
3. Place a little water in tray to a depth of approximately 2 cm.
4. Sprinkle pears with cinnamon and sugar.
5. Bake in slow oven at approximately 100–130°C for 45 minutes or until cooked.

Baked Banana (Thai Style)

	25	50	100
Bananas	25	50	100
Lemon juice	150 mL	300 mL	600 mL
Coconut cream	500 mL	1 L	2 L
Sugar	250 g	500 g	1 kg
Butter	as required		

1. Lightly grease deep-sided baking tray with butter.
2. Peel and half bananas and place on tray.
3. Sprinkle with sugar.
4. Mix lemon juice and coconut cream together and pour over bananas.
5. Place in oven preheated to slow to moderate and bake for 15–20 minutes until cooked.

Fruit Salads

Fruit salads can be made from any combination of fruits depending on what is available and in season. The amounts of total prepared fruit for servings are: 2.5 kg for 25 people, 5 kg for 50 people and 10 kg for 100 people.

	25	50	100
Pineapples, peeled, cored, diced	1	2	4
Apples, peeled, cored, diced	4	8	16
Pears, peeled, cored, diced	4	8	16
Melons, peeled, diced	6	12	24
Bananas, peeled, diced	1 kg	2 kg	4 kg
Oranges, peeled, segments	5	10	20
Sugar	500 g	1 kg	2 kg
Orange juice	300 mL	600 mL	1.2 L

1. Mix together and leave to stand for approximately 1 hour.
2. Chill before service.

NOTE: Due to variation in sizes of fruits, this recipe cannot be guaranteed to reach serving size. Weights should be increased beyond those listed if necessary to achieve required portions, by the addition of a little available fruit.

Fruit Flans

	25	50	100
Pastry, sweet crust	see p 278		
Fruit of your choice, prepared	1.5 kg	3 kg	6 kg
Sugar	250 g	500 g	1 kg
Water	450 mL	900 mL	1.8 mL
Gelatine, powdered	40 g	80 g	160 g

1. Line lightly greased pastry dishes with pastry rolled to ½ cm thickness.
2. Prick with fork and place in oven preheated to a moderate setting for 15–20 minutes.
3. Boil sugar and water together until slightly thickened.
4. Add fruit to syrup and simmer until fruit is soft.
5. Soak gelatine in a very little cold water.
6. Gently strain all juice from fruit.
7. Add gelatine to juice and stir well until all gelatine is dissolved.
8. Arrange fruit neatly into pastry.
9. When gelatine mixture is almost set, pour onto fruit gently.
10. Place in refrigerator until set.
11. Portion and serve.

NOTE: Tinned fruits and fresh banana do not need to be cooked.

ALTERNATIVELY

Spread thickened custard (or custard flavoured with vanilla essence) to pastry before addition of fruit.

Custard Tart

	25	50	100
Pastry, sweet crust	see p 278		
Eggs	12	24	48
Milk	2 L	4 L	8 L
Sugar	200 g	400 g	800 g
Vanilla essence	1 tablespoon	2 tablespoons	4 tablespoons
Nutmeg	as required		

1. Line lightly greased deep-sided baking tray with pastry rolled to ½ cm thickness and prick with fork.
2. Place in oven preheated to a moderate setting for approximately 15–20 minutes.
3. Beat eggs and sugar together and add to milk, salt (sultanas see below) and vanilla essence.
4. Pour mixture into pastry to a depth of 3–4 cm.
5. Sprinkle lightly with nutmeg.
6. Bake in slow oven at temperature of 100–130°C for approximately 30–35 minutes or until custard has set.
7. Serve hot or cold.

Custard and Sultana Tart

As for custard tart with the addition of:

	25	50	100
Sultanas	**100 g**	**200 g**	**400 g**

Add at step 3.

Banana Fritters

	25	50	100
Bananas, small, peeled	25	50	100
Flour, self-raising	1 kg	2 kg	4 kg
Eggs	3	6	12
Milk	1 L	2 L	4 L
Sugar	250 g	500 g	1 kg
Flour	as required to coat bananas		

1. Mix self-raising flour, milk, eggs and sugar in mixer at medium speed until mix is of thick smooth, pouring consistency. If too thick, add a little milk and an extra egg. If too thin, add a little more flour.
2. Preheat deep-fryer to 165°C.
3. Coat each banana in flour.
4. Pass bananas through batter mix and gently place in oil.
5. Cook until golden brown, approximately 2–3 minutes.
6. Drain well and toss in a little caster sugar.
7. Serve as required.

Pineapple Fritters

As above substituting for bananas, the same amount of prepared pineapple rings, making sure that pineapple has been drained of any excess moisture.

Apple Fritters

As for banana fritters substituting peeled, cored apples cut into 2 cm thick rings for bananas.

Apple Strudel

	25	50	100
Flour	750 g	1.5 kg	3 kg
Eggs	2	4	8
Water approx	70 mL	140 mL	280 mL
Margarine	170 g	340 g	680 g
Apples, peeled, cored, sliced	2 kg	4 kg	8 kg
Sugar	350 g	700 g	1.4 kg
Breadcrumbs	110 g	220 g	440 g
Lemon juice	50 mL	100 mL	200 mL
Mixed spice	10 g	20 g	40 g
Cinnamon	5 g	10 g	20 g
Salt	1 teaspoon	2 teaspoons	4 teaspoons

1. Sift salt with flour and gently incorporate margarine by rubbing flour and margarine through fingers.

2. Add beaten eggs to flour mixture and then water slowly until a smooth dough has been made.

3. Divide pastry into four equal pieces and roll out on floured board to rectangles of desired thickness, usually approximately 5 mm.

4. Spread apples evenly on pastry leaving a space of 2–3 cm from edges.

5. Sprinkle apples with mixed breadcrumbs, cinnamon, sugar and mixed spice.

6. Sprinkle with lemon juice.

7. Brush edges of pastry with a little water.

8. Carefully roll pastry and give a little pressure with your hands to the finished roll to compact slightly.

9. Place rolls on lightly greased trays in oven preheated to a moderate setting for approximately 40–50 minutes until golden brown.

10. Sprinkle with icing sugar, portion and serve.

Apple and Sultana Strudel

As for apple strudel with the addition of:

	25	50	100
Sultanas	100 g	200 g	400 g

Place sultanas on apples at step 4.

Apple and Cherry Strudel

As for apple strudel with the addition of:

	25	50	100
Cherries, quartered	100 g	200 g	400 g

Place cherries on apples at step 4.

Mixed Fruit Strudel

As for apple strudel omitting apples and adding:

	25	50	100
Cherries, halved	**150 g**	**300 g**	**600 g**
Apples, peeled, cored, sliced	**700 g**	**1.4 kg**	**2. 8 kg**
Sultanas	**150 g**	**300 g**	**600 g**
Bananas, peeled, sliced	**700 g**	**1.4 kg**	**2.8 kg**
Pineapple, peeled, halved, sliced	**300 g**	**600 g**	**1.2 kg**

Blancmanges

Basic Blancmanges

	25	50	100
Milk	**2.25 L**	**4.5 L**	**9 L**
Cornflour	**225 g**	**450 g**	**900 g**
Sugar	**160 g**	**320 g**	**640 g**
Bay leaves	**2**	**4**	**8**
Lemon rind	**2 lemons**	**4 lemons**	**8 lemons**

1. Using a little milk, mix with cornflour until blended.
2. Place remainder of milk in pan on stove with bay leaves and lemon rind and bring to the boil.
3. Remove from heat and strain, discarding bay leaves and lemon.
4. Stirring vigorously, add cornflour and milk mixture to hot milk.
5. Bring back to the boil and allow to simmer for 3–4 minutes.
6. Add all sugar and stir mix until dissolved.
7. Place required amount of mixture in portion-sized moulds and allow to cool.
8. Refrigerate until set.

Chocolate Blancmange

As for basic recipe omitting lemon rind and bay leaves and adding:

	25	50	100
Cocoa powder	**120 g**	**240 g**	**480 g**
Vanilla essence	**1 teaspoons**	**2 teaspoons**	**4 teaspoons**
Sugar, extra	**100 g**	**200 g**	**400 g**

Add at step 6.

Coffee Blancmange

As for chocolate blancmange omitting vanilla essence and substituting coffee essence for cocoa powder. Add in small amounts until correct strength is reached.

Lemon Blancmange

As for basic blancmange omitting bay leaves with the addition of:

	25	50	100
Lemon juice	3	6	12
Lemon rind	1	2	4
Omit			
Milk	250 mL	500 mL	1 L

1. Add extra rind of lemon at step 2.
2. Add juice of lemon at step 6.

Other Variations

Most essences can be used in moderation with blancmange as well as ground and chopped nuts.

Blancmanges can also be layered to give a rainbow effect by placing a little chocolate blancmange in the bottom of a mould and allowing to set, then on top of this, say a lemon blancmange mix, and then a basic blancmange mix coloured with red food colouring.

Rice Pudding

	25	50	100
Rice, short grain	400 g	800 g	1.6 kg
Milk	3.75 L	7.5 L	15 L
Sugar	425 g	850 g	1.7 kg
Nutmeg	10 g	20 g	40 g
Butter	50 g	100 g	200 g

1. In deep-sided baking or roasting tray, place milk, rice, sugar and butter.
2. Place in oven preheated to a moderate setting.
3. After 1 hour stir all ingredients.
4. Cook for approximately another 40–45 minutes or until rice is soft and creamy.
5. Remove skin from top of pudding and sprinkle with nutmeg.
6. Serve hot or cold.

Creamed Rice Pudding

As for rice pudding with the addition of:

	25	50	100
Cream	**200 mL**	**400 mL**	**800 mL**

Add 5 minutes before cooking time is completed.

Coconut and Rice Pudding

As for rice pudding with the addition of:

	25	50	100
Coconut, desiccated	**150 g**	**300 g**	**600 g**

Add coconut at step 1.

Creamed Raisin and Almond Rice Pudding

As for creamed rice pudding with the addition of:

	25	50	100
Almond essence	**to taste**		
Sultanas	**75 g**	**150 g**	**300 g**
Raisins	**75 g**	**150 g**	**300 g**

Add at step 1.

Banana and Yoghurt Cake

	25	50	100
Butter	375 g	750 g	1.5 kg
Sugar, caster	600 g	1.2 kg	2.4 kg
Eggs	3	6	12
Bananas, mashed	700 g	1.4 kg	2.8 kg
Walnuts, chopped	125 g	250 g	500 g
Yoghurt, natural	600 g	1.2 kg	2.4 kg
Flour, self-raising	750 g	1.5 kg	3 kg

Icing

	25	50	100
Sugar, icing	800 g	1.6 kg	3.2 kg
Butter	20 g	40 g	80 g
Passionfruit, pulp	5	10	20

1. Grease suitable cake pan/pans.
2. Combine butter and sugar and whisk thoroughly.
3. Add eggs and thoroughly incorporate.
4. Add sifted flour and all other ingredients.
5. Place mix into cake pan and place into oven preheated to a moderate setting for approximately 40 minutes or until cooked.
6. Remove from oven, allow to cool for 10 minutes and turn out onto cake stand. Allow to cool for a further hour.
7. To prepare icing, combine all ingredients and whisk thoroughly.
8. Using a pallet knife, spread icing evenly over surface of cake.
9. Cut into required size portions.
10. Serve as required.

Pears Poached in White Wine / Red Wine

	25	50	100
Pears, peeled	1 per portion		
Sugar	1.25 kg	2.5 kg	5 kg
Water	1 L	2 L	4 L
Wine	1 L	2 L	4 L
Lemon juice	100 mL	200 mL	400 mL
Cloves	4	8	16
Vanilla essence	1 tablespoon	2 tablespoons	3 tablespoons

1. Place sugar, water, wine, lemon juice, cloves and vanilla essence into suitable pan and bring to the boil.
2. Poach pears in wine stock for approximately 10–15 minutes.
3. Remove pears and allow to cool.
4. Reduce stock by two-thirds, remove from heat and allow to cool.
5. Strain stock.
6. Pears can be served whole, or quartered and cored, with a little of the reduced stock syrup.

Creme Caramel

	25	50	100
Caramel			
Sugar	**625 g**	**1.25 kg**	**2.5 kg**
Water	**575 mL**	**1.15 L**	**2.3 L**
Custard			
Milk	**1.15 L**	**2.3 L**	**4.6 L**
Cream	**1.15 L**	**2.3 L**	**4.6 L**
Eggs	**15**	**30**	**60**
Sugar	**300 g**	**600 g**	**1.2 kg**
Vanilla essence	**1 tablespoon**	**2 tablespoons**	**3 tablespoons**
Egg yolks	**10**	**20**	**40**

1. To make caramel, combine sugar and water in suitable saucepan over low heat.

2. Once sugar has dissolved, increase heat and boil until mix turns a caramel colour. Remove from heat.

3. Pour a little caramel into well-greased dariole moulds.

4. To make custard, combine eggs, egg yolks, vanilla essence and sugar and beat lightly.

5. Combine milk and cream in saucepan and bring to the boil.

6. Reduce heat, allow to cool slightly and pour in egg mix stirring continuously.

7. Remove from heat and strain custard.

8. Fill each mould with custard mix.

9. Place moulds in roasting tray.

10. Fill tray with approximately 2 cm of water and place into oven preheated to a moderate setting.

11. Cook for approximately 30 minutes or until custard is set.

12. Remove from oven and allow to cool before turning out of moulds.

13. Serve as required.

Chocolate Mousse

	25	50	100
Chocolate, dark	750 g	1.5 kg	3 kg
Eggs	24	48	96
Cream	2.4 L	4.8 L	9.6 L
Brandy	30 mL	60 mL	120 mL
Sugar, caster	250 g	500 g	1 kg
Vanilla essence	1 tablespoon	2 tablespoons	3 tablespoons

1. Separate yolks from whites of eggs.
2. Break chocolate into small pieces and melt using a double saucepan.
3. Remove chocolate from heat and allow to cool.
4. Mix egg yolks into chocolate gradually.
5. Whip cream, sugar and vanilla until firm.
6. Whip egg whites until firm.
7. Add brandy to chocolate mix and carefully fold in whipped cream.
8. Carefully fold in whipped egg whites and refrigerate mousse until firm.
9. Serve as required.

Mango Mousse

	25	50	100
Mangoes, ripe	20	40	80
Gelatine, powdered	5 tablespoons	10 tablespoons	20 tablespoons
Water, cold	290 mL	575 mL	1.15 L
Lemon juice	100 mL	200 mL	400 mL
Sugar, caster	1 kg	2 kg	4 kg
Cream	3 L	6 L	12 L

1. Peel mangoes, cut away flesh and mash to a puree.
2. Soften gelatine in cold water and dissolve over low heat.
3. Add gelatine, lemon juice and sugar to mango puree.
4. Whip cream and fold into mango puree.
5. Portion as required.
6. Refrigerate until set.
7. Serve as required.

NOTE: Tinned drained mangoes can be used.

Scones with Strawberry Jam and Cream

	25	50	100
Flour, self-raising	500 g	1 kg	2 kg
Salt	5 g	10 g	20 g
Sugar, caster	440 g	880 g	1.75 kg
Butter	60 g	120 g	240 g
Milk	430 mL	860 mL	1.7 L

1. Sift flour and salt into a bowl.

2. Add sugar and incorporate butter until a fine breadcrumb-like texture is achieved.

3. Add all liquid and mix into a dough.

4. Place dough onto lightly floured work surface and roll out to a thickness of approximately 3 cm.

5. Cut required amount of scones using a 5 cm pastry cutter.

6. Place scones onto lightly greased baking tray and brush lightly with a little milk.

7. Place into oven preheated to a moderate setting and bake for 10–15 minutes until golden brown.

8. Remove from oven and place scones onto cooling racks for approximately 10 minutes.

9. When scones are cool, cut in half evenly and spread with strawberry jam and whipped cream.

10. Allow one scone per portion and serve as required.

Lemon Shortbreads

	25	50	100
Butter, at room temperature	500 g	1 kg	2 kg
Sugar, caster	110 g	220 g	440 g
Lemon juice	120 mL	240 mL	480 mL
Lemon rind, grated	1 teaspoon	2 teaspoons	4 teaspoons
Flour, plain	375 g	750 g	1.5 kg

1. Whisk butter and sugar until light and fluffy.

2. Add lemon juice and lemon rind.

3. Add sifted flour and mix thoroughly.

4. Place mixture in piping bag with star nozzle.

5. Pipe small swirls onto lightly greased baking trays allowing a little room between each swirl to allow for mixture spreading while in oven.

6. Place into oven preheated to a moderate setting for approximately 10–15 minutes or until golden brown.

7. Remove from oven and allow to cool for 20 minutes.

8. Allow two biscuits per portion.

9. Serve as required.

Anzac Biscuits

	25	50	100
Oats, rolled	160 g	320 g	640 g
Flour, plain	250 g	500 g	1 kg
Sugar, caster	440 g	880 g	1.75 kg
Coconut, desiccated	180 g	360 g	720 g
Butter	250 g	500 g	1 kg
Golden syrup	120 mL	240 mL	480 mL
Bicarbonate of soda	5 g	10 g	20 g
Water, boiling	40 mL	80 mL	160 mL

1. Combine butter and syrup in pan over gentle heat until butter is melted.

2. In a mixing bowl, combine butter and syrup mixture with all other ingredients.

3. Divide mixture into biscuit-sized pieces and roll and press gently onto lightly greased baking trays allowing a little room between each biscuit to allow for spreading during cooking.

4. Place into oven preheated to a moderate setting for approximately 20 minutes.

5. Remove from oven and allow to harden on baking trays for at least 15 minutes.

6. Allow two biscuits per portion.

7. Serve as required.

Individual Passionfruit Meringues

	25	50	100
Egg whites	5	10	20
Lemon juice	10 mL	20 mL	40 mL
Sugar, caster	330 g	660 g	1.3 kg
Cream, whipped	500 mL	1 L	2 L
Passionfruit pulp	500 g	1 kg	2 kg

1. Whisk egg whites, lemon juice and sugar at high speed for 15 minutes or until peaks form.

2. Place mixture into piping bag with star nozzle and pipe onto lightly greased baking tray with small nest shapes approximately 9 cm in diameter.

3. Place into oven preheated to 100°C and cook for approximately 1 hour or until cooked through.

4. Remove from oven and allow to cool.

5. Fill individual meringues with cream and top with passionfruit pulp.

6. Allow one meringue per portion.

7. Serve as required.

NOTE: Any other available fruit can be substituted for passionfruit.

Chocolate Éclairs

	25	50	100
Choux pastry	see p 279		
Chocolate, cooking	750 g	1.5 kg	3 kg
Golden syrup	200 mL	400 mL	800 mL
Cream, whipped	750 mL	1.5 L	3 L

1. Place choux pastry mix into piping bag fitted with a 1 cm plain nozzle.
2. Pipe mix into 5 cm lengths onto lightly greased baking trays.
3. Place into oven preheated to a moderate setting for approximately 10–15 minutes or until golden brown.
4. Remove from oven and allow to cool.
5. Make small incision along the base of éclair.
6. Pipe in whipped cream.
7. In pan over boiling water, melt chocolate.
8. Add golden syrup to melted chocolate and remove from heat.
9. Dip filled éclairs into chocolate so that only top of éclair is coated.
10. Allow chocolate to set.
11. Allow one éclair per portion.
12. Serve as required.

Chocolate Fudge Profiteroles

Ingredients as for chocolate éclairs.

1. Pipe choux pastry into small swirls approximately 2–3 cm in diameter as for chocolate éclairs.
2. Cook as for chocolate éclairs.
3. Fill with cream and top with chocolate as for éclairs.
4. Allow three to four profiteroles per portion.
5. Serve as required.

Bread and Butter Pudding

	25	50	100
Milk	2.5 L	5 L	10 L
Sugar	250 g	500 g	1 kg
Bread, sliced, buttered	30 slices	60 slices	120 slices
Eggs	20	40	80
Vanilla essence	20 mL	40 mL	80 mL
Sultanas	150 g	300 g	600 g

1. Prepare egg custard by mixing milk, sugar, eggs and vanilla essence and whisking thoroughly.

2. Cut bread into quarters.

3. Place one layer of bread in suitable baking dish.

4. Sprinkle bread with sultanas and repeat process until all bread and sultanas are used.

5. Carefully pour custard mix over bread.

6. Allow to stand for 10 minutes.

7. Place into oven preheated to a moderate setting and cook for 45 minutes to 1 hour or until firm to the touch.

8. Portion and serve as required.

Pastry

Short Crust Pastry

		25	50	100
Margarine		350 g	700 g	1.4 kg
Flour, plain		700 g	1.4 kg	2. 8 kg
Water	approx	500 mL	1 L	2 L
Salt		1 teaspoon	2 teaspoons	4 teaspoons

1. Sift flour and salt.

2. Incorporate softened margarine by passing through fingers lightly until sandy texture is reached.

3. Add water gradually and mix into a stiff dough.

4. Place mix on lightly floured surface and leave to rest for 20 minutes before use.

Sweet Crust Pastry

As for short crust pastry with the addition of:

	25	50	100
Sugar	250 g	500 g	1 kg

Add sugar at end of step 2.

Puff Pastry

		25	50	100
Flour, plain		700 g	1.4 kg	2.8 kg
Margarine		700 g	1.4 kg	2.8 kg
Water	approx	300 mL	600 mL	1.2 L
Lemon juice		1 teaspoon	2 teaspoons	4 teaspoons
Salt		1 teaspoon	2 teaspoons	4 teaspoons

1. Sift flour and salt.

2. Add one-quarter of softened margarine by passing through fingers lightly until sandy texture is reached.

3. Make a well in centre of flour, add lemon juice and water and mix until a smooth dough is achieved.

4. Place mix on lightly floured surface and leave to rest for 30 minutes.

5. Roll dough into a square approximately 2 cm deep.

6. Shape margarine into smaller square approximately 2 cm deep and place on centre of rolled out dough.

7. Fold sides of dough to completely enclose margarine.

8. Roll dough to about 1 cm thickness (length to be twice width).

9. Fold bottom third in and top third over.

10. Turn dough so that folded edges are on left and right sides.

11. Repeat steps 8–10 four times leaving pastry to rest for 15 minutes between each process.

12. When process is completed, rest pastry for 1 hour before use.

Choux Pastry

	25	50	100
Water	700 mL	1.4 L	2.8 L
Butter	225 g	450 g	900 g
Flour, plain	250 g	500 g	1 kg
Eggs	8	16	32

1. Place water and butter in suitable pan, heat until all butter has melted and remove from heat.

2. Add sieved flour and mix thoroughly with wooden spoon until mix leaves sides of pan.

3. Add eggs gradually, mixing well until all are incorporated.

4. Allow to cool slightly and use as required.

Homemade Custard Sauce / Sauce a l'Anglaise

	25	50	100
Milk	**1.5 L**	**3 L**	**6 L**
Caster sugar	**150 g**	**300 g**	**600 g**
Egg yolks	**12**	**24**	**48**
Vanilla essence	**to taste**		

1. Mix together yolks, sugar and essence in large bowl using a whisk.
2. Bring milk to the boil.
3. Pour boiling milk into bowl containing egg mixture.
4. Return sauce to clean thick-bottomed pan.
5. On low heat stir sauce with a wooden spoon until correct coating consistency has been reached.
6. Pass sauce through a sieve if required.
7. Serve as required.

NOTE: Sauce must not be allowed to boil.

Most establishments will use custard powder which is very acceptable and also time-saving.

Custard Sauce using Custard Powder

	25	50	100
Milk	**1.5 L**	**3 L**	**6 L**
Caster sugar	**150 g**	**300 g**	**600 g**
Custard powder	**60 g**	**120 g**	**240 g**

1. Mix a little of the milk with the custard powder and caster sugar until a thick liquid is achieved.
2. Bring remaining milk to the boil.
3. Whisk in custard mixture, and bring to the boil stirring constantly.
4. Serve as required.

NOTE: Some custard powder mixes may vary. This recipe gives a rough guide to the weights of ingredients, though it must be stressed that you read the manufacturer's instructions because methods and weights may vary with different brands.

Honey and Sultana Custard

	25	50	100
Custard sauce	**1.5 L**	**3 L**	**6 L**
Sultanas	**200 g**	**400 g**	**800 g**
Honey	**100 mL**	**200 mL**	**400 mL**

When custard is made, mix in honey and sultanas.

Almond Sauce

As for custard sauce with the addition of almond essence to taste.

Vanilla Sauce

As for custard sauce with the addition of vanilla essence to taste.

Sweet Lemon Sauce

As for custard sauce with the addition of lemon essence to taste.

Rum Sauce

As for custard sauce with the addition of rum or rum essence to taste.

Whipped Cream

Place required amount of whipping cream into a large mixing bowl and whisk until peaks form and cream is of a piping consistency. If cream is to be served with a very sweet dish do not add sugar to the cream.

Chantilly Cream

As for whipped cream adding caster sugar and vanilla essence to taste before whisking.

Flavoured Cream

Any suitable flavourings can be used with cream, in moderation. Also a little food colouring can be added for extra effect.

Accompaniments

Sage Butter

	25	50	100
Butter	500 g	1 kg	2 kg
Sage, chopped	10 g	20 g	30 g

1. Allow butter to reach room temperature.

2. Add sage to butter and incorporate thoroughly.

3. Roll into cylinder shapes approximately 3–4 cm in circumference.

4. Place onto aluminium foil, roll so butter is completely covered and twist ends closed.

5. Refrigerate for at least 1 hour.

6. Remove from refrigerator as close to service time as possible.

7. Remove butter from foil.

8. Slice into required portion sizes.

9. Serve as required.

Yorkshire Pudding

	25	50	100
Flour, self-raising	500 g	1 kg	2 kg
Milk	1.25 L	2.5 L	5 L
Eggs	5	10	20
Salt and pepper	to taste		
Oil	as required		

1. Combine sieved flour, milk and eggs and whisk thoroughly until a smooth consistency is reached.
2. Season to taste and allow mix to stand for half an hour.
3. Place well-oiled Yorkshire pudding trays into oven preheated to a moderate setting for 10 minutes.
4. Remove trays and ladle a little mix into each compartment to a depth of approximately 2–3 cm.
5. Return to oven and cook for approximately 15 minutes.
6. Serve as required.

Basic Stuffing

	25	50	100
Breadcrumbs	375 g	7.5 g	1.5 kg
Onions, minced or finely chopped	1 medium	2 medium	4 medium
Parsley, chopped	5 g	10 g	20 g
Salt and pepper	to taste		
Liquid, stock or water	as required		
Oil	50 mL	100 mL	200 mL

1. Place breadcrumbs, onion, parsley and salt and pepper into a large bowl or pan.
2. Add small amounts of warm liquid, mixing well until ingredients can be moulded with the hand.
3. Mix in oil.
4. Grease a baking tray and press mixture into it to a depth of 3 cm.
5. Brush top with a little oil and place into oven preheated to a moderate setting until mixture is cooked through.
6. Remove from oven and allow to stand for approximately 20 minutes.
7. Portion and use as required.

Alternative Method

To mixture add:

	25	50	100
Eggs, beaten	2	4	8

1. Add at step 3 and mix in thoroughly.
2. Grease 300 cm strips of aluminium foil and place a little mixture along length of foil.
3. Fold aluminium foil over mixture and lightly roll to achieve a roll of mixture with a diameter of approximately 6 cm.
4. Secure foil and repeat process until all mixture is used.
5. Place all packages of stuffing mixture onto a tray suitable for a steamer.
6. Place into steamer and cook for approximately 2 hours.
7. Remove from steamer and allow to stand for approximately 30–40 minutes.
8. Gently remove foil and slice portions as required.

Chestnut and Onion Stuffing

As for basic stuffing with the addition of:

	25	50	100
Chestnut puree, tinned	**250 g**	**500 g**	**1 kg**

Combine chestnut puree with other ingredients and cook as for basic stuffing.

Sage and Onion Stuffing

As for basic stuffing with the addition of:

	25	50	100
Sage, chopped	**10 g**	**20 g**	**40 g**

Combine sage with other ingredients and cook as for basic stuffing.

Parsley and Thyme Stuffing

As for basic stuffing with the addition of:

	25	50	100
Parsley, chopped	**10 g**	**20 g**	**40 g**
Thyme, chopped	**10 g**	**20 g**	**40 g**

Combine herbs with other ingredients and cook as for basic stuffing.

Herb Breads

Herb breads are best made from crusty rolls or French sticks and are an ideal way to cut back on wastage. Herb breads can be an accompaniment to many different dishes and many variations are available.

Weights for herb breads will vary according to the amount of bread available and also the portion size required.

If margarine is being used instead of butter, add a little salt to the mixture.

Garlic Bread

The following ingredients make 500 g of garlic butter:

Butter	**500 g**
Garlic cloves, chopped	**3**
Parsley, chopped	**5 g**

1. Melt butter in small saucepan and add garlic (make sure butter does not burn).
2. Cut into bread to about 1 cm of base at 3 cm intervals.
3. Gently open cuts in bread being careful not to break slices away from roll.
4. Using pastry brush, coat inside of each slice with garlic butter.
5. When all slices have been coated, brush a little butter over top of bread and then seal bread in aluminium foil.
6. Place onto trays and into oven preheated to a moderate setting until outside of bread is crisp.
7. Serve as required.

Garlic and Oregano Bread

As for garlic bread with the addition of:

Oregano, chopped	**5 g**

Herb Bread

Butter	**500 g**
Basil, chopped	**5 g**
Mint, chopped	**5 g**
Parsley, chopped	**5 g**

As for garlic bread omitting garlic and adding herbs at step 1.

Cheesy Garlic Bread

As for garlic bread with the addition of:

Parmesan cheese, grated   100 g

1. Add parmesan cheese at step 1.
2. Brush bread with garlic butter, sprinkle a little parmesan cheese over bread and wrap bread in foil.

——————— ◇ ———————

Garnishes

The garnishes listed below can be prepared in advance and will remain fresh for several hours if stored in a refrigerator. Illustrations of these garnishes appear in Chapter 10, pp 75–6.

Chilli Flowers

For curries, chilli con carne, and most Asian dishes.

1. Using small red and green chillis, slit the chillis lengthwise from the tip end to within 2 cm of stalk at six equal intervals.

2. Scrape out excess seeds and place chillis in bowl of chilled water in refrigerator for one hour or until ends have curled sufficiently.

Tomato Rose

Very versatile garnish for salads and fish dishes.

1. Select firm ripe tomato and holding stem downwards, cut skin in 2 cm wide spiral from top and rotate tomato removing all skin from flesh of tomato.

2. Roll skin tightly ensuring flesh side of skin is facing towards the centre of the rose.

3. Gently separate layers to create a rose petal effect.

NOTE: Skinned tomatoes can be used for soup, or seeded and diced and used as a garnish.

Radish Flower

For salads and meat platters.

1. Select firm radish and trim both ends.
2. Make four curved cuts on each side of radish running from top to bottom leaving attached at base.
3. Place in bowl of chilled water and refrigerate for one hour until petals have opened sufficiently.

Turned Mushrooms

For fish and beef dishes.

1. Remove stalk from small mushroom and peel skin gently with a small knife.
2. Using a cantaloupe cutter, start at the top of the mushroom and cut downwards in gentle spiralling motion up to six times.

NOTE: Trimmings should be used for stocks and sauces.

Cucumber Fan

For Indian dishes and sandwich platters.

1. Wash and trim either end of cucumber.
2. Cut into 5 cm pieces.
3. Cut piece in half lengthwise.
4. Lay flesh side down on chopping board and slice through three-quarters width of cucumber approximately 10 times.
5. Curl alternate slices into centre of cucumber.

Spun Shallot

Very versatile garnish. Can be used for most savoury dishes.

1. Wash and remove outer skin and trim both ends.
2. Cut into 6 cm pieces.
3. Cutting lengthwise at both ends for 2 cm make approximately eight cuts.
4. Place in bowl of chilled water and refrigerate for one hour or until ends have curled.

Cucumber Crown

For most cold dishes.

1. Wash and cut cucumber into 10 cm pieces.
2. Continuously make 'V' shaped cuts around the middle of the cucumber piercing to the centre.
3. Split into two pieces gently and scoop away a little of the centre with a teaspoon handle and fill with a little sour cream and paprika or fill with sprigs of fresh herbs.

Tomato Sail

For most meat dishes.

1. Cut a large firm tomato into eight wedges and, using a knife, separate the skin from the tomato flesh cutting two-thirds the length of the tomato wedge.
2. Gently pull back the skin from the flesh to form a sail.

Tomato and Orange Baskets

For large platters of hot or cold foods.

1. Using a large firm tomato or orange place the stem side down on work surface.
2. Make two cuts half way down fruit leaving a 1 cm gap in between centre of fruit to form the handle of the basket.
3. From one end of basket handle make small zigzag incisions to other side of handle removing wedge. Repeat operation on other side of fruit.
4. Scoop out excess flesh and seeds and fill with chilli flowers and sprigs of fresh herbs, or fill with a sauce, for example tomato or mayonnaise.

Lamb

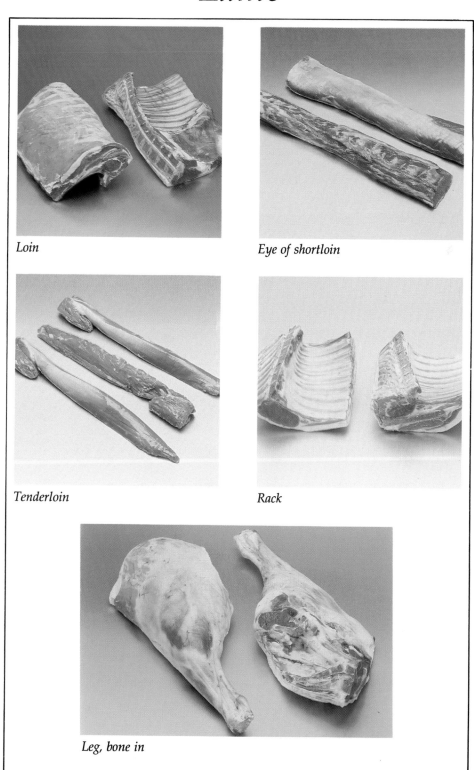

Loin

Eye of shortloin

Tenderloin

Rack

Leg, bone in

Beef

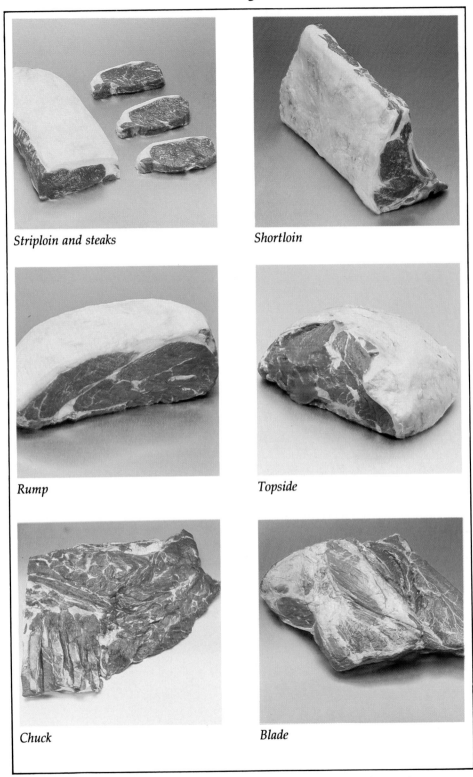

Striploin and steaks

Shortloin

Rump

Topside

Chuck

Blade

Veal

Loins

Tenderloin
(sidestrap off, silverskin removed)

Rack

Backstrap

Topside and trimmed topside

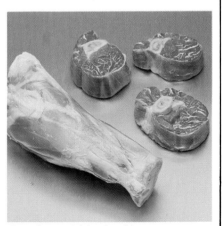

Osso bucco (shin shank)

Pork

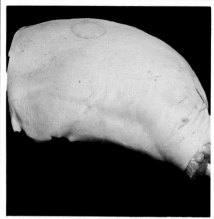

Standard roasting leg

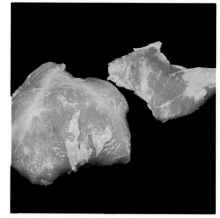

Round and rump

Midloin roasts

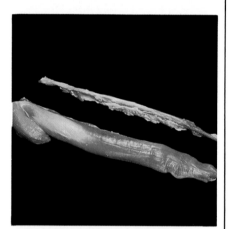

Pork fillet (sidestrap removed)

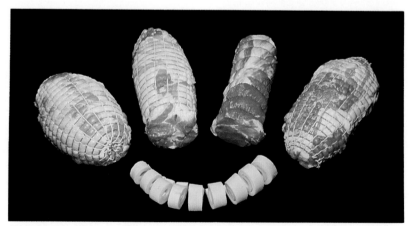

Forequarter joints — Rind (crackling) in foreground

Photographs reproduced by permission of the Australian Pork Corporation

Appendix

- Conversion Charts
- Oven Temperatures

Conversion Charts

Liquids

Imperial Fluid ounces (fl oz)	Exact metric Millilitres (mL)	Rounded metric Millilitres (mL)
⅛	3.551	3.5
¼	7.103	7
⅓	9.471	9.5
⅜	10.654	10.5
½	14.206	14
⅝	17.758	18
⅔	18.942	19
¾	21.309	21.5
⅞	24.861	25
1	28.413	30
1½	42.619	42.5
2	56.826	55
2½	71.023	71
3	85.239	85
3½	99.445	100
4	113.652	115
4½	127.858	128
5	142.065	140
5½	156.271	155
6	170.478	170
6½	184.684	185
7	198.891	200

Liquids — cont.

Imperial Fluid ounces (fl oz)	Exact metric Millilitres (mL)	Rounded metric Millilitres (mL)
7½	213.097	215
8	227.304	230
8½	241.511	242
9	255.718	255
9½	269.924	270
10	284.131	285
10½	298.337	300
11	312.544	310
11½	326.750	325
12	340.957	340
12½	355.163	355
13	369.370	370
13½	383.576	385
14	397.783	400
14½	411.989	410
15	426.196	425
15½	440.402	440
16	454.609	455
16½	468.815	470
17	483.022	485
17½	497.228	500
18	511.435	510
18½	525.641	525
19	539.848	540
19½	554.054	555
20 (1 pint)	568.261	570

Pints (pt)	Litres (L) + Millilitres (mL)		Litres (L)
2 (40 fl oz)	1 L	136 mL	1.1 L
3 (60 fl oz)	1 L	704 mL	1.7 L
4 (80 fl oz)	2 L	273 mL	2.3 L
5 (100 fl oz)	2 L	841 mL	2.8 L
6 (120 fl oz)	3 L	409 mL	3.4 L
7 (140 fl oz)	3 L	977 mL	4 L
8 (160 fl oz)	4 L	546 mL	4.5 L

Gallons (gal)	Litres (L)	Litres (L)
1	4.546	4.5
2	9.092	9
3	13.638	13.5
4	18.184	18
5	22.730	22.750
6	27.276	27
7	31.822	32
8	36.368	36.5

Weights

Imperial	Exact metric	Rounded metric
Ounces (oz)	Grams (g)	Grams (g)
⅛	3.543	3.5
¼	7.087	7
⅜	10.631	10.5
½	14.147	14
⅝	17.718	17.5
¾	21.262	21
⅞	24.805	25
1	28.349	28.5
1½	42.524	42.5
2	56.699	56.5
2½	70.873	71
3	85.048	85
3½	99.223	99
4	113.398	113
4½	127.572	128
5	141.747	140
5½	155.922	155
6	170.097	170
6½	184.271	185
7	198.446	200
7½	212.621	215
8	226.796	225
8½	240.970	240
9	255.145	255
9½	269.320	270
10	283.495	285
10½	297.670	300
11	311.844	310
11½	326.019	325
12	340.194	340
12½	354.369	355
13	368.543	370
13½	382.718	380
14	396.893	395
14½	411.068	410
15	425.221	425
15½	439.417	440
16 (1 pound)	453.592	455

Pounds (lbs)	Kilograms (kg)	Kilograms (kg)
2	0.907	0.9
3	1.360	1.3
4	1.814	1.8
5	2.267	2.2
6	2.721	2.7
7	3.175	3.1
8	3.628	3.6

Weights — cont.

Pounds (lbs)	Kilograms (kg)	Kilograms (kg)
9	4.082	4
10	4.535	4.5
20	9.071	9
30	13.607	13.5
40	18.143	18
60	27.215	27

Weights and Measures for Small Quantities

Liquids

1 teaspoon	5 mL
1 tablespoon	20 mL
½ cup	125 mL
1 cup	250 mL
4 cups	1 L

Food

Butter	1 cup	250 g
Cream	1 cup	300 mL
Flour	1 cup	125 g
Nuts	1 cup	120 g
Rice	1 cup	200 g
Sugar	1 cup	250 g

Food	Teaspoon	Tablespoon
Chopped herbs	2 g	5 g
Cornflour	3 g	12 g
Oil	3 g	20 g
Salt	3 g	10 g

Oven Temperatures

The temperatures given below are approximate only, and may vary according to the oven used.

	Celsius	Fahrenheit
Very slow	110–120	225–250
Slow	120–150	250–300
Moderate	150–175	300–350
Hot	175–230	350–450
Very hot	230–270	450–500

Glossary

Accompaniments: Anything offered separately with a dish.

A la: In the style of.

Aspic: A jelly made from meat, fish, fowl, fruit or vegetables used for decorative work.

Au beurre: With butter.

Au gratin: Sprinkled with grated cheese and browned.

Bacteria: Micro-organisms, some of which are harmful.

Bain-marie: Container of boiling water to keep foods hot without burning.

Barding (Larding): Covering breast of poultry with pork fat to help keep moist.

Blanche: (a) To place in boiling water, to remove skin.

(b) To make white as in meat.

(c) To set colour of vegetables.

(d) To cook without colour before frying, for example potatoes.

Bouquet garni: Parsley, thyme and bay leaf tied inside a piece of leek or celery.

Canapé: Cushion of toast or bread upon which hot or cold foods are placed.

Casserole: Earthenware heatproof dish with lid.

Chinois: Conical strainer.

Clarify: To make clear.

Compote: Stewed fruit.

Concasse: Coarsely chopped.

Cook out: Process of cooking flour in a roux.

Correcting: Adjust seasoning and consistency.

Court bouillon: Flavoured cooking stock for fish.

Croquettes: Cylinder shaped cooked foods.

Crouton: A square of toasted bread.

Dilute: To mix with water, for example custard powder, cornflour.

Drain: To remove excess liquid.

Egg mix: Beaten egg, or beaten egg and milk.

Escalope: thin slice.

Flake: To break into segments free from bone and skin, for example fish.

Flan: Shallow pastry case.

Garnish: To enhance the look of a dish.

Gateau: Elaborate cake of several layers.

Gelatine: Product to help assist the setting of food.

Glaze: (a) To coat a flan, for example with jam.

(b) To colour a dish under the grill.

Hors d'oeuvre: Variety of dishes served at the start of a meal.

Julienne: Cut in fine strips.

Marinade: Seasonings and spices used in conjunction with wine/oil/vinegar and water to make tender.

Menu: List of available food.

Mousse: Light dish, served hot or cold.

Navarin: Browned stew of lamb and vegetables.

Parsley butter: Butter containing lemon juice and chopped parsley.

Pass: To push through a sieve or strainer.

Prove: The expansion of a yeast dough in a warm place.

Pulse: Vegetables grown in pods.

Ragout: Stew.

Réchauffer: To reheat.

Reduce: To reduce in quantity so as to thicken or improve flavour.

Refresh: To make cold under running water.

Roux: Cooked fat and flour for thickening.

Salamander: Grill that heats from above.

Salmonella: Food poisoning bacteria found in poultry and eggs.

Sauté: To cook quickly in frying pan.

Seasoned flour: With the addition of salt or herbs and spices.

Set: To seal the outside of food.

Stuffing: Mixture of breadcrumbs, onions and herbs (also known as seasoning).

Sweat: To cook slowly without colour under a lid.

Velouté: Basic sauce or thick soup.

Vol-au-vent: Puff pastry case of varying size.

Index

Index to Recipes